Joey Green's
MEALTIME magic

Other Books by Joey Green

Joey Green's MEALTIME magic

MORE THAN 250 OFFBEAT RECIPES USING BELOVED BRAND-NAME PRODUCTS

JOEY GREEN

Rodale books may be purchased for business or promotional use or for special sales. For information, please write to: Special Markets Department, Rodale, Inc., 773 Third Avenue, New York, NY 10017

The manufacturers have generously granted permission to reprint recipes as cited on page 285.

Printed in the United States of America
Rodale Inc. makes every effort to use acid-free ⊗, recycled paper ♻.

Illustrations by Jason Schneider

Book design by Anthony Serge

Library of Congress Cataloging-in-Publication Data

Green, Joey.
 Joey Green's mealtime magic : more than 250 offbeat recipes using beloved brand-name products / Joey Green.
    p.   cm.
 Includes bibliographical references and index.
 ISBN-13 978–1–59486–581–7   hardcover
 ISBN-10 1–59486–581–7   hardcover
 1. Cookery, American.   2. Brand name products—United States.   I. Title.
TX715.G811478   2007
641.5973—dc22   2006100599

Distributed to the book trade by Holtzbrinck Publishers

2   4   6   8   10   9   7   5   3   1   hardcover

We inspire and enable people to improve their lives and the world around them
For more of our products visit **rodalestore.com** or call 800-848-4735

For Amy Sue

Ingredients

But First, A Word from Our Sponsor

Every Thanksgiving, my sister Amy fills a casserole dish with canned green beans, pours Campbell's Cream of Mushroom Soup all over them, and tops them with French's Original French Fried Onions. My family goes crazy over her green bean casserole. And they're not alone. Every year, more than 30 million Americans cook up the dish, following the recipe on the back of a can of America's favorite soup or a canister of French's Original French Fried Onions.

America's love affair with brand-name products doesn't stop there.

My mother cooks up an incredible brisket using Coca-Cola. She covers the meat with onion soup mix and tomato sauce, and then pours a liter of Coke over the meat. Although the recipe sounds kooky, the brisket tastes out of this world. The Coke tenderizes the meat and adds a caramel flavor so the brisket truly melts in your mouth. It's so amazing that my wife, Debbie, begged her for the recipe, so she could cook it up at our house. The French may drown their meals in extravagant sauces that take days to prepare and shake their heads at us in derision, but if they would just come down off their high horse and get a taste of American ingenuity at its finest, they'd realize that Americans have devised some of the most ingenious food combinations on the planet.

Who else but resourceful Americans could whip up delectable meals using items from the back reaches of the kitchen pantry? We're innovative, ingenious, and inventive—and justifiably proud of it. We not only originated condensed soup, but we figured out how to whip up a delicious meal by pouring a can of Campbell's Cream of Mushroom Soup over a chicken. Only a plucky American would have the daring-do to devise a taste sensation as bold as Cheez Whiz. And who else but a creative American would have the panache to take Cheez Whiz to the next level by pouring it all over a steak sandwich? While it may not appear on the menus at any of the posh, hoity-toity restaurants in Paris, who can truly deny the exquisite deliciousness of Kellogg's Rice Krispies Treats?

Yes, America's love affair with Jell-O, Tabasco Pepper Sauce, and Marshmallow Fluff is truly one of the greatest culinary gifts to the world. From sea to shining sea, Americans have cooked up some astonishingly yummy dishes.

Hawaiians make SPAM sushi, one of the most popular dishes in the Hawaiian islands. The Ala Moana Poi Bowl restaurant in Honolulu serves SPAM musubi and SPAM, eggs, and rice. The average Hawaiian eats twelve cans of SPAM a year, followed by the average Alaskan with six cans, and Texans, Alabamians, and Arkansans with three cans.

The residents of Utah proudly consume twice as much Jell-O as the average American. A local favorite—a scrumptious ambrosia Jell-O salad made with lime Jell-O, crushed pineapple, and Cool Whip—may sound weird, but this emerald green concoction is truly heaven on earth, a tasty treat that would make even the most haughty French connoisseur shout "Ooh-la-la!" with unreserved glee.

The Philadelphia Cheese Steak Sandwich, smothered with melted Cheez Whiz, has become a venerable institution for aspiring presidential candidates, who seem ritually obligated to make a campaign stop in South Philly to chow down a proper cheese steak sandwich for the television cameras. In 2004, Democratic candidate John Kerry made the unpardonable faux pas of asking for Swiss cheese on his steak sandwich, cementing his image with Philadelphians as a cultural snob. On the television show *The West Wing*, Democratic presidential candidate Matt Santos, played by actor Jimmy Smits, accidentally drips Cheez Whiz all over his clean white shirt in front of the cameras and actually raises his standing in the polls.

This book is a celebration of America's passion for adding honest-to-goodness zest to life. In these pages, you'll learn how to use Fritos Corn Chips as an excellent substitute for croutons. You'll discover how to marinade meats in Wish-Bone Italian Dressing, how to bread veal with Lay's Potato Chips, and how to make potato salad with Carnation Instant Nonfat Dry Milk. You'll find out how to make Iced Tea Cookies with Nestea, oatmeal soup with Quaker Oats, and Hot 'n Nutty Cookies with Tabasco Pepper Sauce. And you'll learn how to cook a salmon in a dishwasher, shrimp in the clothes dryer, and chicken salad in a coffeemaker. Now what could be more American than that?

As the guru of offbeat uses for brand-name products, I contacted dozens of companies and waded through thousands of recipes, experimenting with scores of brand-name products we all know and love to select the most unusual and delicious recipes I could find, with help from food specialists at several corporate kitchens. During my quest, I journeyed to the Culinary Institute of America, spent a week cooking with Jell-O, and served my willing family exotic dishes like Orangey Pancakes made with Tang.

But I had to know more. Who invented the Cuisinart? Who originated the egg beater? Who's great idea was the Mixmaster? And what courageous American invented the microwave oven, enabling us to cook a gourmet family dinner in less than three minutes?

This book is the result of my pilgrimage to unlock a secret cache of recipes that make America the land of extraordinary culinary delight. Inside you'll discover hundreds of ways to excite your taste buds. Hey America! Dinner is served! Come and get it!

Argo® Corn Starch

Easy Chocolate Pudding

Makes 4 (½-cup) servings

WHAT YOU NEED

- ⅔ cup sugar
- ¼ cup Argo Corn Starch
- 3 tablespoons unsweetened cocoa
- ⅛ teaspoon salt

- 2¾ cups milk
- 2 tablespoons unsalted butter or margarine
- 1 teaspoon vanilla extract

WHAT YOU DO

In medium saucepan combine sugar, corn starch, cocoa, and salt. Gradually stir in milk until smooth.

Stirring constantly, bring to boil over medium heat and boil 1 minute. Remove from heat. Stir in butter (or margarine) and vanilla. Pour into serving bowls. Cover; refrigerate.

Easy Gravy

Makes 2 cups

WHAT YOU NEED

- 2 tablespoons fat drippings
- 2 cups broth or bouillon
- 2 tablespoons Argo Corn Starch

- ¼ cup cold water
- Desired seasonings

WHAT YOU DO

Remove all but 2 tablespoons fat drippings from roasting pan. Stir in broth (or bouillon). Cook over medium heat, stirring to loosen browned bits. Remove from heat.

In small bowl stir corn starch and water until smooth; stir into pan. Add seasonings. Stirring constantly, bring to a boil over medium heat and boil 1 minute.

Lemon Meringue Pie

Makes 8 servings

WHAT YOU NEED

- 1⅓ cups sugar, divided
- ¼ cup Argo Corn Starch
- 1½ cups cold water
- 3 egg yolks, slightly beaten

- Grated peel of 1 lemon
- ¼ cup lemon juice
- 1 tablespoon unsalted butter or margarine
- 1 baked pie crust (9-inch)

WHAT YOU DO

Preheat oven to 350 degrees Fahrenheit.

In medium saucepan combine 1 cup sugar and corn starch. Gradually stir in water until smooth. Stir in egg yolks.

Stirring constantly, bring to a boil over medium heat and boil 1 minute. Remove from heat. Stir in lemon peel, lemon juice, and butter (or margarine).

Spoon hot filling into pie crust.

In small bowl with mixer at high speed, beat egg whites until foamy. Gradually beat in remaining ⅓ cup sugar; continue beating until stiff peaks form.

Spread meringue evenly over hot filling, sealing to edge of crust.

Bake 15 to 20 minutes, or until golden. Cool on wire rack completely; refrigerate.

Mandarin Hot & Sour Soup

Makes 6 servings

WHAT YOU NEED

- 3 dried wood ear mushrooms
- ¼ to ⅓ cup rice vinegar
- 3 tablespoons light soy sauce
- 1 tablespoon dark soy sauce
- 2 teaspoons chili garlic sauce
- 1 teaspoon sesame oil

- 1 teaspoon sugar
- ½ teaspoon white pepper
- 6 cups chicken broth
- ½ pound boneless lean pork, julienned
- ½ pound soft tofu, drained and diced
- 1 can (8 ounces) bamboo shoots, julienned

- ½ cup Argo Corn Starch mixed with ¾ cup water
- 2 eggs, lightly beaten

- 1 green onion, thinly sliced
- 1 tablespoon chopped fresh cilantro

WHAT YOU DO

In small bowl, cover mushrooms in warm water and let soak for 15 minutes, or until softened; then discard the liquid.

In another small bowl, combine rice vinegar, light soy sauce, dark soy sauce, chili garlic sauce, sesame oil, sugar, and pepper; set aside.

Bring broth to a boil in large pot.

Add wood ear mushrooms, seasonings, pork, tofu, and bamboo shoots. Stir corn starch mixture until smooth. Add to soup, stirring, for 3 minutes, or until soup boils and thickens.

Remove soup from heat. Slowly drizzle eggs into soup, stirring gently in a circular motion until it forms short threads.

Sprinkle with green onion and cilantro and serve.

✴

Raspberry Creme Brûlée

Makes 6 servings

WHAT YOU NEED

Pudding:
- ⅓ cup sugar
- ¼ cup Argo Corn Starch
- ⅓ teaspoon salt
- 2¾ cups milk
- 2 tablespoons unsalted butter or margarine
- 1 teaspoon vanilla extract

- ½ teaspoon grated orange peel
- 2 cups raspberries

Topping:
- ¼ cup sugar
- 1 tablespoon light corn syrup

WHAT YOU DO

To make the Pudding: In heavy 2-quart saucepan, combine sugar, corn starch, and salt. Gradually stir in milk. Stirring constantly, bring to boil over medium heat and boil 1 minute. Remove from heat. Stir in butter (or margarine), vanilla, and orange peel.

Place raspberries in shallow 8- to 9-inch round serving dish. Pour pudding over raspberries. Cover with plastic wrap. Refrigerate 3 to 4 hours, or until chilled.

To make the Topping: In small saucepan combine sugar and corn syrup. Cook over medium heat, stirring constantly, until light golden. Quickly drizzle over pudding. Chill 15 minutes longer.

To serve, crack topping with back of spoon. Spoon pudding and raspberries into dessert dishes and top with some of the cracked sugar.

Vanilla Pudding

Makes 2 cups

WHAT YOU NEED

- ⅓ cup sugar
- ¼ cup Argo Corn Starch
- ⅛ teaspoon salt
- 2¾ cups milk
- 2 tablespoons butter or margarine
- 1 teaspoon vanilla extract

WHAT YOU DO

In medium saucepan combine sugar, corn starch, and salt. Gradually stir in milk until smooth.

Stirring constantly, bring to boil over medium heat and boil 1 minute. Remove from heat. Stir in butter (or margarine) and vanilla.

Pour into serving bowls. Cover; refrigerate.

✳ Strange Facts ✳

- Corn starch, a natural and odorless carbohydrate found in corn kernels, can be used as a thickener for smooth gravies, sauces, glazes, soups, stews, casseroles, pies, puddings, custards, and cake fillings.
- Corn starch is gluten-free, making it an ideal substitute in cooking and baking when flour and other glutinous starches must be avoided.
- Corn starch can be used as spray starch for clothing, a powder to cure athlete's foot, and a substitute for baby powder or talcum powder.

- As early as 1000 b.c.e. Egyptian Pharaohs and wealthy nobility used starch derived from various grains (not corn, which had not yet been discovered) in cosmetics and as an adhesive to hold papyrus pages together.
- As early as 500 b.c.e., upper-class Romans used starch to give their togas a crisp, neat look.
- In 1842, naturalized British citizen Thomas Kingsford discovered how to isolate starch from kernels of corn using technology he learned from a wheat starch plant in Jersey City, New Jersey. Kingsford perfected the process, making a pure laundry starch from corn.
- In 1846, Thomas Kingsford founded the T. Kingsford and Son company in Bergen, New Jersey, to manufacture corn starch. Two years later, the fast-growing company built the Oswego Starch Factory in Oswego, New York.
- In 1892, a Nebraska corn milling plant, later called Argo Manufacturing, launched Argo Corn Starch. The name *Argo* may refer to the constellation or to the ship made famous by the Greek myth of Jason and the Argonauts. The company owners may have chosen the name so that on customer price lists (printed in alphabetical order), the name Argo would appear above the name of its chief competitor at the time, Kingsford's.
- In 1899, Argo, Kingsford's, and two other starch companies merged to form the United Starch Company, a forerunner of the Corn Products Refining Co.
- While Kingsford's Corn Starch is still available in some parts of the country, Argo has become the largest selling brand of corn starch in the United States.

For More Recipes

Visit www.argostarch.com

Aunt Jemima® Original Syrup

Glazed Carrots

Makes 6 (½-cup) servings

WHAT YOU NEED

- 8 medium carrots, peeled and sliced ¼-inch thick, or 5 cups whole baby carrots
- ¼ cup water
- 3 tablespoons butter or margarine
- ¼ cup Aunt Jemima Original Syrup
- ½ teaspoon ground ginger

WHAT YOU DO

Add carrots and water to medium saucepan. Cover and steam 5 to 7 minutes, or until carrots are crisp tender; drain.

In small pan, melt butter (or margarine). Add syrup and ginger; mix well. Add syrup mixture to carrots; toss until well combined. Cook over low heat 1 to 2 minutes, or until carrots are glazed.

Glazed Roasted Salmon

Makes 7 to 8 servings

WHAT YOU NEED

- 2 tablespoons fresh ginger, peeled and grated or finely chopped
- ¼ cup white wine vinegar
- ¼ cup plus 2 tablespoons Aunt Jemima Original Syrup, divided
- 2½ pounds fresh salmon fillet, skin on
- 6 small shallots, peeled and halved lengthwise, or 2 small onions, peeled and sliced into wedges
- ½ teaspoon salt
- ¼ teaspoon ground black pepper
- ¼ cup fresh parsley, chopped (optional)

WHAT YOU DO

Combine ginger, vinegar, and ¼ cup syrup in large resealable flat container. Add salmon, skin side up, to ginger mixture. Cover tightly and marinate in refrigerator 30 minutes. Remove fish from marinade.

Preheat oven to 450 degrees Fahrenheit.

Place jelly roll pan in oven 5 minutes. Carefully remove pan from oven. Place fish in pan, skin side down; add shallots (or onions). Sprinkle with salt and pepper. Drizzle fish with 1 tablespoon syrup. Bake 10 minutes. Remove from oven and drizzle with remaining 1 tablespoon syrup. Return to oven and bake 8 to 10 minutes, or until fish flakes easily when tested with fork. Sprinkle with parsley, if desired.

Mashed Sweet Potatoes with Syrup

Makes 6 (½-cup) servings

WHAT YOU NEED

- 2¼ pounds sweet potatoes, peeled and cut into 1-inch cubes
- ¼ cup butter or margarine
- 2 tablespoons Aunt Jemima Original Syrup
- ½ teaspoon ground cardamom or ground ginger

WHAT YOU DO

Add sweet potatoes to large pot of boiling water. Cook over medium heat for 10 to 15 minutes, or until sweet potatoes are tender; drain well.

In mixer bowl, add sweet potatoes; mix on medium speed 1 minute, or until fluffy. Add butter (or margarine), syrup, and cardamom (or ginger). Mix until well combined. Serve warm.

Overnight French Toast

Makes 6 (2-slice) servings

WHAT YOU NEED

French Toast:
- ¼ cup unsalted butter or margarine, softened
- 12 slices French bread (¾ inch each)
- 6 eggs, slightly beaten
- 1½ cups milk
- ¼ cup granulated sugar
- 2 tablespoons Aunt Jemima Original Syrup
- 1 teaspoon vanilla extract

Walnut Syrup:
- 2 cups Aunt Jemima Original Syrup
- 1 cup walnuts, chopped and toasted (see *Note*)
- ¼ cup confectioners' sugar

WHAT YOU DO

To prepare French Toast: Coat 9- x 13-inch baking pan with butter (or margarine). Arrange bread slices in pan, side by side. Do not overlap.

Combine eggs, milk, granulated sugar, syrup, and vanilla in medium bowl and whisk until well blended; pour evenly over bread.

Turn bread slices over to coat. Cover with plastic wrap and refrigerate overnight. The next day, preheat oven to 450 degrees Fahrenheit. Remove plastic wrap. Bake 13 to 15 minutes, or until light golden brown.

To prepare Walnut Syrup: Combine syrup and walnuts in medium saucepan. Bring to a boil over medium heat; reduce heat to low and simmer 8 to 10 minutes.

To serve French toast, arrange 2 slices on plate; sprinkle with confectioners' sugar. Top with warm walnut syrup.

Note: To toast walnuts, preheat oven to 350 degrees Fahrenheit; spread walnuts in single layer on baking sheet; bake 7 to 9 minutes until fragrant and lightly browned.

Stovetop "Baked" Beans

Makes 8 (½-cup) servings

WHAT YOU NEED

- 1 tablespoon butter or margarine
- 1¼ cups chopped onion
- ¾ cup chopped green bell pepper
- 2 garlic cloves, minced
- 1 cup ketchup
- ¼ cup packed brown sugar
- ¼ cup Aunt Jemima Original Syrup

- 2 tablespoons Worcestershire sauce
- 2 teaspoons liquid smoked seasoning (such as Hickory Seasoning Liquid Smoke)
- 2 teaspoons prepared mustard
- 1 can (15½ ounces) red beans, rinsed and drained
- 1 can (15½ ounces) Great Northern beans, rinsed and drained

WHAT YOU DO

Melt butter (or margarine) in medium saucepan over medium-high heat. Add onions, green pepper, and garlic; sauté 4 minutes, or until crisp tender.

In medium bowl, whisk together ketchup, brown sugar, syrup, Worcestershire sauce, liquid smoked seasoning, and mustard until well combined. Add beans and ketchup mixture to onion mixture. Reduce heat to low; simmer 30 minutes, stirring occasionally.

Recipe Variation: Oven Baked Beans: Preheat oven to 350 degrees Fahrenheit. After combining the beans, ketchup mixture, and onion mixture, pour into ungreased 2-quart casserole dish. Bake uncovered 45 to 50 minutes, or until hot and bubbly.

Syrup Vinaigrette

Makes 6 to 7 servings

WHAT YOU NEED

- ½ cup vegetable oil
- 2 tablespoons Aunt Jemima Original Syrup
- 2 tablespoons red wine vinegar
- 1 teaspoon Dijon mustard
- ½ teaspoon salt
- ¼ teaspoon ground black pepper

WHAT YOU DO

In small bowl, whisk together oil, syrup, vinegar, mustard, salt, and pepper or shake in a salad dressing mixing container to combine. Serve immediately.

✴ Strange Facts ✴

- Pancakes made their debut in the 1400s, with Pancake Day, also known as Shrove Tuesday or Mardi Gras, the French term for Fat Tuesday. Shrove Tuesday marks the last day before Lent, a religious period of fasting and abstinence preceding Easter that strictly forbids the consumption of fat and eggs. To avoid wasting food, families would make pancakes to mark the start of Lent and to use up all the "forbidden" ingredients.
- In 1889, Chris Rutt and Charles Underwood of the Pearl Milling Company developed Aunt Jemima, the first self-rising pancake mix, and had the Aunt Jemima trademark designed.
- In 1890, the Pearl Milling Company sold the Aunt Jemima trademark and formula to the R.T. Davis Milling Company.
- The R.T. Davis Mill and Manufacturing Company promoted Aunt Jemima pancake mix at the World's Columbian Exposition in Chicago in 1893 by hiring Nancy Green, a famous African-American cook born in Montgomery County, Kentucky, to play the

part of Aunt Jemima and demonstrate the pancake mix. As Aunt Jemima, Green made and served more than one million pancakes by the time the fair closed, prompting buyers to place more than 50,000 orders for Aunt Jemima pancake mix. For the next thirty years, Green played the part of Aunt Jemima at expositions all over the country.

- In 1914, the R.T. Davis Milling Company renamed itself the Aunt Jemima Mills Company.
- In 1923, Nancy Green died in an automobile accident at the age of 89.
- In 1926, the Quaker Oats Company purchased the Aunt Jemima Mills Company and began production at its new plant in St. Joseph, Missouri.
- A caricature of Nancy Green as a black mammy was pictured on packages of Aunt Jemima Pancake mix. In 1917, Aunt Jemima was redrawn as a smiling, heavy-set black housekeeper with a bandanna wrapped around her head. In 1968, Aunt Jemima received a make-over to look younger and thinner, and a headband replaced her bandana. In 1989, the company removed Aunt Jemima's headband, updated her hairstyle, and gave her pearl earrings and a lace collar.
- Aunt Jemima is not and never was a real person. She is a fictional character created to symbolize someone loving and caring.
- In 1979, Aunt Jemima introduced the first light syrup. Today, Aunt Jemima Lite and Butter Lite combined account for some 40 percent of the total Aunt Jemima syrup sales.

For More Recipes

Visit www.auntjemima.com

Bumble Bee® Tuna

Baked Tuna Croquettes with Dill Sauce

Makes 4 (2-croquette and ¼-cup sauce) servings

WHAT YOU NEED

Tuna Croquettes:

- 2 tablespoons butter
- 1 tablespoon all-purpose flour
- ½ cup low-fat milk
- 1 can (12 ounces) Bumble Bee Tuna, drained and finely flaked
- 1 cup grated zucchini or yellow squash
- 2 tablespoons minced green onion
- 1 tablespoon lemon juice
- 1 teaspoon dried thyme, crushed

- ¼ teaspoon black pepper
- ½ cup buttermilk or low-fat milk
- 1 egg
- 1½ cups crushed cornflakes
- ⅓ cup grated Parmesan or Romano cheese

Dill Sauce:

- 1 cup plain low-fat yogurt
- ⅓ cup finely minced cucumber
- ½ teaspoon dill weed

WHAT YOU DO

To make the Tuna Croquettes: Preheat oven to 350 degrees Fahrenheit.

In medium saucepan, melt butter; stir in flour and cook for 1 minute, stirring continuously. Add milk. Cook and stir until mixture thickens and bubbles. Cook for 2 minutes more. Remove from heat. Stir in tuna, zucchini (or squash), onion, lemon juice, thyme, and pepper until well combined. Cover and chill mixture for 30 minutes. Shape chilled mixture into eight 2-inch balls.

In shallow dish, stir together buttermilk (or milk) and egg.

In another shallow dish, combine cornflakes and cheese. Roll balls first in egg mixture, then in cornflake mixture. Repeat procedure to coat well. Spray baking sheet with nonstick cooking spray and arrange croquettes on baking sheet. Bake, uncovered, about 30 minutes, or until heated through.

To make the Dill Sauce: In small bowl, stir together yogurt, cucumber, and dill. Serve sauce with croquettes.

THE START OF CUISINART

While attending a Paris housewares show in 1971, retired physicist Carl Sontheimer, a graduate of MIT and an accomplished cook, and his wife, Shirley, witnessed a demonstration of the Magimix, a compact food processor invented by French chef Pierre Verdun. Eager to distribute the food processor in the United States, Sontheimer founded the Cuisinart company and began importing the Magimix into the United States. The following year, Sontheimer began building a prototype of his own vastly improved version of the food processor, extending the feed tube, enhancing the cutting blade and discs, and adding safety features to meet American standards. In 1973, the Sontheimers introduced the "Food Processor" at the National Housewares Exposition in Chicago. Using a Cuisinart food processor, Sontheimer demonstrated how to turn eggs into a puff pastry dough in fifteen seconds instead of fifteen minutes, chop a pound of meat in less than sixty seconds, and create flavored spreads, pastries, and dough faster and with less cleanup than ever before.

In 1975, Sontheimer gave Cuisinarts to culinary experts James Beard, Julia Child, Craig Claiborne, Jacques Pépin, and Helen McCully, who extolled the virtues of the food processor in such esteemed publications as *Gourmet* and the *New York Times*. Within two years, sales of Cuisinart's food processor skyrocketed to a half-millions machines a year, inspiring scores of imitations and prompting Cuisinart to continually improve and expand its product line.

In 1988, the Sontheimers, having made Cuisinart the premier housewares brand, sold their company to a group of investors, who turned around a year later and sold Cuisinart to Conair Corporation in Stamford, Connecticut, a leading nationwide manufacturer of consumer appliances, personal care products, and consumer electronics.

Over the years, Cuisinart has expanded its line of kitchenware products, including blenders, coffeemakers, hand mixers, toasters, textiles, nonstick cookware, citrus juicers, slow cookers, and cutlery.

In 1998, Cuisinart founder Carl Sontheimer died at the age of eighty-three.

Mac 'n Cheese 'n Tuna

Makes 4 servings

WHAT YOU NEED

- 1 can (6 ounces) Bumble Bee Chunk White or Chunk Light Tuna in Water, well drained
- 2 green onions, thinly sliced (optional)

- 1 carton (7.25 ounces) macaroni and cheese mix
- ¼ cup butter or margarine
- ⅓ cup milk

WHAT YOU DO

Place tuna in bowl; separate into bite-size pieces with fork. Toss with green onions, if desired; set aside.

Bring water to boil in large saucepan, stir in macaroni noodles, and boil 7 to 9 minutes. Drain noodles thoroughly, but do not rinse. Return to saucepan and stir in butter (or margarine) until barely melted. Sprinkle with cheese sauce packet and stir in milk until sauce is creamy. Gently stir in tuna mixture until evenly coated.

Tuna and Cheese Pie

Makes 6 servings

WHAT YOU NEED

- 3 large eggs
- 3 green onions, thinly sliced (including tops)
- 1 cup half-and-half
- 1 clove garlic, minced or pressed
- 2 cups (8 ounces) shredded Swiss or Jack cheese
- 1 cup chopped fresh broccoli flowerets and tender stems

- Salt
- Ground black pepper
- 1 can (12 ounces) Bumble Bee Chunk White Albacore in Water, drained
- 1 pie shell (9-inch), baked until barely golden

WHAT YOU DO

Preheat oven to 350 degrees Fahrenheit and position rack in the bottom of the oven.

In large bowl, beat eggs, onions, half-and-half, and garlic until blended. Mix in cheese and broccoli; season to taste with salt and pepper. Flake tuna and arrange in layer in pie shell, mounding slightly in center, Pour egg mixture over tuna. Bake, uncovered, until filling appears puffed and lightly browned (about 50 minutes). Let stand for about 5 minutes, then cut into wedges.

Tuna Loaf

Makes 4 to 6 servings

WHAT YOU NEED

- 1 cup grated peeled potato
- 1 cup grated carrots
- 1 can (12 ounces) Bumble Bee Tuna, drained and finely flaked
- ½ cup chopped green onions
- 1 tablespoon chopped fresh parsley
- 1 tablespoon chopped, drained pimiento

- 1 clove garlic, minced
- 2 eggs
- 1 teaspoon dried thyme, crushed
- ¼ teaspoon ground sage
- 2 tablespoons cornstarch
- ⅔ cup shredded low-fat mozzarella or Cheddar cheese

WHAT YOU DO

Preheat oven to 350 degrees Fahrenheit. Spray 8- x 4- x 2½-inch loaf pan with nonstick cooking spray.

In saucepan, steam potato and carrots over simmering water for 5 minutes, or until tender.

In large bowl, stir together potato, carrots, tuna, onions, parsley, pimiento, and garlic until well combined.

In small bowl, stir together eggs, thyme, and sage; stir in cornstarch. Add to tuna mixture and combine well. Transfer mixture to loaf pan. Cover with foil. Bake 20 minutes. Uncover; bake 10 minutes more, or until heated through. Sprinkle cheese over top; bake 1 to 2 minutes, or until cheese is melted. Let stand 5 minutes; slice.

Tuna Melt

Makes 6 servings

WHAT YOU NEED

- 1 can (12 ounces) Bumble Bee Solid White or Chunk Light Tuna, drained and flaked
- ⅓ cup mayonnaise
- 1½ tablespoons sweet pickle relish
- 1½ tablespoons chopped onion
- ½ tablespoon prepared mustard

- 3 English muffins, split and toasted
- 6 tomato slices, halved
- 6 slices American, Cheddar, Swiss, or Monterey Jack cheese
- Fresh fruit (optional)

WHAT YOU DO

Preheat broiler.

In medium bowl, combine tuna, mayonnaise, pickle relish, onion, and mustard; mix well. Spread about ⅓ cup on each muffin half. Top each with tomato slice and cheese slice. Broil 4 to 5 minutes, or until cheese melts. Serve with fresh fruit, if desired.

Note: For a festive look, cut each slice of cheese into strips. Arrange in a decorative pattern over sandwiches.

Tuna Noodle Casserole

Makes 4 servings

WHAT YOU NEED

- 2 cups medium egg noodles
- 1 can (6 ounce) Bumble Bee Solid White Albacore in Oil, drained and flaked
- 1 cup fresh or thawed frozen peas
- ¾ cup finely chopped onion
- 1 can (10¾ ounce) cream of mushroom soup

- 1 can (10¾ ounce) cream of celery soup
- ½ cup milk
- ½ teaspoon ground black pepper, or more to taste
- ¼ pound (1 sleeve) saltine crackers, crushed
- 1 cup freshly grated Parmesan cheese

WHAT YOU DO

Preheat oven to 375 degrees Fahrenheit. Coat 2-quart casserole with nonstick cooking spray.

Cook egg noodles according to the package directions. Drain the noodles and place in large bowl. Add the tuna, peas, and onion and toss to combine.

In medium bowl, whisk together the mushroom soup, celery soup, milk, and pepper. Pour over noodle mixture, carefully mixing all of the liquid throughout the noodles. Spread the mixture evenly into prepared casserole. Sprinkle the saltines and cheese over the top. Bake until the casserole is piping hot throughout and the top is golden, about 45 minutes. Let cool slightly before serving.

Strange Facts

- In 1899, a group of seven canners in Astoria, Oregon, formed the Columbia River Packers Association, determined to pool their resources to fish and process salmon successfully. The following year, the association purchased several sailing ships and began building a cannery on Alaska's Bristol Bay.
- In 1910, the Columbia River Packers Association introduced the Bumble Bee brand, one of hundreds of its marketed labels.
- In 1920, after albacore tuna was discovered in seasonal abundance off the Oregon coast, the Columbia River Packers Association began expanding its cannery in Astoria, Oregon, to capitalize on this new resource of albacore. In the 1930s, albacore surpassed salmon as the association's principal product, and the company began to use the Bumble Bee brand on more of its products, becoming a recognized leader in the seafood industry.
- By 1950, the Columbia River Packers Association had developed the Bumble Bee brand into one of the most respected premium labels for canned seafood. By the end of the decade Castle & Cooke, a prominent Hawaii-based seafood company, acquired 61 percent ownership in the company.
- In 1960, Bumble Bee Seafoods, Inc., became a wholly owned subsidiary of Castle & Cooke and was later merged into the parent company as an operating division.
- In 1997, International Home Foods Inc. acquired Bumble Bee and Orleans Seafoods, Inc., enabling Bumble Bee to launch a new line of products, including shrimp, oysters, clams, smoked scallops, and anchovies.

- In 1999, Bumble Bee acquired Clover Leaf, the leading brand of tuna and salmon in Canada, and began distributing King Oscar sardines.
- ConAgra Foods acquired Bumble Bee in 2000; Bumble Bee became Bumble Bee Seafoods, LLC, in 2003; and the following year, the company merged with Connors Bros. Income Fund to become the largest branded seafood company in North America.
- Bumble Bee has canning facilities in Mayaguez, Puerto Rico, and Santa Fe Springs, California.
- Today, Bumble Bee Seafoods sells canned tuna and salmon throughout the world under the Bumble Bee Label and in Canada under the Clover Leaf brand name.
- The first Bumble Bee mascot was a real bee. Today, the Bumble Bee bee doesn't have a tail, stinger, or stripes. Instead, the bee wears a striped shirt.

For More Recipes

Visit www.bumblebee.com

Campbell's® Condensed Cream of Mushroom Soup

Baked Tuna 'n Noodles

Makes 20 (1-cup) servings

WHAT YOU NEED

- 2 cups thinly sliced celery
- ½ cup chopped onion
- ¼ cup shortening
- 6 cans (10¾ ounces each) Campbell's Condensed Cream of Mushroom Soup
- 3 cups milk
- 6 cups cooked medium noodles
- 6 cans (7 ounces each) tuna, drained and flaked
- ½ cup diced pimiento
- ½ cup buttered bread crumbs

WHAT YOU DO

Preheat oven to 375 degrees Fahrenheit.

In medium saucepan, cook celery and onion in shortening until tender. Blend in soup and milk. Add noodles, tuna, and pimiento. Pour into 12- × 18- × 2-inch baking pan. Sprinkle bread crumbs on top. Bake 45 minutes, or until bubbling and brown.

Chicken à la King

Makes 4 servings

WHAT YOU NEED

- ¼ cup chopped onion
- 2 tablespoons chopped green bell pepper
- 2 tablespoons butter or margarine
- 1 can (10¾ ounces) Campbell's Condensed Cream of Mushroom Soup
- ⅓ to ½ cup milk
- 1 cup cubed cooked chicken or turkey
- 2 tablespoons diced pimiento
- Dash ground black pepper
- 4 slices toast

WHAT YOU DO

In medium saucepan, cook onion and green pepper in butter (or margarine) until tender. Blend in soup and milk; add chicken (or turkey), pimiento, and pepper. Heat slowly; stir often. Serve over toast.

Easy Eggs Benedict

Makes 6 servings

WHAT YOU NEED

- 1 can (10¾ ounces) Campbell's Condensed Cream of Mushroom Soup
- ⅓ cup milk
- 6 thin slices ham, fried
- 6 slices buttered toast or English muffin halves
- 6 eggs, poached
- 1 tablespoon minced parsley

WHAT YOU DO

In medium saucepan, blend soup and milk. Heat. Meanwhile, place a slice of ham on each slice of toast (or muffin half); top with poached egg. Pour sauce over eggs. Sprinkle with parsley.

Green Beans with Mushroom-Cheese Sauce

Makes 4 servings

WHAT YOU NEED

- 1 can (10¾ ounces) Campbell's Condensed Cream of Mushroom Soup
- ½ cup shredded American cheese
- 2 cups cut green beans, cooked and drained

WHAT YOU DO

In saucepan, combine soup and cheese; heat slowly, stirring constantly until cheese is melted. Add green beans; heat thoroughly and serve immediately.

Horseradish Souperburger

Makes 8 servings

WHAT YOU NEED

- 1 pound ground beef
- 1 can (10¾ ounces) Campbell's Condensed Cream of Mushroom Soup
- ½ cup sour cream
- 1 teaspoon prepared horseradish
- ¼ cup chopped green bell pepper or pimiento
- 8 buns, split and toasted

WHAT YOU DO

Brown beef in skillet; stir often to separate meat particles. Add soup, sour cream, horseradish, and green pepper (or pimiento). Simmer about 10 minutes. Serve on buns.

Marvelous Muffins

Makes 12 muffins

WHAT YOU NEED

- 2 cups sifted flour
- 1 tablespoon baking powder
- 1 tablespoon sugar
- ½ teaspoon salt
- 1 can (10¾ ounces) Campbell's Condensed Cream of Mushroom Soup
- 1 egg, beaten
- ¼ cup melted shortening

WHAT YOU DO

Preheat oven to 400 degrees Fahrenheit. Spray 12-cup muffin pan with nonstick cooking spray.

In large bowl, sift together flour, baking powder, sugar, and salt; make a well in the center. Set aside.

In another bowl, combine soup, egg, and shortening; pour into flour well. Stir until just mixed. (If you overmix the batter, your muffins will be tough.) Fill prepared muffin pans two-thirds full. Bake 20 minutes. Serve warm.

Scrumptious Scalloped Potatoes

Makes 6 servings

WHAT YOU NEED

- 1 can (10¾ ounces) Campbell's Condensed Cream of Mushroom Soup
- ½ cup milk
- ½ teaspoon salt
- Dash ground black pepper
- 1 tablespoon minced onion
- 5 cups sliced potatoes
- 2 tablespoons butter

WHAT YOU DO

Preheat oven to 375 degrees Fahrenheit. Coat 2-quart casserole with nonstick cooking spray.

In saucepan, stir soup well; blend in milk and heat. Add salt, pepper, and onion. Arrange a layer of half the potatoes in casserole; pour on half the mushroom sauce; repeat layers. Dot with butter; cover and bake 30 minutes.

Strange Facts

- In 1869, fruit merchant Joseph Campbell and icebox manufacturer Abraham Anderson teamed up to form the Joseph A. Campbell Preserve Company in Camden, New Jersey. The company produced canned tomatoes, vegetables, jellies, soups, condiments, and minced meats.

- In 1897, the company's general manager, Arthur Dorrance, hired his eager 24-year-old nephew, Dr. John T. Dorrance, a chemist who agreed to buy his own laboratory equipment and accept a token salary of just $7.50 per week. That same year, Dr. Dorrance invented condensed soup—eliminating the water in canned soup and lowering the costs for packaging, shipping, and storage. The company could then offer a ten-ounce can of Campbell's condensed soup for ten cents, versus more than thirty cents for a typical thirty-two-ounce can of soup.

- In 1898, company executive Herberton Williams attended the traditional football game between rivals Cornell University and the University of Pennsylvania.

Impressed by Cornell's brilliant new red and white uniforms, Williams convinced the company to adopt the colors on the labels on cans of Campbell's Soups.

- In 1916, Campbell's published a cookbook entitled *Helps for the Hostess*, originating the idea of using condensed soup in recipes.
- In 1922, the Campbell Company formally adopted "Soup" as its middle name.
- In the 1930s, Campbell began sponsoring radio shows and introducing the highly memorable "M'm! M'm! Good!" jingle.
- Americans use more than 440 million cans of Campbell's Soup each year to prepare recipes.
- Campbell's introduced Cream of Mushroom Soup in 1934.
- Ronald Reagan, Johnny Carson, Jimmy Stewart, Orson Welles, Helen Hayes, Donna Reed, Robin Leach, George Burns, and Gracie Allen have served as spokespeople for various Campbell products.
- Campbell products are sold in practically every country in the world. Consumers can buy Watercress and Duck-Gizzard Soup in China and Cream of Chili Poblano soup in Mexico.

For More Recipes

Visit www.campbellkitchen.com

Campbell's® Condensed Tomato Soup

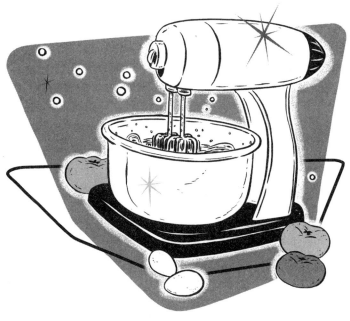

All-Round Tomato-Barbecue Sauce

Makes 1½ cups sauce

WHAT YOU NEED

- 1 can (10¾ ounces) Campbell's Condensed Tomato Soup
- 2 to 4 tablespoons sweet pickle relish
- ¼ cup chopped onion
- 1 tablespoon brown sugar
- 1 tablespoon vinegar
- 1 tablespoon Worcestershire sauce

WHAT YOU DO

Combine all ingredients in small saucepan. Cover; simmer until onion is cooked and flavors are blended.

Chili Con Carne

Makes 6 servings

WHAT YOU NEED

- 2 tablespoons shortening
- 1 medium onion, finely chopped
- 2 cloves garlic, minced
- 1 pound ground beef
- 1 to 2 tablespoons chili powder
- ½ teaspoon salt
- ¼ teaspoon cayenne pepper
- ⅛ teaspoon ground black pepper
- 2 cans (10¾ ounces each) Campbell's Condensed Tomato Soup
- 1 can (20 ounces) red kidney beans

WHAT YOU DO

Melt shortening in saucepan; add onion, garlic, and beef; brown slightly. Add chili powder, salt, cayenne pepper, black pepper, soup, and kidney beans. Cover and cook over low heat slowly about 30 minutes, stirring occasionally.

Serving Suggestion: Serve hot with crisp crackers and relishes.

Glorified Spaghetti with Meatballs

Makes 6 servings

WHAT YOU NEED

- 1 pound ground beef
- ½ cup bread crumbs
- ⅔ cup milk
- 1 egg
- 1 tablespoon minced fresh parsley
- 1¼ plus ½ teaspoon salt, divided
- ⅛ teaspoon ground black pepper
- 1 pound thin spaghetti
- 2 large cloves garlic
- 2 medium onions, minced

- ⅓ cup olive oil
- 2 cans (10¾ ounces each) Campbell's Condensed Tomato Soup
- 2 tablespoons lemon juice
- ½ teaspoon dried sweet basil
- ½ teaspoon dried sage
- ¼ teaspoon dried thyme
- ¼ teaspoon cayenne pepper
- Parmesan cheese (optional)

WHAT YOU DO

In large bowl, combine beef, bread crumbs, milk, egg, parsley, salt, and black pepper; form into balls.

Cook spaghetti according to package directions.

Mash garlic in large heavy skillet; add onion and oil. Brown meat balls, garlic, and onion in oil. Blend in soup, 2 soup cans of water, lemon juice, basil, sage, thyme, and cayenne pepper; simmer 1 hour. Serve immediately on hot spaghetti. Sprinkle with cheese, if desired.

Lamb Ragout

Makes 4 to 6 servings

WHAT YOU NEED

- 1½ pounds lamb cubes
- 2 tablespoons flour
- ¼ cup shortening
- 1 can (10¾ ounces) Campbell's Condensed Tomato Soup
- 1 teaspoon salt
- ⅛ teaspoon ground black pepper
- 1 clove garlic, minced
- ⅛ to ¼ teaspoon caraway seed (optional)
- 3 medium potatoes, quartered (about 2 cups)
- ½ medium cabbage, cut into wedges

WHAT YOU DO

Dust lamb with flour; brown in shortening in large heavy kettle or pot. Add soup, one soup can of water, salt, pepper, garlic, and caraway seed (if desired). Cover; simmer 1 hour; stir often. Add potatoes to broth; cover and cook 15 minutes. Lay cabbage on top. Cover; cook 30 minutes more, or until meat and vegetables are tender.

Master Meat Loaf

Makes 6 servings

WHAT YOU NEED

- 2 cans (10¾ ounces each) Campbell's Condensed Tomato Soup, divided
- 1 pound ground beef
- ½ pound ground pork
- 1½ cups soft bread cubes
- ¼ cup chopped onion
- ¼ cup chopped fresh parsley
- 1 egg, slightly beaten
- 1 tablespoon Worcestershire sauce
- 1 teaspoon salt
- ¼ teaspoon ground black pepper

WHAT YOU DO

Preheat oven to 350 degrees Fahrenheit. Coat loaf pan with nonstick cooking spray.

Combine ½ cup of soup with other ingredients. (Save rest of soup for sauce.) Shape into loaf and pack lightly into prepared pan. Bake 1 hour. Remove loaf from pan; pour in remaining soup and simmer about 5 minutes. Pour hot sauce over loaf.

Tomato French Dressing

Makes about 2⅔ cups dressing

WHAT YOU NEED

- 2 tablespoons sugar
- 2 teaspoons dry mustard
- 1 teaspoon salt
- 1 teaspoon paprika
- ½ teaspoon ground black pepper
- 1 can (10¾ ounces) Campbell's Condensed Tomato Soup
- ½ soup can vinegar (½ cup plus 2 tablespoons)
- ½ soup can olive oil (½ cup plus 2 tablespoons)
- 2 tablespoons minced onion

WHAT YOU DO

Combine sugar, mustard, salt, paprika, and pepper in 1-quart jar with tight fitting lid; add soup, vinegar, oil, and onion and shake well. Store in refrigerator until needed; shake well before using.

Tomato Soup Cake

Makes 8 servings

WHAT YOU NEED

- 2 cups sifted cake flour
- 1 tablespoon baking powder
- 1 tablespoon baking soda
- ½ teaspoon ground cloves
- ½ teaspoon cinnamon or mace
- ½ teaspoon ground nutmeg
- 1 cup seedless raisins
- ½ cup shortening
- 1 cup sugar
- 2 eggs, well beaten
- 1 can (10¾ ounces) Campbell's Condensed Tomato Soup

WHAT YOU DO

Preheat oven to 375 degrees Fahrenheit. Spray two 8-inch layer pans with nonstick cooking spray and dust them with flour.

In medium bowl, sift together flour, baking powder, baking soda, cloves, cinnamon (or mace), and nutmeg. Wash raisins briefly, drain, chop, and roll in a small amount of the flour mixture.

In large bowl, cream shortening; add sugar gradually; then eggs, mixing thoroughly. Add flour mixture alternately with soup; stir until smooth. Fold in raisins. Pour into prepared pans; bake about 35 minutes, or until a wooden pick inserted into the center of the cake comes out clean. Frost as desired.

Strange Facts

- In 1893, the United States Supreme Court designated the tomato as a vegetable for trade purposes, though it is technically a fruit.
- The Campbell Company introduced its Tomato Soup in 1897.
- The original label on cans of Campbell's canned tomatoes portrayed two men hauling a tomato the size of an ice box.
- In the 1900s, Campbell's first magazine advertisement boasted twenty-one varieties of soup, each selling for a dime.
- In 1904, Philadelphia illustrator Grace Wiederseim drew the cherubic Campbell's Soup Kids, modeling the chubby-faced kids after herself. Like the Campbell Soup Kids, Wiederseim had a round face, wide eyes, and a turned up nose. Over the years, the Campbell Soup Kids grew taller and lost a little baby fat. The Campbell's Soup Kids were introduced in a series of trolley car advertisements, as a way to appeal to working mothers.
- In the 1960s, pop artist Andy Warhol immortalized the classic red-and-white Campbell's soup can labels in his classic pop art painting.
- Combined, Americans consume approximately 2.5 billion bowls of Campbell's three most popular soups—Tomato, Cream of Mushroom, and Chicken Noodle—each year.

For More Recipes

Visit www.campbellkitchen.com

Campfire® Marshmallows

Classic Marshmallow Cereal Squares

Makes 12 to 16 squares

WHAT YOU NEED

- ¼ cup (½ stick) butter or margarine
- 1 package (10½ ounces) Campfire Miniature Marshmallows
- 1 box (12½ to 13 ounces) cereal of your choice (fruit flavored rice cereal, chocolate puffed rice cereal, chocolate rice cereal, sugar frosted corn flakes, or corn flakes)

WHAT YOU DO

Line 13- x 9-inch pan with foil; lightly coat foil with nonstick cooking spray.

Microwave butter (or margarine) in 4-quart microwavable bowl on high 45 seconds, or until melted. Add marshmallows, mix to coat. Microwave 1½ minutes, or until marshmallows are melted and smooth, stirring after 45 seconds. Add cereal; mix to coat well.

Press firmly into prepared pan. Cool and cut into squares. Store in airtight container.

Cranberry Fluff

Makes 8 to 10 servings

WHAT YOU NEED

- 2 cups fresh cranberries, ground
- 3 cups Campfire Miniature Marshmallows
- ¾ cup sugar
- ½ cup shelled walnuts, crushed
- 2 cups diced unpared tart apples (such as Granny Smith)
- ½ cup seedless green grapes, plus additional for garnish (optional)
- ¼ teaspoon salt
- 1 cup heavy cream, whipped
- 8 to 10 leaves lettuce
- Green grapes (optional)

WHAT YOU DO

In medium bowl, combine cranberries, marshmallows, and sugar. Cover and chill overnight. Add walnuts, apples, grapes, and salt.

Fold in whipped cream. Chill. Turn into serving bowl or spoon into individual lettuce leaves. Trim with a cluster of green grapes, if desired.

Hawaiian Salad

Makes 6 to 8 servings

WHAT YOU NEED

- 1 bag (10½ ounces) Campfire Miniature Marshmallows
- 1 can (11 ounces) mandarin orange segments, drained
- 1 can (8 ounces) pineapple chunks in juice, drained
- 1 medium banana, peeled and sliced
- 1 cup flaked coconut
- ½ cup sour cream
- ½ cup whipping cream, whipped

WHAT YOU DO

In mixing bowl, combine marshmallows, oranges, pineapple, banana, coconut, and sour cream. Fold in whipped cream. Chill uncovered, several hours.

Heavenly Hash

Makes 8 servings

WHAT YOU NEED

- 2 cups cold cooked rice
- 2 cups Campfire Miniature Marshmallows
- 1⅓ cups drained pineapple tidbits
- ½ cup maraschino cherries
- ¼ cup slivered almonds, toasted (see *Note*)
- 1 cup heavy cream
- ¼ cup sugar
- 1 teaspoon vanilla extract

WHAT YOU DO

In medium bowl, combine rice, marshmallows, pineapple, cherries, and almonds.

In separate bowl, whip cream, gradually adding sugar and vanilla. Fold into rice mixture. Chill.

Note: To toast almonds, preheat oven to 350 degrees Fahrenheit, spread slivered almonds in an ungreased baking pan, and bake 5 to 10 minutes, or until almonds are light brown, stirring the almonds once or twice to ensure even browning.

Marshmallow Acorn Squash

Makes 4 servings

WHAT YOU NEED

- 2 medium acorn squash, halved lengthwise and seeded
- 2 tablespoons butter or margarine
- 4 teaspoons brown sugar
- 1 cup Campfire Miniature Marshmallows

WHAT YOU DO

Preheat oven to 375 degrees Fahrenheit.

Place squash halves in microwavable dish; cover with vented plastic wrap (see *Note* for cooking in conventional oven). Microwave on high 12 to 14 minutes, or until tender, turning after 6 minutes. Let stand, covered, 5 minutes.

Scoop squash from shells into large bowl, leaving ¼-inch-thick shells. Mash squash with butter (or margarine); spoon into shells. Place on baking sheet; top each squash half with 1 teaspoon of the sugar and ¼ cup of the marshmallows.

Bake 12 to 15 minutes, or until squash is heated through and marshmallows are lightly browned.

Note: To cook the squash in the oven rather than a microwave, place unfilled squash halves, cut sides down, in 13- x 9-inch baking pan filled with ½ inch water. Bake at 375 degrees Fahrenheit for 40 to 50 minutes, or until squash is tender. Scoop squash from the shells and continue as directed.

Marshmallow-Banana Salad

Makes 6 to 8 servings

WHAT YOU NEED

- 6 large apples, pared and cut into bite-size pieces
- 3 bananas, peeled and cut into bite-sized pieces
- 12 regular size Campfire Marshmallows
- ¼ cup sugar
- ¼ cup cream
- 1 tablespoon mayonnaise
- ¼ cup walnuts

WHAT YOU DO

In large bowl, combine apples, bananas, and marshmallows. Add sugar, cream, mayonnaise, and walnuts. Stir thoroughly and serve immediately.

Waldorf Salad

Makes 6 to 8 servings

WHAT YOU NEED

- 2 cups diced unpeeled apple
- ½ teaspoon lemon juice
- 1 cup Campfire Miniature Marshmallows
- ½ cup chopped celery

- ¾ cup coarsely chopped walnuts, divided
- ½ cup vanilla low-fat yogurt
- ¼ cup mayonnaise

WHAT YOU DO

In bowl, toss apples lightly with lemon juice. Add marshmallows, celery, and ½ cup nuts; mix well.

   In separate bowl, combine yogurt and mayonnaise. Fold into salad mixture. Sprinkle with remaining nuts.

✳ Strange Facts ✳

- Marshmallows, one of the world's oldest confections, date back to ancient Egypt around 2000 b.c.e. A delicacy reserved for royalty, marshmallows are believed to have been named after the mallow plant, a pink-flowered European perennial herb (*Althaea officinalis)* that grew wild in marshes and contains a sweet, sticky substance that could be made into a confection.
- In the mid-1800s, French candy makers made marshmallows by mixing the gummy sap from the mallow root with eggs and sugar, whipping this concoction, and molding it—by hand. The high demand for marshmallows prompted candy makers to develop the "starch mogul" system, enabling candy makers to create marshmallows in molds made of modified cornstarch. Today, marshmallows do not contain any

mallow. They are made from a combination of corn syrup, modified cornstarch, sugar, and gelatin.

- Doctors also extracted sap from the root of the mallow plant, cooked it with egg whites and sugar, and whipped it into a meringue that hardened into a medicinal candy to soothe sore throats, suppress coughs, and heal wounds.

- Doumak, Inc., began making Campfire marshmallows in 1917 and introduced the classic advertising icon Campy in 1960.

- In 1948, marshmallow maker Alex Doumakes discovered the "extrusion process," which revolutionized marshmallow production. The fluffy mixture of corn syrup, modified cornstarch, sugar, and gelatin is piped through long tubes, and the tubular shape is then cut into equal pieces, cooled, and packaged.

- Freezing marshmallows prevents them from going stale.

- Americans buy more than 90 million pounds of marshmallows each year.

- The Ligonier Marshmallow Festival, the world's only marshmallow festival, is held annually over Labor Day weekend in Noble County, Indiana, attracting more than 10,000 marshmallow lovers who roast, toast, cook with, eat, and enjoy marshmallows.

- While no one knows the origin of toasting marshmallows, the 1927 Girl Scout handbook first documented the recipe for the S'more—a combination of graham crackers, chocolate, and toasted marshmallows. Although the origin of the name *s'more* remains mystery, the name most likely stems from the phrase "I want some more."

For More Recipes

Visit www.campfiremarshmallows.com

Cheerios®

Cheerios Breakfast Bars

Makes 24 (2-inch) bars

WHAT YOU NEED

- 1¼ cups sugar
- ½ cup butter or margarine, softened
- ½ cup peanut butter
- ¼ cup water
- 1 tablespoon vanilla extract
- 1 egg

- 1½ cups all-purpose or whole wheat flour
- 1 cup old-fashioned or quick-cooking oats
- 1 cup raisins
- 1½ teaspoon baking soda
- 1½ teaspoon salt
- 4 cups Cheerios cereal

WHAT YOU DO

Preheat oven to 375 degrees Fahrenheit.

Stir together sugar, butter (or margarine), peanut butter, water, vanilla, and egg in large bowl. Stir in flour, oats, raisins, baking soda, and salt. Gently stir in cereal.

Pour into ungreased 13- × 9-inch pan.

Bake 15 to 20 minutes, or until golden brown. Cool. Cut into bars.

Cheerios Breakfast Smoothie

Makes approximately 2 cups

WHAT YOU NEED

- 1 cup yogurt (any flavor)
- ¾ cup Cheerios cereal
- ½ cup fresh, frozen, or canned fruit (such as strawberries, raspberries, blueberries, kiwi, pineapple, mandarin oranges)

- ½ cup milk
- ½ banana, sliced
- 2 to 3 teaspoons sugar, or as desired
- 2 ice cubes

WHAT YOU DO

Place all ingredients in blender. Cover and blend on high speed for 10 seconds; scrape sides. Cover and blend about 20 seconds longer, or until smooth. Serve immediately.

Crunchy Apple Salad

Makes 4 servings

WHAT YOU NEED

- 1 large apple, cut into bite-size pieces
- 1 large stalk celery, sliced
- ¼ cup light mayonnaise or salad dressing
- ¼ cup salted peanuts or raisins (optional)
- Lettuce leaves
- 1 cup Cheerios cereal

WHAT YOU DO

In bowl, stir together apple, celery, mayonnaise (or salad dressing), and peanuts (or raisins) if desired. Refrigerate until ready to serve.

Place lettuce leaves on 4 salad plates. Divide salad mixture among salad plates. Top each with ¼ cup cereal. Serve immediately.

WHIPPING UP THE SUNBEAM MIXMASTER

In 1928, Swedish immigrant and mechanical engineer Ivar Jepson, the head designer at Sunbeam in Chicago, invented the Mixmaster. Unlike the single-beater, milkshake mixer patented by L.H. Hamilton, Chester Beach, and Fred Osius in 1911, Jepson's mixer featured two detachable beaters with interlocking blades and a quiet, more stable motor encased in a perpendicular, sleekly-designed pivoting arm that extended out over the mixing bowl. Sunbeam first mass marketed the Mixmaster in 1930, which became an enormous success, miraculously turning Sunbeam into a household name during the worst years of the Great Depression.

Over the successive years, Jepson continually refined the Mixmaster, enhancing the motor and controls and adding attachments. By 1940, homemakers could use the Sunbeam Mixmaster to make juice, peel fruit, shell peas, press pasta, grind coffee, open tin cans, sharpen knives, and polish silverware. In 1990, Sunbeam released the sixtieth Anniversary Edition of the Mixmaster, which differed only slightly from Jepson's original model.

Today, Sunbeam markets more than 250 appliances, including irons, tea kettles, toasters, fry pans, electric blankets, and massagers.

Crunchy Chicken Nuggets

Makes 30 nuggets

WHAT YOU NEED

- 3 cups Cheerios cereal, finely crushed
- ¾ teaspoon salt
- ½ teaspoon ground black pepper
- ¼ cup milk
- 2 tablespoons honey

- 1 tablespoon prepared mustard
- 1 pound boneless, skinless chicken breast, cut into 1-inch pieces
- 2 tablespoons butter or margarine, melted (optional)
- Favorite dipping sauce

WHAT YOU DO

Preheat oven to 400 degrees Fahrenheit. Spray 13- x 9- x 2-inch pan with nonstick cooking spray.

In bowl, stir together cereal, salt, and pepper; set aside.

Stir together milk, honey, and mustard in medium bowl until blended. Dip chicken into milk mixture, shake off excess; coat with cereal mixture. Place chicken in prepared pan; drizzle with butter (or margarine), if desired. Bake 10 to 15 minutes, or until crust is golden and chicken is no longer pink in center. Serve with favorite dipping sauce.

Crunchy Frozen Bananas

Makes 8 servings

WHAT YOU NEED

- 4 firm ripe bananas
- 8 wooden craft sticks with rounded ends

- 1 to 2 containers (6 ounce) fat-free yogurt (any flavor)
- 3 cups Cheerios cereal

WHAT YOU DO

Cover baking sheet with waxed paper. Peel bananas; cut bananas crosswise in half. Insert wooden stick into cut end of each banana. Roll in yogurt; sprinkle with cereal. Place on baking sheet.

Freeze about 1 hour, or until firm. Wrap each banana in plastic wrap or aluminum foil. Store in freezer.

Lemon Dessert

Makes 6 plated desserts or 16 small squares

WHAT YOU NEED

- 3 cups Cheerios cereal, finely crushed
- ⅓ cup butter or margarine, melted
- 1 tablespoon sugar
- 1 teaspoon ground cinnamon
- ⅔ cup boiling water
- 1 package (3 ounces) lemon-flavored gelatin powder
- 2¼ cups lemon- or vanilla-flavored yogurt

WHAT YOU DO

Preheat oven to 350 degrees Fahrenheit.

In bowl, stir together cereal, butter (or margarine), sugar, and cinnamon. Reserve 2 table-spoons and set aside for the topping. Press remaining cereal mixture into ungreased 8- or 9-inch-square baking dish. Bake 9 minutes. Cool.

Pour boiling water on gelatin powder in bowl; stir until gelatin is dissolved. Place in bowl of ice and water 2 to 5 minutes, or until chilled. Stir yogurt into gelatin mixture until blended. Pour over baked layer.

Sprinkle with reserved cereal mixture. Refrigerate 1½ to 2 hours, or until firm. Refrigerate any remaining dessert.

Strange Facts

- Research shows that when people eat cereal such as Cheerios for breakfast, they eat less fat and cholesterol during the rest of the day than when they eat other types of breakfasts. On days when people eat cereal, they also take in significantly higher amounts of essential vitamins and minerals.
- Eating three grams of soluble fiber daily from whole grain oat foods, in a diet low in saturated fat and cholesterol, can help lower blood cholesterol, which can help reduce the risk of heart disease. Cheerios is among the few breakfast cereals that contain soluble fiber from whole grain oats. The soluble fiber in whole grain oats Cheerios (1 gram per cup) helps prevent cholesterol from being absorbed from your digestive system into the bloodstream.

- Cheerios can be substituted for croutons on salads.
- In 1941, General Mills launched Cheeri Oats as the first ready-to-eat oat cereal. The following year, the company introduced Cheeri O'Leary, the first mascot for the cereal.
- In 1945, the Quaker Oats Company claimed to own the exclusive right to use the word *oats* in a commercial name, prompting General Mills to change the name of Cheeri Oats to Cheerios.
- Cheerios sponsored *The Lone Ranger* on radio from 1941 to 1949 and then on television.
- From 1953 to 1973, television commercials for Cheerios featured the Cheerios Kid, who rescued his friend Sue from cartoon-world dangers by "feelin' his Cheerios."
- In 1964, cartoon star Bullwinkle appeared in Cheerios ads, and Cheerios introduced a new slogan, "Go with the Goodness of Cheerios."
- In 1974, Cheerios began advertising its cereal as food for toddlers. Today, four out of five pediatricians who recommend finger foods for toddlers recommend Cheerios.
- In 1977, Cheerios introduced Cheeriodle, its yodeling spokesperson.
- General Mills introduced Honey Nut Cheerios in 1979, Apple Cinnamon Cheerios in 1988, MultiGrain Cheerios in 1992, Frosted Cheerios in 1995, and Berry Burst Cheerios in 2003.
- In 1985, Snoopy appeared on the Cheerios box as Joe Cool.
- In 1999, Cheerios was clinically proven to be the only leading cold cereal to help lower cholesterol in a low-fat diet.

For More Recipes

Visit www.cheerios.com

Cheesy Beef Stew

Makes 8 servings

WHAT YOU NEED

- 3 pounds beef stew meat
- 1 onion, chopped
- 4 medium russet potatoes, cut into chunks
- 1 jar (15 ounces) Cheez Whiz
- 1 cup mushrooms, sliced in half
- Cooked rice (optional)

WHAT YOU DO

Preheat oven to 350 degrees Fahrenheit.

Mix all ingredients except rice in oven bag and secure closed. Place bag in casserole dish. Roast for 45 minutes, or until meat is brown. Serve over rice, if desired.

Cheesy Greek Spinach Pie

Makes 24 servings

WHAT YOU NEED

- 1 cup Cheez Whiz
- 1 small onion, diced and drained of liquid
- ¼ teaspoon cumin
- 1 tablespoon lemon juice
- 1 box (9 ounces) frozen spinach, thawed
- 1 can (13 ounces) ready-mixed bread dough
- 1 cup vegetable oil

WHAT YOU DO

Preheat oven to 350 degrees Fahrenheit. Lightly coat baking pan with nonstick cooking spray.

In large bowl, mix Cheez Whiz, onion, cumin, and lemon juice.

Drain all water from spinach and squeeze well to remove excess water. Add spinach to cheese mixture and mix well.

Slice bread dough into 24 ½-inch thick slices. Lightly oil cutting board. Flatten one slice to a circle approximately 6 inches in diameter. Place 1 heaping tablespoon of cheese-spinach mixture in the center of dough circle. Fold edges of the dough into center to cover the cheese-spinach mixture and form a triangle. Press edges firmly to secure in place and pinch each corner together. Repeat to make 24 dough triangles.

Place triangles in prepared baking pan, leaving at least 1 inch between each one. Brush the top of each triangle of dough with a thick coat of oil. Bake 30 minutes, or until golden.

Cheesy Welsh Rabbit

Makes 4 servings

WHAT YOU NEED

- 1 tablespoon butter
- ½ teaspoon salt
- Pinch ground black pepper
- 1 jar (15 ounces) Cheez Whiz

- ⅓ cup beer
- 1 egg, well beaten
- 4 pieces bread, toasted

WHAT YOU DO

In small saucepan, melt butter. Add salt, pepper, Cheez Whiz, and beer. Stir continually until mixture is smooth. Quickly beat in egg. Serve over toast.

Cheez Nachos

Makes 8 servings

WHAT YOU NEED

- 1 package (8 ounces) tortilla chips
- 1 jar (16 ounces) bean dip

- 1 jar (8 ounces) salsa
- 1 cup Cheez Whiz

WHAT YOU DO

Preheat oven to 350 degrees Fahrenheit. Line baking sheet with aluminum foil.

Place single layer of tortilla chips on baking sheet. Spread bean dip over chips, spoon thin layer of salsa over chips, and spread layer of Cheez Whiz over chips. Bake 5 to 10 minutes.

Note: To cook nachos in microwave oven, use 10-inch casserole dish and microwave 1 minute on high.

Cheez Whiz Soup

Makes 6 (1-cup) servings

WHAT YOU NEED

- 1 large onion, chopped
- 1 carrot, grated
- 2 tablespoons butter or margarine
- 2 tablespoons flour
- 1 teaspoon paprika

- Pinch salt
- 4 cups chicken broth
- 1 jar (15 ounces) Cheez Whiz
- Chopped fresh parsley

WHAT YOU DO

In large saucepan, sauté onion and carrot in butter (or margarine) until soft. Add flour and cook until the mixture bubbles. Add paprika and salt. While stirring, slowly add chicken broth. Bring to a boil, lower heat, and simmer 10 minutes. Add Cheez Whiz, stirring continually over low heat for 5 minutes. Garnish with parsley and serve immediately.

Philadelphia Cheese Steak Sandwich

Makes 4 servings

WHAT YOU NEED

- ¼ tablespoon vegetable oil
- 1 large onion, sliced thin
- 1 pound tri-tip beef, sliced thin
- 1 green bell pepper, sliced thin

- 1 red bell pepper, sliced thin
- 1 jar (15 ounces) Cheez Whiz
- 4 sourdough rolls (6 inch), sliced open

WHAT YOU DO

In large skillet, heat the oil over medium-high heat. Sauté onion until soft, about 3 to 5 minutes, then add beef and cook thoroughly. Add peppers and cook another 3 to 5 minutes, until the peppers are soft. Drain fat from the pan. Lower heat, pour in Cheez Whiz, stir to blend ingredients, and immediately remove from heat. Spoon the cheese-steak mixture into rolls and serve immediately.

Sassy Cheese Coleslaw

Makes 4 servings

WHAT YOU NEED

- 2 cups shredded cabbage
- ½ cup shredded carrots
- 1 teaspoon grated onion
- 2 tablespoons mayonnaise
- 2 tablespoons vegetable oil
- 1 tablespoon vinegar
- ¼ cup Cheez Whiz
- 1 teaspoon prepared horseradish
- Salt
- Ground black pepper

WHAT YOU DO

In bowl, mix all ingredients together well.

Strange Facts

- In 1903, James Lewis Kraft started J.L. Kraft and Bros. Co., a cheese wholesaling business in Chicago. After developing Kraft Singles (individually wrapped slices of cheese), Kraft scientists formulated Cheez Whiz, a spreadable cheese product with its own distinct flavor, the ability to melt smoothly without clumping, and a cheerful orange color, slightly more pale than Cheddar cheese.
- Kraft launched Cheez Whiz in 1952 with the advertising slogan "Spoon it, Spread it, Heat it."
- Unlike natural cheese, Cheez Whiz is spreadable and has no aroma.
- President George Herbert Walker Bush enjoys snacking on pork rinds in Tabasco Pepper Sauce, Shredded Wheat mixed with crushed Butterfinger bars, and pigs-in-a-blanket smothered with Cheez Whiz.
- In 1992, forty years after the launch of Cheez Whiz, Kraft introduced Cheez Whiz Light.
- The advent of the microwave oven dramatically rejuvenated interest in Cheez Whiz

because of its wonderful ability to microwave so gooily. When melted in a micro-wave, Cheez Whiz will not resolidify.

- In 2003, Kraft produced more than 20 million jars of Cheez Whiz. If you stacked those jars one on top of each other, they would reach a height 58,000 times taller than Niagara Falls.

For More Recipes

Visit www.kraftfoods.com/cheezwhiz

Chex Brittle

Makes 10 cups

WHAT YOU NEED

- 8 cups Rice Chex cereal
- 1 cup salted peanuts

- 1 can (14 ounces) sweetened condensed milk
- 1 teaspoon vanilla extract

WHAT YOU DO

Preheat oven to 325 degrees Fahrenheit. Coat two jelly roll pans, 15½- × 10½- × 1-inch, with nonstick cooking spray.

Stir all ingredients in large bowl until evenly coated. Spread in pans in single layer. Bake 12 minutes. Remove from pans; cool on waxed paper. Break into pieces. Store in airtight container.

Chocolate-Peanut Butter Pie

Makes 8 servings

WHAT YOU NEED

- 3 cups Multi-Bran Chex cereal
- 3 tablespoons butter or margarine
- 5 tablespoons peanut butter

- 1 package (2 ounces) chocolate pudding and pie filling mix (not instant)
- 2 cups milk

WHAT YOU DO

Preheat oven to 350 degrees Fahrenheit.

Crush cereal; set aside. Microwave butter (or margarine) and 1 tablespoon peanut butter in microwavable pie plate, 9 × 1¼ inches, uncovered on high 30 seconds; stir until blended. Stir in cereal until evenly coated. Press evenly on bottom and up side of pie plate. Bake 10 minutes. Cool enough to handle, then place in freezer while preparing filling.

Prepare pudding mix as directed on package for pie, except after cooling 5 minutes, add 2 tablespoons of the peanut butter and stir a few times until melted and marbled throughout. Pour into crust. Microwave remaining 2 tablespoons peanut butter in microwavable measuring cup uncovered on high 30 seconds; drizzle over pie. Refrigerate at least 3 hours but no longer than 24 hours until filling is set.

Deep Dish Chicken Pie

Makes 8 servings

WHAT YOU NEED

- 2 cups cut-up cooked chicken
- ½ cup milk
- 1½ teaspoons instant minced onion
- 1 package (10 ounces) frozen mixed vegetables, rinsed to separate
- 1 can (10¾ ounces) condensed cream of chicken soup

- 1 can (4 ounces) mushrooms, drained
- 4 cups Rice Chex cereal
- 3 tablespoons butter or margarine, melted (see *Note*)
- ⅓ cup grated Parmesan cheese

WHAT YOU DO

Preheat oven to 350 degrees Fahrenheit.

Stir together chicken, milk, onion, vegetables, soup, and mushrooms. Spread in ungreased square baking dish, 8- x 8- x 2-inches.

Stir together cereal and butter (or margarine) in medium bowl until cereal is evenly coated. Stir in cheese until evenly coated. Spoon over chicken mixture. Bake uncovered 35 minutes.

Note: If using margarine, use only a stick that has more than 65 percent vegetable oil.

Muddy Buddies

Makes 9 cups

WHAT YOU NEED

- 9 cups Chex cereal (any variety)
- 1 package (6 ounces) semisweet chocolate chips (about 1 cup)
- ½ cup peanut butter
- ¼ cup butter or margarine (see *Note*)
- 1 teaspoon vanilla extract
- 1½ cups powdered sugar

WHAT YOU DO

Measure cereal into large bowl; set aside.

Microwave chocolate chips, peanut butter, and butter (or margarine) in 1-quart microwavable bowl, uncovered on high 1 minute; stir. Microwave 30 seconds longer, or until mixture can be stirred smooth. Stir in vanilla. Pour chocolate mixture over cereal in bowl, stirring until evenly coated. Pour into large, resealable plastic food-storage bag; add powdered sugar. Seal bag; shake until well coated. Spread on waxed paper to cool. Store in airtight container in refrigerator.

Note: Do not use spread or tub products.

Porcupine Meatballs

Makes 30 meatballs

WHAT YOU NEED

- 1½ cups Multi-Bran Chex cereal, crushed
- 1 pound ground beef
- ⅔ cup uncooked parboiled (converted) rice
- ½ cup milk
- 1 envelope (1 ounce) onion soup mix
- 1 egg
- 1 cup water
- 2 cans (11½ ounces each) tomato juice

WHAT YOU DO

Preheat oven to 425 degrees Fahrenheit.

Mix cereal, beef, rice, milk, soup mix, and egg in large bowl. Shape mixture into 30 meatballs, using wet hands. Place in ungreased rectangular baking dish (13- × 9- × 2-inches), 3-quart casserole, or ovenproof bowl. Pour water and tomato juice over meatballs; stir gently. Cover and bake 50 to 55 minutes, or until rice is tender and beef is no longer pink in center.

Tuna Vegetable Casserole

Makes 5 servings

WHAT YOU NEED

- 2 cups Corn Chex cereal
- 1 package (7 ounces) elbow macaroni
- 1 cup milk
- ½ teaspoon salt
- ¼ teaspoon ground black pepper
- 1 can (10¾ ounces) condensed cream of mushroom soup

- 1 package (10 ounces) frozen mixed vegetables, thawed and drained
- 1 can (6 ounces) tuna in water, drained
- 1 tablespoon butter or margarine, melted (see *Note*)
- ½ cup shredded Cheddar cheese

WHAT YOU DO

Preheat oven to 400 degrees Fahrenheit.

Crush cereal; set aside. Cook macaroni as directed on package.

Stir together milk, salt, pepper, soup, vegetables, tuna, and macaroni in ungreased 2-quart casserole.

In bowl, mix cereal and butter (or margarine) with fork; sprinkle over mixture in casserole. Bake uncovered about 30 minutes, or until bubbly around edge and heated through. Sprinkle with cheese; let stand 5 minutes.

Note: If using margarine, use only a stick that has more than 65 percent vegetable oil.

White Candy Fantasy Clusters

Makes about 24 clusters

WHAT YOU NEED

- 4 cups Rice Chex cereal
- 2 cups pretzel sticks, coarsely broken
- 1 cup cashews, coarsely chopped
- ½ package (16-ounce size) vanilla-flavored candy coating
- ½ cup semisweet chocolate chips, melted

WHAT YOU DO

Coat rectangular pan, 13- x 9- x 2-inches, with nonstick cooking spray.

Mix cereal, pretzels, and cashews in large bowl; set aside.

Melt candy coating in 2-quart saucepan over low heat, stirring constantly. Pour over cereal mixture, stirring until evenly coated. Press in pan; cool slightly. Drizzle with chocolate chips; let stand until chocolate is firm. Break into clusters. Store in airtight container.

Strange Facts

- In 1937, the Ralston-Purina Company introduced Wheat Chex cereal.
- From the original Wheat Chex, the line of Chex cereals has grown to include Corn Chex, Rice Chex, Multi-Bran Chex, Honey Nut Chex, Chex Morning Mix, and Frosted Mini Chex.
- In 1955, Ralston-Purina, concocted the recipe for Chex Party Mix and cleverly introduced the homemade party mix to the public, creating an instant hit. The company printed the recipe for Chex Party Mix on boxes of Chex cereal, and Chex later introduced a prepackaged Chex Mix.

For More Recipes

Visit www.chex.com

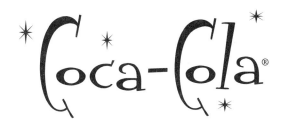

Coca-Cola Brisket

Makes 6 to 8 servings

WHAT YOU NEED

- Center cut beef brisket, 2 pounds
- 1 envelope (1 ounce) instant onion soup/dip mix
- 2 cans (4 ounces each) tomato sauce
- Ground ginger
- 1 bottle (2 liters) Coca-Cola
- Small potatoes, peeled
- Carrots, peeled and cut
- 1 fresh loaf challah

WHAT YOU DO

Preheat oven to 350 degrees Fahrenheit.

In roasting pan, place beef brisket fat side up.

Sprinkle onion soup/dip mix on top of brisket and pour tomato sauce on top.

Sprinkle with ginger. Pour half of the Coca-Cola over meat. Place potatoes and carrots around the sides of the pan. Add enough water to cover meat.

Roast 3½ to 4 hours, occasionally spooning sauce over meat. If necessary, add a little more Coca-Cola or water to keep the meat covered.

Meat is done when fork tender.

To serve, remove meat from pan and slice fat cap off the top. Carefully cut meat across the grain into ¼-inch slices and place in casserole dish covering with some of the sauce.

Reserve the remaining pan sauce to serve as gravy.

Serve with the potatoes, carrots, and challah for sopping up the gravy.

Coca-Cola Ham

Makes 6 servings

WHAT YOU NEED

- ½ ham (5 to 6 pounds)
- 1 cup brown sugar
- 1½ cups Coca-Cola
- 1 cup crushed pineapple (optional)

WHAT YOU DO

Preheat oven to 450 degrees Fahrenheit.

Wash ham thoroughly. Rub fat side with brown sugar. Place ham in roasting pan and pour Coca-Cola over ham. Pour crushed pineapple over ham, if desired. Bake 3 hours.

Easy Coca-Cola Chicken

Makes 4 servings

WHAT YOU NEED

- 1 cut-up chicken
- Salt

- 1 can (12 ounces) Coca-Cola
- 1 cup ketchup

WHAT YOU DO

Preheat oven to 350 degrees Fahrenheit.

Season chicken lightly with salt. Carefully put chicken pieces in an electric frying pan.

In small bowl, combine Coca-Cola and ketchup and pour over chicken.

Cover the chicken. Bake 1 hour, or until chicken is tender.

French Onion Soup

Makes 4 (about 1¼-cup) servings

WHAT YOU NEED

- ¼ cup butter or margarine
- 4 cups thinly sliced onions
- 2 cans (10½ ounce each) beef broth
- ¾ cup Coca-Cola, at room temperature
- 1 teaspoon salt

- ½ teaspoon white vinegar
- ⅛ teaspoon ground black pepper
- Slices French bread, about ½-inch thick
- 4 tablespoons grated Parmesan cheese

WHAT YOU DO

Preheat broiler.

Melt butter (or margarine) in large heavy saucepan over medium heat. Add onion and cook until golden, about 8 to 10 minutes; do not brown. Add broth, 1 soup can of water, Coca-Cola, salt, vinegar, and pepper. Cover, reduce heat to low, and simmer 20 to 25 minutes.

Arrange bread slices on baking sheet and broil until toasted and browned, about 1 to 2 minutes. Turn slices, generously sprinkle with cheese, and toast until browned, about 1 to 2 minutes more. Set aside.

Ladle soup into deep bowls and top with toast, cheese side up.

THE CAN OPENER'S GRAND OPENING

In 1810, British merchant Peter Durand invented the metal can so he could supply rations to the Royal Navy. Unfortunately, Durand failed to invent a device to open the cans. During the war of 1812, British soldiers used pocketknives or bayonets to tear open canned rations—sometimes resorting to gunfire. The War of 1812 popularized the metal can in England, despite the absence of an efficient can opener. Americans, while familiar with the can, had little use for it—until 1861 when soldiers fighting the Civil War needed preserved rations, necessitating canned foods.

In 1858, Ezra J. Warner of Waterbury, Connecticut, invented and patented the first can opener—a fierce-looking device with a large curved blade like a sickle that the user stabbed into the can and then worked around the rim. In 1870, American inventor William W. Lyman developed a can opener with a cutting wheel that rolled around the rim of the can. In 1925, the Star Can Opener Company of San Francisco added a serrated "feed wheel" to Lyman's can opener so the can rotated against the wheel—the design used to this very day.

- On an Arctic expedition in 1824, British explorer Sir William Parry carried a can of veal printed with the instructions: "Cut round on the top with a chisel and hammer."
- Some warfare historians claim that the bayonet was originally designed by a blacksmith in the French city of Bayonne as a can opener.
- The electric can opener was invented in 1931.

Hungarian Goulash

Makes 6 servings

WHAT YOU NEED

- 2 tablespoons butter or margarine
- 3 pounds lean beef chuck, cubed
- 2 cups chopped onion
- 1 clove garlic, minced
- 1 tablespoon paprika
- 2½ teaspoons salt

- ½ teaspoon caraway seeds
- ½ cup Coca-Cola
- ¼ cup dry red wine
- 1 can (14½ ounces) peeled, diced tomatoes
- 3 tablespoons flour
- Hot cooked noodles

WHAT YOU DO

In Dutch oven, melt butter (or margarine) and add beef, stirring to brown on all sides. Remove beef cubes as they brown. Sauté onion and garlic in the drippings until they are soft. Stir in paprika, salt, and caraway seeds; cook 1 minute. Stir in beef, Coca-Cola, wine, and tomatoes. Cover tightly; simmer about 1¼ hours, or until beef is fork-tender.

In small bowl, blend flour with a little water to make a smooth paste; stir into goulash. Stir and cook 3 to 5 minutes until gravy is thickened. Serve with hot noodles.

Matchless Meat Loaf

Makes 6 to 8 servings

WHAT YOU NEED

- 1½ pounds ground beef
- 1½ cups fresh bread crumbs
- ¼ cup minced onion
- 2 tablespoons minced fresh parsley
- 1 egg
- ½ cup Coca-Cola

- 2 tablespoons ketchup
- 1½ tablespoons prepared mustard
- 1 teaspoon salt
- ½ teaspoon dried basil
- ⅛ teaspoon ground black pepper

WHAT YOU DO

Preheat oven to 350 degrees Fahrenheit.

In large bowl, break up beef with a fork. Add bread crumbs, onion, and parsley, mixing well.

In small bowl, beat egg. Add Coca-Cola, ketchup, mustard, salt, basil, and pepper and mix well. Pour over beef. With fork, toss lightly to blend thoroughly. (Mixture will be soft. Be careful not to overmix the meat—this loaf will be moist and tender if you mix it lightly.)

Turn into 9- x 5- x 3-inch loaf pan. Bake 1 hour. Let set about 10 minutes before slicing.

Twin Cheese Dip

Makes about 3 cups

WHAT YOU NEED

- ¾ pound (12 ounces) sharp Cheddar cheese
- 1 package (4 ounces) Roquefort cheese
- 1 clove garlic
- ¾ cup Coca-Cola, divided
- 2 tablespoons butter or margarine

- 1 tablespoon grated onion
- 1½ teaspoons Worcestershire sauce
- 1 teaspoon dry mustard
- ¼ teaspoon salt
- ⅛ teaspoon Tabasco Pepper Sauce

WHAT YOU DO

Grate Cheddar into large mixing bowl. Add crumbled Roquefort. Mince or press garlic; add to cheeses with ½ cup of the Coca-Cola and butter (or margarine), onion, Worcestershire sauce, mustard, salt, and pepper sauce. Beat with electric mixer on low speed until blended. Gradually add remaining Coca-Cola, then beat on high speed until mixture is fairly smooth, light, and fluffy. Pack into container and cover. Chill, preferably overnight.

Serving Suggestion: This dip keeps very well for a week or more. Serve it with raw vegetables, as a spread for cocktail breads or crackers, or even as a sandwich filling.

- In July 1985, Coca-Cola became the first soft-drink consumed in space aboard a space shuttle mission.

- The 1971 Coca-Cola television commercial, featuring the song "I'd Like to Buy the World a Coke," was filmed on a hilltop in Rome, Italy, and featured five hundred young people from around the world, hired from embassies and schools in Rome. The close-up shots, however, were filmed at a racetrack in Rome. For the commercial, the British group the New Seekers sang the song—written by Bill Backer, Billy Davis, Roger Cook, and Roger Greenaway—and recorded a retitled version of the song for national release as "I'd Like to Teach the World to Sing (in Perfect Harmony)," which became a Top Ten hit. The Coca-Cola Company donated the first $80,000 of royalties earned from the song to UNICEF.

- Since 1920, the Coca-Cola sign has been a continuously changing landmark in New York City's Times Square. The sign has featured neon lighting since 1923. The Coca-Cola bottle unveiled on the billboard in 1991 and displayed for thirteen years was the world's largest Coca-Cola bottle. The Coca-Cola billboard unveiled in 2004 is one of the largest digital canvases in the world, measuring more than six stories high and illuminating more than 2.6 million light-emitting diodes.

- The 1961 madcap comedy *One, Two, Three* stars James Cagney as a Coca-Cola bottler in West Berlin during the Cold War, who tries to prevent his American boss's daughter from marrying an East Berlin communist.

- In the 1964 Stanley Kubrick movie *Dr. Strangelove (or How I Learned to Stop Worrying and Love the Bomb)*, Peter Sellers instructs his sidekick to shoot the lock off of a Coca-Cola vending machine to get the change to make a phone call to the president to prevent a nuclear war. The sidekick warns him, "You're gonna have to answer to the Coca-Cola Company."

- The 1980 South African comedy *The Gods Must Be Crazy* follows the adventures of a remote Bushman who mistakes an empty Coke bottle tossed from an airplane as a gift from the gods.

- The 1985 Australian movie *The Coca-Cola Kid* stars Eric Roberts as an American Coca-Cola executive from Georgia sent to the Australian outback to market the soft drink.

For More Recipes

Visit www2.coca-cola.com/heritage/recipes.html

COOKING WITH A DISHWASHER

Chef Bob Blumer, creator and host of the television show *The Surreal Gourmet* on the Food Network and the author of four cookbooks, devised this recipe (based on an urban legend) for a moist and perfectly cooked salmon fillet. Since then, Bob has poached salmon in more than 100 dishwashers on 3 continents.

Dishwasher Salmon

What You Need

- Heavy-duty aluminum foil
- 2 tablespoons olive oil
- 4 salmon fillets (6-ounce)
- 4 tablespoons freshly squeezed lime juice
- Salt
- Freshly ground black pepper
- 2 sprigs fresh dill

What You Do

Cut two 12-inch pieces of heavy duty aluminum foil.

Grease the shiny side of the foil with the oil. Place 2 fillets side by side on each square and fold up the outer edges.

Pour 1 tablespoon lime juice over each fillet. Season with salt and pepper and top with dill.

Fold and pinch the aluminum foil extra tightly to create a watertight seal around each pair of fillets.

Make sure the packet is airtight by pressing down on it gently with your hand. If air escapes easily, repackage. And make sure that your dishwasher is on the regular cycle (economy settings will undercook the fish).

Place foil packets on the top rack of the dishwasher for the entire wash and dry cycle.

When cycle is complete, take out salmon, discard foil, and place one fillet on each plate.

Reprinted from *Off the Eaten Path: Inspired Recipes for Adventurous Cooks* by Bob Blumer, a.k.a The Surreal Gourmet (Ballantine Books)

Crisco® All-Vegetable Shortening

Almond Cookies

Makes about 4 dozen cookies

WHAT YOU NEED

- 1 cup Crisco All-Vegetable Shortening
- 1 cup sugar
- 1 large egg, lightly beaten
- 3 tablespoons almond extract
- 2¼ cups all-purpose flour

- 1½ teaspoons baking powder
- ¼ teaspoon salt
- 2 ounces whole almonds (approximately 48)

WHAT YOU DO

Combine shortening and sugar in large bowl. Beat at medium speed with electric mixer until well blended. Beat in egg and almond extract until well blended.

Combine flour, baking powder, and salt in medium bowl. Add to creamed mixture; blend well. Wrap dough in plastic wrap and refrigerate 2 hours.

Preheat oven to 350 degrees Fahrenheit.

Roll rounded tablespoonfuls of dough into balls. Place on ungreased cookie sheets about 2 inches apart; flatten slightly with fingertips. Gently press an almond into center of each.

Bake 10 to 12 minutes, or until cookies are just done but not brown. Cool on cookie sheet 4 minutes; transfer to cooling racks.

✳

Blended Carrot Dinner Muffins

Makes 8 to 10 muffins

WHAT YOU NEED

- 1¾ cups sifted all-purpose flour
- 2½ teaspoons baking powder
- 1 teaspoon salt
- ⅔ cup milk

- ⅓ cup Crisco All-Vegetable Shortening, melted
- 1 egg
- ¼ cup sugar
- 2 medium carrots, peeled and sliced

WHAT YOU DO

Preheat oven to 425 degrees Fahrenheit. Coat 12-cup muffin pan with nonstick cooking spray.

In bowl, combine flour, baking powder, and salt; set aside.

In blender container, combine milk, Crisco, egg, sugar, and carrots; blend till the carrots are very finely chopped. Pour the carrot mixture over dry ingredients. Mix just till moistened. Fill muffin pan two-thirds full. Bake about 25 minutes.

Hot Mustard Sauce

Makes ½ cup

WHAT YOU NEED

- 1 tablespoon Crisco Butter Flavor All-Vegetable Shortening
- 1 tablespoon all-purpose flour
- 1 tablespoon dry mustard
- ¼ teaspoon salt

- Dash ground black pepper
- ½ cup milk
- 2 teaspoons prepared mustard
- 1 teaspoon white vinegar

WHAT YOU DO

In small saucepan, melt shortening. Remove from heat. Stir in flour, dry mustard, salt, and pepper. Blend in milk. Cook over medium heat until mixture thickens, stirring constantly. Blend in prepared mustard and vinegar. Serve warm or cold.

Lemon Dill Sauce

Makes 1 cup

WHAT YOU NEED

- 2 tablespoons Crisco Butter Flavor All-Vegetable Shortening
- 1 tablespoon all-purpose flour
- 1 teaspoon grated lemon peel

- ¼ teaspoon dried dill weed
- ¼ teaspoon salt
- 1 cup half-and-half or milk
- 1 egg yolk, beaten

WHAT YOU DO

In 1-quart saucepan, melt shortening. Remove from heat. Stir in flour, lemon peel, dill weed, and salt. Blend in half-and-half (or milk). Cook and stir over medium heat until mixture thickens and just comes to a boil. Remove from heat.

Place egg yolk in medium bowl. Blend small amount of hot mixture into egg. Blend back into hot mixture, stirring to combine. Cook and stir until mixture just comes to a boil. Cook and stir for 1 minute longer.

Serving Suggestion: Serve with fish.

Sour Cream Coffee Cake

Makes 8 servings

WHAT YOU NEED

- 2 cups sugar, divided
- 2 teaspoons ground cinnamon
- ¾ cup finely chopped walnuts
- ¾ cup Crisco All-Vegetable Shortening
- 1 teaspoon vanilla extract
- 3 eggs

- 3 cups all-purpose flour
- 1½ teaspoons baking powder
- 1½ teaspoons baking soda
- 1 teaspoon salt
- 1½ cups sour cream

WHAT YOU DO

Preheat oven to 350 degrees Fahrenheit. Coat 10-inch tube pan with nonstick cooking spray.

In bowl, combine ¾ cup sugar, cinnamon, and walnuts. Set aside.

Cream Crisco, remaining 1¼ cups sugar, and vanilla in large bowl at medium to high speed with electric mixer. Add eggs, one at a time, beating well after each addition.

In another bowl, combine flour, baking powder, baking soda, and salt. Add alternately with sour cream to creamed mixture, mixing until blended after each addition. (Batter will be thick.) Spread half of batter in prepared pan. Spoon three-fourths of nut mixture over batter. Repeat with remaining batter and nut mixture. Bake 1 hour, or until wooden pick inserted into center comes out clean. Cool 20 minutes in pan on rack. Gently run a knife around the side of the tube pan to loosen the cake from the sides. Place upside-down plate on cake and turn both over. Remove pan. Turn cake topside up on rack. Cool completely. Slide onto cake plate to serve.

Tropical Banana Bread

Makes 1 loaf

WHAT YOU NEED

- ½ cup Crisco All-Vegetable Shortening
- 1 cup sugar
- 2 eggs, well beaten
- 1 cup mashed bananas (2 to 3 medium)
- ½ cup sour cream

- 2 cups all-purpose flour
- 1 teaspoon baking soda
- ½ teaspoon salt
- ½ cup chopped pecans or walnuts

WHAT YOU DO

Preheat oven to 350 degrees Fahrenheit. Coat 8½- × 4½- × 2½-inch loaf pan with nonstick cooking spray and dust with flour.

Combine Crisco and sugar in large bowl. Beat at medium speed with electric mixer until creamed. Add eggs, bananas, and sour cream. Beat until well blended.

Add flour, baking soda, and salt. Mix at low speed until blended. Stir in pecans (or walnuts). Spread in pan. Bake 50 to 60 minutes, or until wooden pick inserted into center comes out clean. Cool in pan 10 minutes. Remove from pan to cooling rack. Cool completely before slicing.

Strange Facts

- Procter & Gamble, the company founded in 1837 by candle maker William Procter and soap maker James Gamble in Cincinnati, Ohio, introduced Crisco, the first mass-marketed, 100 percent vegetable shortening, in 1911 to provide an economical alternative to animal fats and butter.
- To emphasize the purity of the product, the first cans of Crisco came inside an additional, removable over-wrap of white paper.
- The first cans of Crisco contained an eight-page circular cookbook cut to fit the lid.
- Procter & Gamble produced Crisco, the first solidified shortening product made entirely of vegetable oil, through a new process called hydrogenation, creating a shortening that stays in solid form year-round, regardless of temperature.

- To teach homemakers how to cook with the new vegetable shortening, Crisco published *Tested Crisco Recipes* in 1911, a cookbook available by mail.
- Starting in 1913, Procter & Gamble hired home economists to run cooking schools around the country, teaching homemakers how to use the all-vegetable shortening.
- In the 1920s, Procter & Gamble began marketing Crisco to a number of different ethnic groups, creating cookbooks in their native languages.
- In 1933, Crisco published a cookbook for kosher homemakers, featuring recipes in both English and Yiddish. Cans of Crisco were packaged with the certification of a prominent Orthodox rabbi and displayed the Parve symbol for kosher food, denoting that Crisco contained nothing animal-based.
- Crisco All-Vegetable Shortening will easily glide out of a bowl or measuring cup that was previously used to beat or measure eggs.
- Although Crisco appears solid, it actually contains more than 80 percent liquid oil. The oil is suspended in the lattice of fat solids much like honey is held in a honeycomb.

For More Recipes

Visit www.crisco.com

Dole® Pineapple

Chicken Sticks with Pineapple-Peanut Sauce

Makes 8 or 9 servings

WHAT YOU NEED

- 8 or 9 wooden or metal skewers
- 3 boneless, skinless chicken breasts
- 1 can (8 ounces) Dole Crushed Pineapple
- ⅓ cup creamy peanut butter

- 3 tablespoons packed brown sugar
- 1 tablespoon lime juice
- 1½ teaspoons curry powder
- ½ teaspoon ground ginger

WHAT YOU DO

Soak wooden skewers, if using, in water for 30 minutes. Coat broiler pan with nonstick cooking spray.

Cut chicken into strips ½ inch wide and 3 to 4 inches long. Thread two or three strips of chicken onto each skewer. Arrange skewers on broiler pan.

Drain pineapple, reserving ¼ cup juice. Combine pineapple, reserved juice, peanut butter, sugar, lime juice, curry powder, and ginger in blender or food processor. Cover; blend until smooth. Reserve ¾ cup sauce for dipping; set aside.

Brush part of the remaining pineapple sauce over chicken. Broil chicken 4 inches from heat about 10 minutes, turning once and brushing with sauce, or until chicken is no longer pink. Discard any remaining sauce used during broiling. Serve chicken with reserved pineapple sauce for dipping.

Mustard-Sauced Pineapple Chicken

Makes 4 servings

WHAT YOU NEED

- 2 tablespoons olive or vegetable oil
- 1 red bell pepper, cut into strips
- 2 leeks, thinly sliced (white parts only)
- 4 boneless, skinless chicken breasts halves
- 1 can (20 ounces) Dole Pineapple Chunks

- ¾ cup half-and-half
- 2 tablespoons mayonnaise
- 1 teaspoon cornstarch
- 2 or 3 teaspoons Dijon mustard
- 2 teaspoons chopped fresh tarragon

WHAT YOU DO

Heat oil in large skillet. Cook pepper and leeks 3 minutes. Remove from skillet.

Add chicken to skillet and cook until browned on all sides. Stir in cooked vegetables and pineapple with juice; heat to boiling. Reduce heat; cook 15 minutes more, or until chicken is no longer pink in center. Remove chicken and vegetables to platter.

Reserve 3 tablespoons juices in skillet; discard remaining juices.

Stir half-and-half, mayonnaise, cornstarch, mustard, and tarragon into skillet. Cook over medium heat, stirring constantly, until boiling. Reduce heat; cook 2 minutes more, or until thickened. Spoon sauce over chicken and vegetables. Serve immediately.

No-Bake Pineapple Squares

Makes 9 servings

WHAT YOU NEED

- 1 cup graham cracker crumbs
- ½ cup plus 2 tablespoons sugar, divided
- ¼ cup butter or margarine, melted
- 1 cup fat-free or light sour cream
- 4 ounces light cream cheese, softened

- 4 tablespoons orange marmalade or apricot fruit spread, divided
- 1 can (20 ounces) Dole Crushed Pineapple
- 1 package (1 ounce) unflavored gelatin

WHAT YOU DO

Combine graham cracker crumbs, 2 tablespoons sugar, and butter (or margarine) in 8-inch square baking dish; pat mixture firmly and evenly onto bottom of pan. Freeze 10 minutes.

Beat together sour cream, cream cheese, ½ cup sugar, and 1 tablespoon marmalade (or fruit spread) in medium bowl until smooth and blended; set aside.

Drain pineapple; reserve ¼ cup juice.

Sprinkle gelatin over reserved juice in small saucepan; let stand 1 minute.

Cook and stir over low heat until gelatin dissolves.

Beat gelatin mixture into sour cream mixture until well blended. Spoon mixture evenly over crust.

Stir together crushed pineapple and remaining 3 tablespoons marmalade (or fruit spread) in small bowl until blended. Evenly spoon over sour cream filling. Cover and refrigerate 2 hours, or until firm.

Pineapple Butterscotch Squares

Makes 12 servings

WHAT YOU NEED

- 2½ cups all-purpose flour
- 2 teaspoons baking powder
- ½ teaspoon salt
- ½ cup unsalted butter or margarine, softened
- 1 cup packed brown sugar
- ½ cup granulated sugar
- 3 eggs
- 1 teaspoon vanilla extract
- 1 can (20 ounces) Dole Crushed Pineapple, well drained
- 1 cup butterscotch chips
- ½ cup chopped walnuts, toasted
- Confectioners' sugar (optional)

WHAT YOU DO

Preheat oven to 350 degrees Fahrenheit. Coat 13- × 9-inch baking pan with nonstick cooking spray. Set aside.

Combine flour, baking powder, and salt in small bowl; set aside.

Beat together butter (or margarine), brown sugar, and granulated sugar in large bowl until creamy. Add eggs and vanilla; beat until blended. Stir in pineapple. Stir in flour mixture, butterscotch chips, and walnuts until blended.

Pour into prepared pan.

Bake 40 to 45 minutes, or until wooden pick inserted into center comes out clean. Cool completely in pan on wire rack. Dust cooled cake with confectioners' sugar, if desired. Cut into squares.

Pineapple-Glazed Pork Chops

Makes 4 servings

WHAT YOU NEED

- 4 pork loin chops, ¾- to 1-inch thick
- 1 clove garlic, finely chopped, or ¼ teaspoon garlic powder
- 1 tablespoon canola oil
- 1 can (8 ounces) Dole Crushed Pineapple
- ½ cup apple jelly
- ¼ teaspoon ground cinnamon
- ¼ teaspoon ground ginger
- 1 tablespoon water
- 1 teaspoon cornstarch

WHAT YOU DO

Brown pork with garlic in oil in large skillet. Remove pork from skillet. Spoon off fat.

Add pineapple, jelly, cinnamon, and ginger to skillet. Cook over medium heat until jelly melts.

Return pork to skillet; spoon sauce over chops. Reduce heat to low. Cover; cook 10 minutes, or until pork is no longer pink in center. Remove pork to serving platter; keep warm.

In small bowl, stir together water and cornstarch; add to skillet. Cook, stirring, until thickened. Spoon sauce over pork.

Three-Cheese Pineapple Pizza

Makes 8 servings

WHAT YOU NEED

- 1½ cups chopped fresh Dole Tropical Gold Pineapple
- 1 tablespoon chopped fresh oregano leaves or 1 teaspoon dried oreganos, crushed
- 1 (12-inch) prepared pizza crust
- ½ cup (2 ounces) shredded mozzarella cheese
- ½ cup (2 ounces) shredded Cheddar cheese
- ½ cup (2 ounces) crumbled feta cheese
- ⅓ cup sliced ripe olives

WHAT YOU DO

Preheat oven to 400 degrees Fahrenheit.

Place pineapple in colander. Stir in oregano; set aside.

Place pizza crust on baking sheet. Sprinkle pizza crust with mozzarella. Spoon pineapple mixture over mozzarella; sprinkle with Cheddar, feta, and olives.

Bake 20 to 25 minutes, or until cheese melts.

✴Strange Facts✴

- In 1851, James Drummond Dole came to Hawaii and, with an initial investment of $1,000, degrees in business and horticulture, and a love of farming, founded the first successful pineapple growing and canning operation, which he called the Hawaiian Pineapple Company.
- Dole developed the pineapple business into Hawaii's second largest industry, making pineapple available in every grocery store in the country,
- Considered an exotic fruit, the pineapple is the symbol of hospitality, and is often depicted on fine furniture.
- Dole popularized the pineapple by advertising with recipes in women's magazines.
- Thailand grows one-quarter of the world's pineapple, and Hawaii supplies virtually all the pineapples for the United States.
- Each flower on a pineapple plant blooms for only one day, and then the flowers collectively develop into a pineapple fruit.

For More Recipes

Visit www.dole.com

Brown Derby Cheese Bread

Makes 2 loaves

WHAT YOU NEED

- 2 cups Dr Pepper, room temperature, divided
- 1 tablespoon sugar
- 2½ teaspoons salt
- 2 tablespoons shortening

- 4 to 6 cups sifted flour, divided
- ½ pound Cheddar cheese, grated
- 3 packages (¼ ounce each) active dry yeast
- ½ cup warm water
- 3 tablespoons vegetable oil

WHAT YOU DO

Preheat oven to 400 degrees Fahrenheit. Coat two 9- x 5- x 3-inch loaf pans with nonstick cooking spray.

In saucepan, heat 1 cup Dr Pepper until it steams; stir in sugar, salt, and shortening. Pour into large bowl; cool to lukewarm. Stir in 2 cups flour; mix until smooth. Sprinkle cheese over dough.

In small bowl, sprinkle yeast over water. Stir until dissolved. Add to flour mixture; stir in 1 cup Dr Pepper and mix well. Add 4 cups flour all at once. Mix until smooth. Add more flour if necessary to make medium-stiff dough. Turn out onto lightly floured board. Knead until smooth and elastic (about 10 minutes). Place in bowl lightly coated with oil. Lightly oil the top of dough. Cover with clean kitchen towel and let rise in warm place, free from draft, about 1 hour, or until doubled in bulk. Punch dough down, cover, and let rest on board 5 minutes.

Divide dough in half. Shape into loaves and place in prepared pans. Cover. Let rise in warm place, free from draft about 30 minutes, or until doubled in bulk. Bake 40 minutes.

✳

Browned Beef Stew

Makes 8 servings

WHAT YOU NEED

- 3 pounds stew meat
- 3 teaspoons salt
- 1 tablespoon ground black pepper

- ¼ cup flour
- 3 tablespoons shortening
- 2 cups beef stock or bouillon

- 2 cups Dr Pepper
- 1½ cups chopped onion
- 1 cup sliced celery
- 1 cup frozen or fresh garden peas

WHAT YOU DO

Sprinkle meat with salt and pepper and dust with flour. In large stock pot or Dutch oven over high heat, brown meat in the shortening. Add stock (or bouillon), Dr Pepper, onion, and celery and reduce heat to low. Cover and cook until meat is tender, about 1½ hours. Add peas and cook at least 10 minutes longer.

Butter Spice Cupcakes

Makes 2 dozen cupcakes

WHAT YOU NEED

- ½ cup butter or margarine
- ½ cup peanut butter (smooth or crunchy)
- 1½ cups light brown sugar
- 2 eggs
- 2 cups all-purpose flour
- 3 teaspoons baking powder
- 3 tablespoons dry milk (optional)
- ⅛ teaspoon baking soda
- ½ teaspoon ground cinnamon
- ½ teaspoon ground cloves
- ½ teaspoon salt
- 1 cup Dr Pepper
- 1 teaspoon vanilla extract

WHAT YOU DO

Preheat oven to 350 degrees Fahrenheit. Coat two 12-cup muffin pans with nonstick cooking spray or line with paper baking cups.

In large bowl, cream butter (or margarine) and peanut butter. Gradually add sugar and beat until fluffy. Add eggs one at a time and beat well after each addition.

In separate bowl, sift together flour, baking powder, dry milk (if desired), baking soda, cinnamon, cloves, and salt. Blend with the creamed mixture alternately with the Dr Pepper and vanilla, starting and ending with the dry ingredients. (Do not over beat, or the cupcakes will be tough.)

Fill prepared pans one-half full. Bake approximately 25 minutes.

Candied Sweet Potatoes

Makes 8 servings

WHAT YOU NEED

- 2 pounds sweet potatoes (4 medium)
- 1 cup Dr Pepper
- ¾ cup brown sugar
- ¼ cup butter
- ½ teaspoon salt

WHAT YOU DO

Preheat oven to 375 degrees Fahrenheit.

In large pot, cover potatoes in cold water and bring to a boil. Boil potatoes 10 minutes. Place in cold water. Peel and slice crosswise and arrange in baking dish.

In small saucepan over high heat, combine Dr Pepper, sugar, butter, and salt. Bring to boil and cook for 10 minutes until the mixture reduces to a syrupy consistency. Pour syrup over potatoes.

Bake uncovered 45 minutes. Baste potatoes several times with syrup as potatoes bake.

Dr Pepper Cocoa

Makes 4 to 6 servings

WHAT YOU NEED

- 2 cups Dr Pepper
- 1½ cups milk
- 2 level tablespoons instant cocoa mix
- Whipped cream or mini marshmallows

WHAT YOU DO

In saucepan, mix Dr Pepper, milk, and cocoa mix well. Warm over moderate heat and serve with whipped cream (or marshmallows).

Heavenly Pumpkin Pie

Makes 8 servings

WHAT YOU NEED

- 12 ounces canned pumpkin
- ¾ cup brown sugar
- ½ teaspoon salt
- ½ teaspoon ground ginger
- 1 teaspoon ground cinnamon
- ¼ teaspoon ground nutmeg
- 3 eggs, slightly beaten
- 1¼ cups (10 ounces) Dr Pepper
- ¾ cup light cream
- 1 pie shell (9-inch), unbaked

WHAT YOU DO

Preheat oven to 400 degrees Fahrenheit.

In large bowl, combine pumpkin, sugar, salt, ginger, cinnamon, and nutmeg. Add eggs, mixing well. Add Dr Pepper and cream. Mix well. Pour into pie shell. Bake about 1 hour and 20 minutes, or until center is set.

Marinated Chuck Roast

Makes 8 servings

WHAT YOU NEED

- 3 to 4 pound chuck roast
- 2 cloves garlic, minced
- 2 tablespoons vegetable oil
- 1 cup Dr Pepper
- ¼ teaspoon dry mustard
- 2 tablespoons ketchup
- 1¼ teaspoons salt
- ¼ teaspoon ground black pepper
- 1 tablespoon white vinegar
- 2 teaspoons soy sauce

WHAT YOU DO

Place roast in large, resealable, plastic food-storage bag.

In separate pan, sauté garlic in oil. Add Dr Pepper, mustard, ketchup, salt, pepper, vinegar, and soy sauce, mixing well. Pour marinade over roast in storage bag and seal. Refrigerate 6 to 24 hours. Turn roast over several times so that both sides are well marinated.

Preheat oven to 325 degrees Fahrenheit.

In roasting pan, place a large piece of heavy aluminum foil. Place roast on foil, bend foil up around roast, leaving top open. Pour marinade over roast. Roast until tender, about 2½ hours. Gently turn roast several times during cooking. Slice roast against the grain.

✶ Strange Facts ✶

- Dr Pepper is the oldest major soft drink in the United States.
- In 1885, Charles Alderton, a young pharmacist educated in England, worked at Wade Morrison's Old Corner Drug Store in Waco, Texas, where he also served carbonated soft drinks at the soda fountain. Realizing that customers grew tired of drinking the same old fruit flavors, Alderton blended together several fruit-based flavors to create a new soft drink. After Wade Morrison tasted and liked the new soda, Alderton offered his new drink to fountain customers, giving birth to the soda known today as Dr Pepper.
- Legend holds that Wade Morrison moved to Texas from Rural Retreat, Virginia, where he had worked as a pharmacist for drugstore owner Dr. Charles Pepper. Patrons of Morrison's Old Corner Drug Store in Waco suggested naming the new fountain drink after the Virginia doctor.
- In the 1920s and 1930s, "Old Doc," a typical country doctor character with monocle and top hat, became the Dr Pepper trademark character. When O'Hara discovered research proving that sugar produces energy and that the average person typically experiences a sense of fatigue during a normal day at 10:30 a.m., 2:30 p.m. and 4:30 p.m., he initiated the highly successful Dr Pepper advertising slogan "Drink a Bite to Eat at 10, 2 and 4."
- In 1950, the company dropped the period after *Dr* to improve legibility on the 6½-inch bottles of the time.
- In the 1960s, Dr Pepper advertised itself as "America's Most Misunderstood Soft Drink."
- In the 1970s, the Dr Pepper Company touted the brand as "the Most Original Soft Drink Ever." In 1977, the company launched its highly memorable "Be a Pepper" campaign.

For More Recipes

Visit www.brandspeoplelove.com/csab

*French's® Mustard

Barbecued Chicken

Makes 8 servings

WHAT YOU NEED

- 2 pounds boneless skinless chicken breast halves or thighs
- ¾ cup packed light brown sugar, divided
- ¾ cup French's Classic Yellow Mustard

- ⅔ cup fresh lemon juice
- 2 tablespoons olive oil
- 2 tablespoons soy sauce

WHAT YOU DO

Place chicken into large, resealable, plastic food-storage bag.

Combine ½ cup brown sugar, mustard, lemon juice, oil, and soy sauce in 4-cup measure or medium bowl; mix well. Pour 1 cup mixture over chicken. Seal bag; marinate in refrigerator 1 hour or overnight.

Pour remaining mustard mixture into small saucepan. Stir in remaining ¼ cup sugar. Bring to a boil. Reduce heat; simmer 5 minutes, or until sugar is dissolved and mixture thickens slightly, stirring often. Reserve for serving sauce.

Preheat grill.

Place chicken on well-oiled rack, reserving marinade. Grill over high heat 10 to 15 minutes, or until chicken is no longer pink in center, turning and basting once with marinade. (Do not baste during last 5 minutes of cooking.) Discard any remaining marinade. Serve chicken with reserved sauce.

Hawaiian Turkey Kabobs

Makes 4 servings

WHAT YOU NEED

- 4 to 6 metal or wooden skewers
- 1 pound thin turkey cutlets
- 1 can (8 ounces) pineapple chunks, drained
- 1 green bell pepper, cut into 1-inch chunks
- 1 cup cherry tomatoes

- 2 green onions, cut into 1-inch pieces
- ⅔ cup French's Classic Yellow Mustard
- ¼ cup honey
- 1 teaspoon ground ginger

WHAT YOU DO

Coat grill rack with nonstick cooking spray and preheat grill. If using wooden skewers, soak them for 30 minutes.

Cut turkey into thin strips. Thread turkey accordion-style alternately with pineapple, peppers, tomatoes, and onions onto skewers.

Combine mustard, honey, and ginger in small bowl; brush half of the mixture onto skewers.

Place skewers on prepared rack. Grill over high heat 15 minutes, or until turkey is no longer pink in center, turning and basing with remaining mustard mixture. Discard unused mustard mixture. Serve warm.

Home-Style Baked Beans

Makes 8 to 10 servings

WHAT YOU NEED

- 1 large green or red bell pepper, chopped, plus additional for garnish
- 1 small onion, chopped
- 2 strips uncooked bacon, finely chopped

- 3 cans (16 ounces each) pork and beans
- ½ cup French's Classic Yellow Mustard
- ½ cup French's Worcestershire Sauce
- ½ cup brown sugar

WHAT YOU DO

Place pepper, onion, and bacon in microwave-safe 3-quart bowl. Cover loosely with waxed paper. Microwave on high 5 minutes, or until bacon is partially cooked.

Stir in pork and beans, mustard, Worcestershire sauce, and sugar. Microwave, uncovered, on high, 20 minutes, or until heated through and mixture is slightly thickened; stirring twice. Top with additional chopped peppers, if desired.

Note: Conventional oven directions: Sauté bacon and vegetables in large nonstick skillet until bacon is cooked; transfer to casserole. Stir in remaining ingredients. Bake at 400 degrees Fahrenheit for 45 to 50 minutes, stirring occasionally.

Marinade Magic

Makes 4 to 6 servings

WHAT YOU NEED

- 1 cup Italian salad dressing
- ⅓ cup French's Classic Yellow Mustard
- 3 pounds chicken or ribs

WHAT YOU DO

In bowl, combine salad dressing with mustard. Marinate chicken (or ribs) in refrigerator for several hours.

Preheat grill. Place chicken (or ribs) on the rack and cook until no longer pink.

Rosemary's Chicken

Makes 4 servings

WHAT YOU NEED

- 4 large boneless, skinless chicken breast halves (1½ pounds)
- ¼ cup French's Classic Yellow Mustard
- ¼ cup orange juice concentrate, undiluted
- 2 tablespoons cider vinegar
- 2 teaspoons dried rosemary leaves, crushed
- 4 strips thick sliced bacon

WHAT YOU DO

Place chicken in large, resealable, plastic food-storage bag.

In bowl, combine mustard, orange juice concentrate, vinegar, and rosemary. Pour over chicken. Seal bag and marinate in refrigerator 30 minutes.

Preheat grill.

Wrap 1 strip bacon around each piece of chicken; secure with wooden toothpicks.

Grill chicken over medium heat 25 minutes, or until chicken is no longer pink, turning and basting often. (Do not baste chicken during last 10 minutes of cooking.) Discard unused marinade. Remove toothpicks before serving.

Southern Barbecue Sauce

Makes 1¼ cups

WHAT YOU NEED

- ¼ cup French's Classic Yellow Mustard
- 1 cup of your favorite barbecue sauce

WHAT YOU DO

In bowl, combine mustard and barbecue sauce.

Tropical Fruit Dip

Makes 1 serving

WHAT YOU NEED

- ¼ cup French's Classic Yellow Mustard
- ¼ cup honey
- ½ cup plain yogurt
- 1 teaspoon brown sugar
- 1 teaspoon grated lime peel
- Fresh strawberries
- Fresh pineapple, sliced and cut into wedges
- Fresh peaches, peeled, pitted, and sliced

WHAT YOU DO

In bowl, combine mustard, honey, and yogurt, blending well. Add sugar and lime peel, stirring thoroughly. Serve with strawberries, pineapple, and peaches.

Zesty Baked Beans

Makes 4 (1-cup) servings

WHAT YOU NEED

- ½ cup French's Mustard
- 2 cans (16 ounces each) pork and beans

WHAT YOU DO

In saucepan, combine mustard and beans. Heat and serve.

Zesty Grilled Asparagus

Makes 6 servings

WHAT YOU NEED

- ¼ cup French's Classic Yellow Mustard
- 3 tablespoons olive oil
- 3 tablespoons minced fresh dill or
    2 teaspoons dried dill weed

- 3 tablespoons lemon juice
- 1 tablespoon grated lemon peel
- ⅛ teaspoon ground black pepper
- 2 pounds asparagus, washed and trimmed

WHAT YOU DO

Preheat grill. Combine mustard, oil, dill, lemon juice, lemon peel, and pepper in small bowl.

Brush mixture on asparagus. Grill over medium-high heat 5 minutes, or until asparagus are fork-tender, turning and basting often with mustard mixture.

Zesty Potato Salad

Makes 8 servings

WHAT YOU NEED

- 1½ pounds small red skin potatoes, quartered
- ⅓ cup olive oil
- ¼ cup French's Classic Yellow Mustard
- 3 tablespoons lemon juice
- ¼ teaspoon ground black pepper

- 1 cup diagonally sliced celery
- 1 bell pepper (green, red, or yellow), cut
    into strips
- 2 green onions, thinly sliced
- ¼ cup minced fresh parsley

WHAT YOU DO

Cook potatoes in boiling, salted water to cover 15 minutes, or until tender but firm; rinse with cold water and drain.

Combine oil, mustard, lemon juice, and black pepper in large bowl. Add potatoes, celery, bell pepper, onion, and parsley; toss well to coat evenly. Cover; refrigerate 1 hour before serving.

✳ Strange Facts ✳

- Around 3000 b.c.e., the ancient Chinese and Indians first cultivated and used mustard.
- According to Greek mythology, Aesculapius, the Greek god of medicine and healing, was credited with having created mustard.
- In the New Testament, Jesus compares the kingdom to God to a mustard seed (Mark 4).
- In his book *Natural History*, Roman author and philosopher Pliny the Elder (33–79 c.e.) outlined numerous medicinal uses of mustard. Hippocrates, the Greek physician and philosopher, used mustard in poultices to treat bronchitis, pneumonia, and rheumatism. Nicholas Culpeper (1616-1654), a famous seventeenth century herbalist and physician, recommended the use of mustard for fevers, sciatica, and rheumatic pains.
- In the first century c.e., retired Roman legionnaire Lucius Junius Moderatus published his book *De Re Rustica* ("On Agriculture"), containing one of the earliest recipes for preparing mustard.
- The Romans turned mustard into a paste by adding grape juice, vinegar, oil, and honey. The Romans are credited with having brought mustard to Gaul (modern-day France), and in the thirteenth century, the Provost of Paris granted the vinegar makers of Dijon the right to make mustard, paving the way for Dijon to become the French capital of mustard.
- In the fourteenth century, Dijon's mustard makers adopted Duke Philip the Bold's motto, *"Mout me Tarde"* ("I ardently desire"). Legend holds that this motto was shortened to *"Moustarde"*—the French name for the condiment.
- King Louis XI of France (1423–83) carried his own personal pot of mustard, made for him by a Dijon mustard maker, wherever he went.
- In William Shakespeare's play *As You Like It*, Touchstone says, "The mustard was good."

- Mustard has been used throughout history as a symbol of fertility because of the mustard plant's prolificacy.
- Around 1720 in Durham, England, a Mrs. Clements developed a process for extracting the husk from mustard seeds and milling a smooth mustard powder, going into full production in 1729.
- In eighteenth century France, Maurice Grey developed a secret recipe for a strong mustard made with white wine. keeping his mustard recipe in a safe. He teamed up with financier Monsuier Poupon, manufacturing what became known as Grey Poupon mustard.
- Colman's, established in Norwich, became synonymous with mustard in Britain.
- In 1880, fifty-seven-year-old Robert T. French founded a spice company in the hopes of providing a livelihood for his three sons. By 1885 the company was operating out of an old flour mill in Rochester, New York, eventually manufacturing mustard. In 1904, the Frenchs concocted a mild, bright-yellow mustard that quickly became a national favorite.
- The R. T. French Company was acquired by Reckitt & Colman, the company formed by the 1938 merger of Reckitt & Sons (a flour milling business started by Isaac Reckitt in England in 1819) and J. and J. Colman (a flour and mustard seed mill founded in Norwich, England, in 1804 by Jeremiah Colman).
- Colonel Mustard is a character in the board game "Clue."
- The Mount Horeb Mustard Museum in Mount Horeb, Wisconsin, houses the largest collection of mustards in the world, with more than 4,400 different types of mustard, and publishes a newsletter called *The Proper Mustard*.
- Colman's Mustard Shop and Museum in Royal Arcade, Norwich, England, displays the history of mustard production and sells a selection of mustards, pots, and mustard paraphernalia emblazoned with the company name.
- The Beatles' album Abbey Road contains the song "Mean Mr. Mustard."
- French's Mustard, the best-selling mustard in the world, is 100 percent natural.

For More Recipes

Visit www.frenchs.com

French's® Original French Fried Onions

Classic Pizza

Makes 8 servings

WHAT YOU NEED

- Cornmeal
- 8 ounces pizza dough
- 1 cup barbecue sauce

- 1½ cups French's Original French Fried Onions
- 8 ounces shredded mozzarella cheese

WHAT YOU DO

Preheat oven to 500 degrees Fahrenheit.

On work surface sprinkled with cornmeal, stretch or pat dough into 16-inch circle. Place on baking sheet. Spread barbecue sauce over dough. Sprinkle onions over sauce and top with cheese. Bake 8 to 10 minutes until bottom of crust is browned and crispy and cheese is melted.

Variations: Top pizza with diced bell peppers, sliced mushrooms, or sliced pepperoni before topping with cheese. For a spicy Southwest taste, try Monterey Jack cheese with jalapeño peppers.

Creamy Mashed Potato Bake

Makes 6 servings

WHAT YOU NEED

- 3 cups mashed potatoes
- 1 cup sour cream
- ¼ cup milk
- ¼ teaspoon garlic powder

- 1⅓ cups French's Original French Fried Onions, divided
- 1 cup shredded Cheddar cheese, divided

WHAT YOU DO

Preheat oven to 350 degree Fahrenheit.

In bowl, combine mashed potatoes, sour cream, milk, and garlic powder.

Spoon half the mixture into 2-quart casserole. Sprinkle with ⅔ cup French Fried Onions and ½ cup cheese. Top with remaining potato mixture.

Bake 30 minutes, or until hot. Top with remaining ⅔ cup onions and ½ cup cheese. Bake 5 minutes, or until onions are golden.

Crispy Lemon-Garlic Fish Fillets

Makes 4 servings

WHAT YOU NEED

- 1⅓ cups French's Original French Fried Onions
- 1 teaspoon grated lemon zest
- 1 teaspoon minced garlic
- 1 egg, beaten
- 4 tilapia or red snapper fish fillets, ½ inch thick

WHAT YOU DO

Preheat oven to 400 degrees Fahrenheit.

Place onions, lemon zest, and garlic in large, resealable, plastic food-storage bag. Seal bag. Lightly crush onions with hands or with rolling pin. Shake to combine.

Place egg in small bowl. Dip fish into egg; then firmly coat with seasoned onion crumbs. Place fish on baking sheet. Sprinkle with additional crumbs, if desired.

Bake 15 to 20 minutes, or until fish flakes easily with fork.

Serving Suggestion: Pair with rice and steamed vegetables.

Crunchy Chicken Caesar Salad

Makes 6 servings

WHAT YOU NEED

- 1⅓ cups French's Original French Fried Onions
- 12 cups salad greens
- 4 cups sliced cooked chicken
- 1 tomato, cut into wedges
- 1 cup Caesar salad dressing

WHAT YOU DO

Place onions in microwave-safe bowl and microwave onions 1 minute on high. Toss salad with chicken and tomato. Top with onions. Serve with dressing.

Crunchy Onion Chicken Bake

Makes 4 servings

WHAT YOU NEED

- 1⅓ cups French's Original French Fried Onions
- ¼ cup grated Parmesan cheese

- 1 egg, beaten
- 4 boneless skinless chicken breast halves

WHAT YOU DO

Preheat oven to 400 degrees Fahrenheit.

Place onions into large, resealable, plastic food-storage bag. Lightly crush onions with hands or with rolling pin.

Place egg in small bowl. Dip chicken into egg; then coat with onion crumbs, pressing firmly to adhere. Place chicken on baking sheet. Sprinkle with additional crumbs, if desired.

Bake 20 minutes, or until chicken is no longer pink in center.

French Onion Bread

Makes 12 breadsticks

WHAT YOU NEED

- 1⅓ cups French's Original French Fried Onions
- ¼ cup grated Parmesan cheese

- 1 container (11 ounces) refrigerated soft bread sticks
- 1 egg white, beaten

WHAT YOU DO

Preheat oven to 350 degrees Fahrenheit.

Place onions into large, resealable, plastic food-storage bag. Lightly crush onions with hands or with rolling pin.

Combine onions and cheese in shallow bowl.

Separate dough into 12 pieces on a sheet of waxed paper.

Brush one side of dough with egg white. Dip pieces wet side down into crumbs, pressing firmly. Baste top surface with egg white and dip into crumbs.

Twist dough to form a spiral. Arrange on an ungreased baking sheet. Repeat with the remaining breadsticks. Bake 15 to 20 minutes, or until golden brown.

Green Bean Casserole

Makes 6 servings

WHAT YOU NEED

- ¾ cup milk
- ⅛ teaspoon ground black pepper
- 1 can (10¾ ounces) cream of mushroom soup

- 2 cans (14½ ounces each) green beans, cut and drained, or 2 packages (9 ounces each) frozen cut green beans, thawed
- 1⅓ cups French's Original French Fried Onions, divided

WHAT YOU DO

Preheat oven to 350 degrees Fahrenheit.

In 1½-quart baking dish, mix milk, pepper, soup, beans, and ⅔ cup onions. Bake 30 minutes, or until hot throughout; stir. Top with ⅔ cup onions. Bake 5 minutes more, or until onions are golden.

Savory Onion Focaccia

Makes 8 servings

WHAT YOU NEED

- 1¼ pounds pizza dough
- 1 tablespoon olive oil, plus more as needed, divided
- 1 clove garlic, minced
- 1½ cups French's Original French Fried Onions

- 6 ounces shredded mozzarella cheese
- 2 Roma tomatoes, thinly sliced
- ¼ cup grated Parmesan cheese
- 2 teaspoons fresh rosemary leaves, chopped

WHAT YOU DO

Preheat oven to 450 degrees Fahrenheit. Lightly coat half sheet pan (18 × 13 inches) with nonstick cooking spray.

Roll or pat dough to fit pan; place into pan. Combine 1 tablespoon oil with garlic in bowl. Brush on dough. Cover with a clean kitchen towel; let rise in warm place 30 minutes.

Bake dough 20 minutes, or until bottom of crust is golden.

Layer half the onions, mozzarella, tomatoes, Parmesan, and rosemary on top of crust. Repeat layers. Bake 5 to 8 minutes until cheese melts and onions are golden. Cut into 3-inch squares to serve.

✶ Strange Facts ✶

- Every Thanksgiving more than thirty million Americans make Green Bean Casserole using French's Original French Fried Onions.
- French's Original French Fried Onions can be substituted for bread crumbs in recipes, making a zesty alternative.
- For a taste treat, sprinkle French's Original French Fried Onions on top of baked or mashed potatoes.
- In 1986, Reckitt & Colman acquired Durkee Famous Foods and renamed Durkee's French Fried Onions as French's Original French Fried Onions.

For More Recipes

Visit www.frenchs.com

Chili Pie Casserole

Makes 4 to 6 servings

WHAT YOU NEED

- 3 cups Fritos Corn Chips, divided
- 1 large onion, chopped
- 1 cup grated American cheese, divided
- 1 can (19 ounces) chili

WHAT YOU DO

Preheat oven to 350 degrees Fahrenheit.

Sprinkle 2 cups corn chips in baking dish. Arrange onion and half of cheese on top. Pour chili over onion and cheese. Top with remaining corn chips and cheese. Bake 15 to 20 minutes until hot and bubbly.

Chocolate Jets

Makes 24 pieces

WHAT YOU NEED

- 1 package (6 ounces) semi-sweet chocolate pieces
- 1½ cups lightly crushed Fritos Corn Chips

WHAT YOU DO

Line baking sheet with waxed paper. Set aside.

Melt chocolate in double boiler. Stir in corn chips until thoroughly covered with chocolate. Drop by spoonfuls onto baking sheet and place in the refrigerator. Serve chilled.

Fix-A-Pizza

Makes 8 servings

WHAT YOU NEED

- 4 cups Fritos Corn Chips
- ½ pound mozzarella cheese, sliced thin
- 1 pound ground beef
- 1 clove garlic, minced
- 1 can (12 ounces) tomato paste
- 1 teaspoon salt
- ¼ teaspoon ground black pepper
- 1 teaspoon dried oregano

- 1 can (3 ounces) mushrooms, drained and sliced
- 3 eggs, beaten
- ½ cup canned tomatoes, drained and cut into pieces
- ½ cup grated sharp Cheddar cheese
- 1 can (2 ounces) anchovies
- ½ cup grated Parmesan cheese

WHAT YOU DO

Preheat oven to 375 degrees Fahrenheit.

Arrange corn chips in 12-inch pizza pan. Cover with mozzarella.

In saucepan, sauté beef with garlic until light brown. Add tomato paste, salt, pepper, oregano, mushrooms, and eggs. Mix well. Spread beef mixture over cheese. Sprinkle with tomatoes, Cheddar, and anchovies. Top with Parmesan. Bake 20 minutes.

Fritos Chili Pie in a Bag

Makes 4 servings

WHAT YOU NEED

- 4 cups Fritos Corn Chips
- 1 can (15 ounces) no-bean chili
- 1½ cups shredded Cheddar cheese

- Sour cream
- Sliced green onions

WHAT YOU DO

Place corn chips in large microwave-safe bowl. Add chili and cheese. Microwave mixture on high 3 to 4 minutes, or until hot. Before serving, toss mixture gently. Serve with sour cream and onions.

Frito Salad

Makes 1 serving

WHAT YOU NEED

- Salad mix
- Salad dressing of choice
- Fritos Corn Chips

WHAT YOU DO

Put desired amount of salad in bowl. Add dressing and top with corn chips.

Mexicana Casserole

Makes 8 servings

WHAT YOU NEED

- 1 pound ground beef
- ½ cup chopped yellow onion
- 1 can (15 ounces) no-bean chili
- 1 can (2¼ ounces) sliced ripe olives
- 1 container (12 ounces) cottage cheese
- 1 cup sour cream
- 1 cup shredded Cheddar cheese, divided
- 1 package (10 ounces) Fritos Corn Chips

WHAT YOU DO

Preheat oven to 350 degrees Fahrenheit.

In large skillet, cook ground beef and onion until lightly browned and cooked through; drain. Stir chili and olives into the ground beef mixture.

In another bowl, combine the cottage cheese, sour cream, and ½ cup Cheddar cheese.

In 9- x 13-inch baking dish, layer one-third of the corn chips; top with half of the ground beef mixture and half of the cheese mixture. Repeat layers. Top with remaining corn chips and sprinkle with remaining Cheddar cheese.

Bake 30 minutes, or until warmed through.

COOKING WITH A HAIR DRYER

- **Frost a cake like an expert.** To give the frosting on your homemade cakes that professional silky look, frost the cake as usual and then set your hair dryer on "warm" and blow-dry the frosting, melting it slightly until the frosting appears smooth.
- **Make the perfect Jell-O mold.** Before you attempt to slide a finished Jell-O mold out of the mold itself, set a hair dryer on "warm" and gently warm the mold. The gelatin will slide out of the mold easily and effortlessly.
- **Prevent clumping in salt and pepper shakers.** After washing salt and pepper shakers, use a hair dryer set on "hot" to dry the insides thoroughly. This way, no moisture will be left inside the shakers to clump up the salt and pepper.
- **Dry salad greens.** Instead of serving wet salad greens, set a hair dryer on "cool" and gently blow the salad greens dry.
- **Soften ice cream to make scooping easier.** Set the hair dyer on "hot" to soften ice cream enough to scoop it out of the container.
- **Remove a cake from a wax-paper lined pan.** Set the hair dryer on "hot" and gently run it along the bottom of the pan to soften the wax from the wax paper. Invert the pan and let the cake slide out.

Strange Facts

- In 1932, Elmer Doolin, an ice cream maker in San Antonio, Texas, stopped for lunch at a small San Antonio café, where he bought a plain package of corn chips made from corn dough, used for centuries as bread by Mexicans. In 1938, Doolin tracked down the maker of the corn chips and for one hundred dollars (which he had to borrow from his mother, who hocked her wedding ring), bought the recipe and the manufacturing equipment—a converted hand-operated potato slicer. In 1945, the Frito Company, distributing Fritos Corn Chips across the Southwest, granted H.W. Lay Company the right to manufacture and distribute Fritos Corn Chips in the Southeast.

- Doolin produced Fritos Corn Chips in his mother's kitchen, making ten pounds of chips per hour, and sold the chips out of the back of his Model T Ford, earning a profit as high as two dollars a day.
- In 1961, the Frito Company merged with the H.W. Lay Company, founded in 1932 by college drop-out Herman W. Lay, to form Frito-Lay.
- In 1959, Vice President Richard Nixon took Fritos to Soviet leader Nikita Krushchev.
- Tex Avery, the legendary animator who created Daffy Duck, Droopy, and a host of other characters, created the Frito Bandito. A Mexican-American group threatened to sue the company for disparaging Mexicans.
- In 1966, Frito-Lay introduced Doritos.

For More Recipes

Visit www.fritolay.com

Glazed Frank Kabobs

Makes 4 (1-kabob) servings

WHAT YOU NEED

- 4 metal or wooden skewers
- ½ cup chili sauce
- 3 tablespoons brown sugar
- 2 tablespoons prepared mustard
- 1 package (12 ounces) Hebrew National Beef Franks, cut into 16 (1½-inch) pieces
- 1 small red onion, cut into ½-inch wedges
- 1 medium red bell pepper, cut into 1-inch pieces
- 1 medium green bell pepper, cut into 1-inch pieces
- 2 medium ears fresh corn, shucked, cut into 1-inch-thick slices

WHAT YOU DO

If using wooden skewers, soak 30 minutes. Coat cold grate of outdoor grill with nonstick cooking spray. Preheat grill to medium heat.

Combine chili sauce, brown sugar, and mustard in small bowl until blended. Set aside.

Thread franks, onion, red pepper, green pepper, and corn alternately on 4 skewers.

Place kabobs on grill. Brush with half of the sauce; grill 5 minutes. Turn kabobs; brush with remaining sauce. Grill 5 minutes more, or until vegetables are tender and franks are hot.

Grilled Dinner Franks with Salsa Cruda

Makes 4 servings

WHAT YOU NEED

- 1 large tomato, seeded and chopped (about 1 cup)
- 2 tablespoons finely chopped green bell pepper
- 2 tablespoons finely chopped red onion
- 2 tablespoons finely chopped fresh cilantro
- 1 jalapeño pepper, seeded and finely chopped
- ¼ teaspoon salt
- 1 package (16 ounces) Hebrew National Beef Franks
- 4 flour tortillas (optional)

WHAT YOU DO

Prepare outdoor grill for medium heat.

Combine tomato, bell pepper, onion, cilantro, jalapeño pepper, and salt in medium bowl. Set aside.

Grill franks 15 minutes, or until heated through and lightly browned, turning occasionally.

Wrap franks in tortillas, if desired. Serve franks topped with salsa.

Sizzling Franks with Grilled Corn and Black Beans

Makes 7 servings

WHAT YOU NEED

- 2 ears fresh corn, shucked
- 2 tablespoons vegetable oil, divided
- 1 package (12 ounces) Hebrew National Beef Franks
- ½ medium red onion, chopped (about ½ cup)

- ½ red bell pepper, chopped (about ½ cup)
- 1 can (15 ounces) black beans, rinsed and drained
- ½ cup chunky salsa
- Chopped fresh cilantro (optional)

WHAT YOU DO

Coat cold grate of outdoor grill with nonstick cooking spray. Prepare grill for medium heat.

Brush corn with 1 tablespoon oil. Grill corn and franks 10 minutes, or until corn is tender and franks are hot.

Heat remaining 1 tablespoon oil in medium saucepan over medium-high heat. Add onion; cook and stir 3 minutes. Stir in pepper; cook and stir 2 minutes. Add beans and salsa. Cover; simmer 5 minutes, or until heated through.

Cut corn from cobs; discard cobs. Stir corn into bean mixture. Serve with grilled franks. Top with cilantro, if desired.

Skillet Franks and Potatoes

Makes 4 servings

WHAT YOU NEED

- 1 package (12 ounces) Hebrew National Beef Franks
- 3 tablespoons vegetable oil, divided
- 4 medium red potatoes, chopped, boiled, and drained (about 3 cups)
- 1 large onion, chopped (about 1 cup)
- 1 medium green bell pepper, chopped (about 1 cup)
- 1 teaspoon ground sage
- ½ teaspoon salt
- ¼ teaspoon ground black pepper
- 2 tablespoons chopped fresh parsley (optional)

WHAT YOU DO

Make shallow cuts in franks (no more than halfway through) about every inch. Heat 1 tablespoon oil in large nonstick skillet over medium heat. Add franks; heat 5 minutes, or until browned, turning occasionally. Remove franks from skillet; set aside.

Add remaining 2 tablespoons oil, potatoes, onion, and bell pepper to skillet. Cook and stir 12 minutes, or until potatoes are golden brown. Stir in sage, salt, and black pepper; mix well.

Return franks to skillet. Cook 5 minutes, or until heated through, turning franks once halfway through cooking time. Sprinkle with parsley, if desired.

Three Bean and Franks Bake

Makes 8 (1-cup) servings

WHAT YOU NEED

- 1 medium onion, chopped (about ½ cup)
- 2 cloves garlic, minced
- 1 tablespoon vegetable oil
- 1 medium red bell pepper, chopped (about 1 cup)
- 1 medium green bell pepper, chopped (about 1 cup)
- 1 can (16 ounces) vegetarian baked beans
- 1 can (15 ounces) butter beans, rinsed and drained
- 1 can (15 ounces) red or kidney beans, rinsed and drained
- ½ cup ketchup
- ½ cup firmly packed brown sugar
- 2 tablespoons cider vinegar
- 1 tablespoon prepared mustard
- 1 package (12 ounces) Hebrew National Beef Franks, cut into 1-inch pieces

WHAT YOU DO

Preheat oven to 350 degrees Fahrenheit.

Cook onion and garlic in oil in large saucepan over medium heat 8 minutes, stirring frequently. Add bell peppers; cook 5 minutes, stirring frequently.

Stir in baked beans, butter beans, red (or kidney) beans, ketchup, sugar, vinegar, and mustard; mix well. Stir franks into bean mixture. Remove from heat.

Spoon mixture into 2-quart casserole or 8- x 8-inch baking dish. Bake 40 minutes, or until hot and bubbly.

Strange Facts

- In 1905, the Hebrew National Kosher Sausage Factory, Inc., located in a six-story walk-up on East Broadway on the Lower East Side of Manhattan, processed kosher meats for New York's numerous delicatessen restaurants and served a predominantly Jewish neighborhood composed of immigrants from Germany and Eastern Europe.

- In 1928, Isadore Pinckowitz (who later changed his last name to Pines), a Romanian immigrant butcher who began his career peddling meat from the back of a horse-drawn wagon, bought the Hebrew National Kosher Sausage Factory and began selling kosher sausages and hot dogs to many of New York's deli restaurants and for Waldbaums, the city's largest grocery chain.
- In 1935, Isadore's son Leonard took over the business.
- During the 1940s, Hebrew National began creating products especially for supermarkets, widening the appeal of kosher foods to mass consumers.
- In 1965, Hebrew National hot dogs launched an advertising campaign featuring the popular slogan "We Answer to a Higher Authority."
- In 1968, Houston-based Riviana Foods purchased the Hebrew National Company. In 1976, Riviana foods was acquired by the Colgate-Palmolive Company. Four years later, Isidore "Skip" Pines, Leonard's son, repurchased the company from Colgate-Palmolive and in 1986 changed the company's name to National Foods.
- ConAgra, Inc. acquired National Foods in 1993, sold off the non-kosher National Deli business in 2001, to focus on developing the kosher product line and the Hebrew National brand.

For More Recipes

Visit www.hebrewnational.com

Creole Sauce

Makes 1 cup

WHAT YOU NEED

- 1 medium onion, halved and thinly sliced
- ¼ cup chopped green bell pepper
- 1 tablespoon butter or margarine
- ½ cup Heinz Ketchup
- 2 tablespoons water
- ¼ teaspoon salt
- Dash hot pepper sauce
- Dash ground black pepper
- 1 tablespoon Worcestershire sauce

WHAT YOU DO

In saucepan, sauté onion and bell pepper in butter (or margarine) until tender. Stir in ketchup, water, salt, hot pepper sauce, black pepper, and Worcestershire sauce. Simmer, uncovered, 10 minutes, stirring occasionally. Serve warm.

Serving Suggestion: Try this sauce over omelets, meat loaf, and baked or broiled fish.

Heinz Ketchup Basic Barbecue Sauce

Makes about ¾ cup

WHAT YOU NEED

- ¼ cup water
- ¼ teaspoon celery seeds
- ½ teaspoon salt
- 1 teaspoon chili powder
- ¼ teaspoon hot pepper sauce
- 2 tablespoons white vinegar
- ½ cup Heinz Ketchup
- 2 tablespoons Worcestershire sauce
- 2 tablespoons brown sugar

WHAT YOU DO

In saucepan, combine all ingredients. Simmer, uncovered, 10 minutes.

Serving Suggestion: Brush this sauce on ribs or chicken during the last 10 minutes of grilling or broiling.

Heinz Ketchup's Love Apple Pie

Makes 8 servings

WHAT YOU NEED

- ⅓ cup Heinz Ketchup
- 2 teaspoons lemon juice
- 6 cups (about 2 pounds) sliced, peeled tart cooking apples, such as Granny Smith
- ⅓ cup sugar, plus more as needed
- ⅔ cup all-purpose flour
- 1 teaspoon cinnamon
- ⅓ cup unsalted butter or margarine, softened
- 1 pie shell (9-inch), unbaked

WHAT YOU DO

Preheat oven to 425 degrees Fahrenheit.

Blend ketchup and lemon juice; combine with apples in medium bowl. If apples are very tart, add 1 to 2 tablespoons sugar to ketchup mixture.

For topping, combine flour, ⅓ cup sugar, and cinnamon; cut in butter (or margarine) until thoroughly mixed.

Fill pie shell with apples; sprinkle topping over apples. Bake 40 to 45 minutes, or until apples are cooked.

Serving Suggestion: Top a warm slice of pie with a scoop of ice cream.

Mocha Brownies

Makes 24 brownies

WHAT YOU NEED

- ½ cup unsalted butter
- ¾ cup Heinz Ketchup
- 2 cups sugar
- 1¼ cups all-purpose flour
- ¾ cup unsweetened cocoa powder
- ½ teaspoon baking soda
- 2 tablespoons instant espresso
- ½ teaspoon salt
- 4 large eggs
- 2 teaspoons vanilla extract
- 1 cup chopped walnuts

WHAT YOU DO

Preheat oven to 350 degrees Fahrenheit. Coat 13- x 9- x 2-inch baking pan with nonstick cooking spray; set aside.

Melt butter in saucepan. Add ketchup to melted butter and stir to combine; set aside.

In medium bowl, whisk together sugar, flour, cocoa powder, baking soda, espresso, and salt. Add to the butter/ketchup mixture and stir until well blended. Stir in eggs and vanilla; mix until smooth. Stir in walnuts. Bake 30 minutes, or until brownies just start to pull away from the edges of the pan. Allow brownies to cool completely in pan on a wire rack. Cut brownies into 2-inch squares.

Secret Spice Cookies

Makes approximately 24 cookies

WHAT YOU NEED

- 1 cup oat flour
- 1 cup all-purpose flour
- 2 teaspoons baking soda
- 2 teaspoons ground ginger
- 1 teaspoon ground cinnamon
- ½ teaspoon ground allspice
- ½ teaspoon salt

- 1 cup sugar, plus more as needed
- ⅓ cup Heinz Ketchup
- ⅓ cup canola oil
- 1 large egg
- ¼ cup molasses
- 1 teaspoon vanilla extract

WHAT YOU DO

Preheat oven to 350 degrees Fahrenheit. Line baking sheet with parchment paper or Silpat baking mat.

Combine oat flour, all-purpose flour, baking soda, ginger, cinnamon, allspice, and salt in medium bowl; whisk to combine and set aside.

In large bowl, combine 1 cup sugar, ketchup, and oil. Using an electric mixer, beat on medium speed for 2 minutes. Add egg, molasses, and vanilla and continue to beat, just until mixture is combined. Reduce speed to low and gradually add flour mixture, until thoroughly combined.

Fill the bottom of shallow bowl with sugar. Using a #40 scoop (approximately 1½ tablespoons), form dough into balls then roll in additional sugar to coat. Arrange dough balls 2 inches apart on prepared baking sheet. Bake 10 to 12 minutes until cookies are golden brown around the edges and cracked on top. Let cool 2 minutes on baking sheet. Transfer to a wire rack to finish cooling.

Tampa Bay Spicy Shrimp

Makes 6 servings

WHAT YOU NEED

- Steamed crab seasoning
- ½ cup vegetable oil
- ¼ cup Heinz Ketchup
- ¼ cup apple cider vinegar
- 2 tablespoons Worcestershire sauce
- 1 tablespoon light brown sugar
- Pinch salt

- ½ teaspoon dry mustard
- Hot pepper sauce
- 3 bay leaves
- 2 pounds uncooked shrimp, peeled and deveined
- 1 cup sliced onion

WHAT YOU DO

Bring pot of water to a boil and season with steamed crab seasoning.

In large bowl, combine oil, ketchup, vinegar, Worcestershire sauce, sugar, salt, mustard, pepper sauce, and bay leaves. Set aside.

Place shrimp in the rapidly boiling water and cook for 3 minutes, or until shrimp are bright pink and cooked. Drain.

Immediately toss shrimp in the marinade. Add onion. Cover and refrigerate for at least 4 hours. Remove from the refrigerator just before serving.

Serving Suggestion: While the shrimp is marinating, grill some garlic bread to serve alongside.

Strange Facts

- In the seventeenth century, English sailors whose ships were docked in Singapore discovered that local natives ate *kechap*—a tangy sauce made from fish brine, herbs, and spices—with their fish and fowl dishes. Upon returning home to Britain, the sailors, yearning for the sauce, tried to recreate it, substituting mushrooms, walnuts, cucumbers, and later, tomatoes, for the ingredients they were missing. *Ketchup*, as the British called the surrogate sauce, became a national favorite.
- In the seventeenth century, Maine sea captains acquired a taste for Singaporean

kechap and for the exotic tomato, relished in Mexico and the Spanish West Indies. Maine families were soon growing tomatoes in their gardens and making ketchup to use on codfish cakes, baked beans, and meat.

- Making ketchup at home required that the tomatoes be parboiled and peeled. The puree had to be continually stirred on the stove to prevent the pulp from sticking to the cauldron and burning.
- In 1876, Henry J. Heinz introduced the first mass-produced, bottled ketchup. Today, ketchup is the best-known condiment in the world, and Heinz's Ketchup is the best-selling ketchup in the United States.
- In the 1950s, after developing aerosol whipped cream, Bunny Lapin, the creator of Reddi-wip, tried to develop aerosol ketchup.

For More Recipes

Visit www.heinz.com

Heinz® Vinegar

Basic Vinaigrette

Makes 6 (about ¾-cup) servings

WHAT YOU NEED

- 1½ teaspoons minced garlic
- ¼ cup Heinz White Vinegar
- 1 teaspoon Dijon mustard
- ¾ teaspoon salt

- Dash ground black pepper
- 1 teaspoon dried herbs, such as dill, thyme, or Italian seasoning
- ½ cup olive oil or vegetable oil

WHAT YOU DO

Combine garlic, vinegar, mustard, salt, pepper, and herbs in small bowl; whisk until well combined. Slowly whisk in oil.

Heinz Malt Vinegar-Peachy Chicken

Makes 4 to 5 servings

WHAT YOU NEED

- 1 can (16 ounce) peaches packed in light syrup
- ¼ cup frozen orange juice concentrate, thawed
- ¼ cup Heinz Malt Vinegar
- 1 tablespoon brown sugar
- 1 teaspoon dried basil
- ½ teaspoon salt

- ¼ teaspoon ground cloves
- ¼ teaspoon ground cinnamon
- ⅛ teaspoon ground black pepper
- 2½ pounds skinless, boneless chicken pieces
- 1 tablespoon vegetable oil
- 2 tablespoons water
- 2 tablespoons cornstarch

WHAT YOU DO

Drain peaches, reserving liquid; set peaches aside.

In small mixing bowl, combine reserved peach liquid, orange juice concentrate, vinegar, brown sugar, basil, salt, cloves, cinnamon, and pepper. Set aside.

In large skillet over high heat, brown chicken in oil. Reduce heat to low and pour peach sauce over chicken. Cover; simmer 25 to 30 minutes, or until chicken no longer pink. Add peaches.

Combine water and cornstarch in small bowl; stir into sauce. Cook, stirring until sauce is thickened.

Refrigerator Pickles

Makes about 8 cups

WHAT YOU NEED

- 8 cups sliced unpeeled cucumbers
- 2 cups sliced onions
- 1 cup thin sliced red bell pepper
- 1 tablespoon salt

- 2 cups sugar
- 1½ cups Heinz White Vinegar
- 2 teaspoons celery seeds
- 2 teaspoons mustard seeds

WHAT YOU DO

In large bowl, combine cucumbers, onion, and bell pepper. Sprinkle with salt and mix well. Let stand 1 hour. Drain.

In medium bowl, combine sugar, vinegar, celery seeds, and mustard seeds; stir until sugar is dissolved. Place cucumber mixture in sealable plastic container. Pour vinegar mixture over cucumbers. Cover and chill for at least 24 hours to blend flavors.

Sweet and Easy Pickled Beets

Makes about 5 cups

WHAT YOU NEED

- 3 cans (16 ounces each) cut beets
- 1 tablespoon mixed pickling spice

- 1¼ cups sugar
- ½ cup Heinz Apple Cider Vinegar

WHAT YOU DO

Drain beets, reserving 1 cup liquid. Tie pickling spice in a spice bag or cheesecloth.

In 3-quart saucepan, combine spice bag, reserved beet liquid, sugar, and vinegar. Bring to a boil over high heat, stirring occasionally. Reduce heat, cover, and simmer 15 minutes. Add beets; simmer 5 minutes. Remove spice bag. Cover and chill overnight, stirring once or twice.

Tomato Vinaigrette

Makes 10 servings

WHAT YOU NEED

- ¼ cup Heinz White Vinegar
- ⅓ cup ketchup
- 3 tablespoons sugar
- ½ teaspoon Worcestershire sauce
- Pinch salt
- ¾ cup olive oil or vegetable oil

WHAT YOU DO

Combine vinegar, ketchup, sugar, Worcestershire sauce, and salt in medium bowl, whisk until well combined. Slowly whisk in oil.

Tricolor Slaw

Makes 4 (about 1-cup) servings

WHAT YOU NEED

- 2 cups shredded green cabbage
- 2 cups shredded red cabbage
- 2 cups grated carrots
- ⅓ cup vegetable oil
- ½ cup Heinz Apple Cider Vinegar
- ⅓ cup sugar
- 1 tablespoon Asian sesame oil
- 1 teaspoon salt

WHAT YOU DO

Combine all ingredients in large bowl. Refrigerate overnight. Stir before serving.

Strange Facts

- The word *vinegar* comes from the French word *vinaigre*, which means "sour wine."
- Around 5,000 b.c.e., ancient Babylonians used vinegar as both a preservative and a condiment and began flavoring vinegar with herbs and spices.
- Ancient Romans dunked bread in vinegar.
- According to Pliny the Elder, Cleopatra dissolved a pearl in a glass of vinegar and drank the resulting liquid to win a bet against Marc Antony that she could consume the most expensive dinner in history.
- The ancient Greek physician Hippocrates extolled vinegar's medicinal qualities. During the Black Plague, doctors rubbed vinegar over their own bodies before treating contagious patients. During the American Civil War, vinegar was used to treat scurvy. During World War I, medics used vinegar to treat wounds.
- Vinegar has an almost indefinite shelf life. The acetic acid in vinegar is self-preserving, and vinegar does not require refrigeration.
- In 1869, Henry John Heinz founded the H. J. Heinz Company to market horseradish that he grew on less than one-acre of land in Sharpsburg, Pennsylvania. Soon after, Heinz and his partner L.C. Noble started the Anchor Pickle and Vinegar Works.
- The International Vinegar Museum in Roslyn, South Dakota, features displays showing how vinegar is made around the world and how to make your own vinegar.
- For cleaning windows and mirrors, mix equal parts Heinz Vinegar and water in a squirt bottle. Wipe clean with paper towel, newspaper, or a microfiber cloth.
- Scrub the bottoms of tarnished pans with a paste made from salt and Heinz Vinegar. Start with about ¼ cup salt and add enough vinegar to form a thick paste.
- For mopping floors, add up to a cup of Heinz Vinegar to a gallon of warm water.
- Soak mineral-stained clay flower pots in a solution that is two parts water to one part Heinz Vinegar to remove the stains.

For More Recipes

Visit www.askhj.com

THE MICROWAVE OVEN WARMS UP

Shortly after World War II, Navy veteran and self-taught electrical engineer Percy Spencer was touring a laboratory at the Raytheon Company where he worked in Waltham, Massachusetts, and stopped in front of a magnetron, an electron tube that generates high-frequency radio waves to power a radar set. Suddenly, Spencer noticed that the chocolate bar in his pocket had begun to melt. Intrigued, Spencer held a bag of unpopped pop-corn next to the magnetron, only to discover that the radio waves popped the kernels into popcorn. The following day, Spencer placed an egg in a pot and held it near the magnetron. The egg exploded. Spencer quickly realized that the microwaves had cooked the egg from the inside out, and the resulting pressure had caused the shell to burst.

In 1945, Spencer used the magnetron—a device invented in 1940 by Sir John Randall and Dr. H.A. Boot at Birmingham University to create radar to help England fight the Nazis—to develop the first microwave oven, weighing 750 pounds and standing five feet, six inches tall. Two years later, Raytheon marketed the Radarange microwave oven (named by an employee in a company contest) to restaurants, passenger railroad dining cars, and cruise ships. Unfortunately, the original microwave oven could not brown meat and left French fries white and limp. Twenty years later, engineers at Raytheon had improved the microwave oven, and the company, having acquired Amana Refrigeration in 1965, began marketing the Amana Radarange microwave ovens to consumers.

- Percy Spencer, born in Howland, Maine, was orphaned at a young age and never graduated from grammar school.
- During his career, Percy Spencer served as senior vice president and a member of the board of directors at Raytheon and received 150 patents for his inventions.
- The United States Navy awarded Percy Spencer the Distinguished Service Medal.
- In 1975, Americans bought more microwave ovens than gas ranges.
- Today, there are more than 200 million microwave ovens in use throughout the world.

Chicken and Potato Salad

Makes 8 servings

WHAT YOU NEED

- 1 pound potatoes, peeled and cut into ½-inch pieces
- 3 cups shredded cooked chicken
- 1 medium Granny Smith apple, peeled, if desired, and chopped
- 1 carrot, chopped
- ⅓ cup chopped celery
- ¼ cup finely chopped onion

- ¾ cup Hellmann's or Best Foods Real Mayonnaise with Lime Juice (or Hellmann's or Best Foods Real Mayonnaise blended with 1 to 2 tablespoons lime juice)
- 15 pimento stuffed green olives, quartered (optional)
- 2 tablespoons sofrito (or 1 tablespoon jarred roasted red peppers, diced; plus 1 tablespoon chopped fresh cilantro)
- ½ teaspoon salt

WHAT YOU DO

In 2-quart saucepan, cover potatoes with water; bring to a boil over medium-high heat. Reduce heat and simmer uncovered 8 minutes, or until potatoes are tender; drain and cool slightly.

Meanwhile, in large bowl, combine chicken, apple, carrot, celery, onion, mayonnaise, olives (if desired), sofrito (or peppers and cilantro), and salt. Add potatoes and toss gently. Serve at room temperature or chilled.

Chocolate Mayonnaise Cake

Makes 12 servings

WHAT YOU NEED

- 2 cups all-purpose flour
- ⅔ cup unsweetened cocoa powder
- 1¼ teaspoons baking soda
- ¼ teaspoon baking powder
- 3 eggs

- 1⅔ cups sugar
- 1 teaspoon vanilla extract
- 1 cup Hellmann's or Best Foods Real Mayonnaise
- 1⅓ cups water

WHAT YOU DO

Preheat oven to 350 degrees Fahrenheit. Coat 9- × 13-inch baking pan with nonstick cooking spray and dust lightly with flour; set aside.

In medium bowl, combine flour, cocoa, baking soda, and baking powder; set aside.

In large bowl, with electric mixer at high speed, beat eggs, sugar, and vanilla for 3 minutes, or until light and fluffy. Beat in mayonnaise at low speed until blended. Alternately beat in flour mixture with water, beginning and ending with flour mixture. Pour batter into prepared pan.

Bake 40 minutes, or until wooden pick inserted into center comes out clean. Place pan on wire racks and cool 10 minutes. Remove cake from pan and cool completely on racks.

Note: You can bake this cake in two 9-inch round cake pans. Decrease cooking time to 30 minutes. Frost, if desired, or sprinkle with confectioners' sugar.

Creamy Spinach Dip
Makes 4 cups

WHAT YOU NEED

- 1 cup Hellmann's or Best Foods Real Mayonnaise
- 1 envelope (1.4 ounces) vegetable soup and recipe mix
- 1 package (10 ounces) frozen chopped spinach, thawed and squeezed dry, or 1 package (10 ounces) fresh baby spinach, chopped
- 1 container (16 ounces) sour cream

WHAT YOU DO

Combine all ingredients in bowl. Chill 2 hours.

Parmesan-Crusted Chicken

Makes 4 servings

WHAT YOU NEED

- ½ cup Hellmann's or Best Foods Real Mayonnaise
- ¼ cup grated Parmesan cheese

- 4 boneless, skinless chicken breast halves (about 1¼ pounds)
- 4 teaspoons Italian seasoned dry bread crumbs

WHAT YOU DO

Preheat oven to 425 degrees Fahrenheit. Coat baking sheet with nonstick cooking spray.

In medium bowl, combine mayonnaise and cheese.

Place chicken on prepared baking sheet. Top each chicken breast with a quarter of the mayonnaise mixture, then sprinkle each with 1 teaspoon bread crumbs.

Bake 20 minutes, or until chicken is thoroughly cooked.

Quick Mayonnaise Biscuits

Makes 24 biscuits

WHAT YOU NEED

- 2 cups all-purpose flour
- 1 tablespoon baking powder
- ½ teaspoon salt

- ⅓ cup Hellmann's or Best Foods Real Mayonnaise
- ¾ cup milk

WHAT YOU DO

Preheat oven to 450 degree Fahrenheit.

In medium bowl, combine flour, baking powder and salt. Stir in mayonnaise and milk. On ungreased baking sheet, drop batter by rounded tablespoonfuls.

Bake 13 minutes, or until slightly golden. Serve warm.

Smokin' Succulent Grilled Chicken

Makes 4 servings

WHAT YOU NEED

- 1 cup Hellmann's or Best Foods Real Mayonnaise
- 2 tablespoon lime juice
- 2 tablespoon chopped fresh cilantro (optional)
- 2 cloves garlic, minced
- 1 teaspoon ground chipotle chile pepper
- 4 boneless, skinless chicken breast halves (about 1¼ pounds)

WHAT YOU DO

In medium bowl, combine all ingredients except chicken. Reserve ½ cup mayonnaise mixture.

Grill or broil chicken, turning once and brushing frequently with remaining mayonnaise mixture, until chicken is thoroughly cooked. Serve chicken with reserved mayonnaise mixture.

Recipe Variation: For a Smokin' Chicken Salad, serve hot sliced chicken over crisp salad greens, then top with thinly sliced onions, shredded Mexican cheese, and tomato wedges. Drizzle with reserved mayonnaise mixture.

The Original Potato Salad

Makes 8 servings

WHAT YOU NEED

- 2 pounds potatoes (5 to 6 medium), peeled and cut into ¾-inch chunks
- 1 cup Hellmann's or Best Foods Real Mayonnaise
- 2 tablespoons white vinegar
- 1½ teaspoons salt
- 1 teaspoon sugar
- ¼ teaspoon ground black pepper
- 1 cup thinly sliced celery
- ½ cup chopped onion
- 2 hard-cooked eggs, chopped (optional)

WHAT YOU DO

In 4-quart saucepot, cover potatoes with water; bring to a boil over medium-high heat. Reduce heat and simmer 10 minutes, or until potatoes are tender. Drain and cool slightly.

In large bowl, combine mayonnaise, vinegar, salt, sugar, and pepper. Add potatoes, celery, onion, and eggs (if desired) and toss gently. Serve at room temperature or chilled.

Strange Facts

- In 1912, Richard Hellmann, a German immigrant who owned a delicatessen in Manhattan, began selling his premixed mayonnaise in one-pound wooden "boats," graduating to glass jars the following year. Hellmann's eventually extended its distribution from the East Coast to the Rocky Mountains.

- Meanwhile, Best Foods, Inc., had introduced mayonnaise in California, calling it Best Foods Real Mayonnaise and expanding distribution throughout the West. Eventually the two companies merged under the Best Foods, Inc. banner, but since both brands of mayonnaise had developed strong followings, neither name was changed.

- Hellmann's Real Mayonnaise and Best Foods Real Mayonnaise are essentially the same, although some people find Hellmann's mayonnaise slightly more tangy.

- Mayonnaise is not salad dressing. Real mayonnaise contains at least 65 percent oil by weight, vinegar, and egg or egg yolks. Salad dressings contain a minimum of 30 percent oil, at least 4 percent egg yolk, cooked starch, water, and vinegar or other specified acid ingredients.

- Mayonnaise provides essential fatty acids, which the body cannot manufacture, and vitamin E. It also aids in the absorption of vitamins A, D, E, and K.

- One tablespoon of Hellmann's Real Mayonnaise contains 5 milligrams cholesterol. That's less than 2 percent of the recommended maximum daily intake of 300 milligrams.

- Mayonnaise jars are not suitable for home canning. The glass used for the jars will not withstand the temperatures required for the canning process, and the lid does not give a proper seal.

For More Recipes

Visit www.mayo.com

Hidden Valley® Original Ranch® Dressing

Fettuccine with Chicken Breasts

Makes 8 servings

WHAT YOU NEED

- 1 package (12 ounces) fettuccine or egg noodles
- 1 cup Hidden Valley Original Ranch Dressing
- ⅓ cup Dijon mustard
- 8 boneless, skinless chicken breast halves, pounded thin
- 8 tablespoons butter, divided
- ⅓ cup dry white wine

WHAT YOU DO

Cook fettuccine according to package directions; drain.

Preheat oven to 425 degrees Fahrenheit. Coat 13- × 9-inch baking dish with nonstick cooking spray.

Stir together dressing and mustard in small bowl; set aside.

Pour fettuccine into prepared baking dish.

In large skillet over medium-high heat, melt 2 tablespoons butter. Sauté chicken in batches until golden, about 2 to 3 minutes per side, melting an additional 2 tablespoons of butter between batches. Transfer cooked chicken to the bed of fettuccine. Add wine to skillet; cook to reduce to desired consistency. Drizzle over chicken. Pour the reserved dressing mixture over the chicken. Bake 10 minutes, or until dressing forms a golden brown crust.

Original Ranch Cheddar Chicken

Makes 4 servings

WHAT YOU NEED

- ½ cup Hidden Valley Original Ranch Dressing
- 1 tablespoon all-purpose flour
- 4 boneless, skinless chicken breast halves (about 1 pound)
- ¼ cup shredded sharp Cheddar cheese
- ¼ cup grated Parmesan cheese

WHAT YOU DO

Preheat oven to 375 degrees Fahrenheit.

Combine dressing with flour in shallow bowl. Coat chicken with dressing mixture. Place on ungreased baking pan.

Combine Cheddar and Parmesan in another bowl; sprinkle on chicken. Bake 25 minutes, or until chicken is no longer pink in center and juices run clear.

Original Ranch Ravioli

Makes 3 to 4 servings

WHAT YOU NEED

- ½ cup roasted red peppers, rinsed and drained if jarred
- 1 package (9 ounces) fresh meat or chicken ravioli
- 1 cup Hidden Valley Original Ranch Dressing
- ¼ cup grated Parmesan cheese

WHAT YOU DO

Blot peppers dry; cut into thin strips. Cook ravioli according to package directions; drain and combine with pepper strips and dressing in large nonstick skillet. Cook and stir over medium heat until mixture is hot. Garnish with cheese.

Potato and Cauliflower Bake

Makes 10 servings

WHAT YOU NEED

- 4 cups country-style frozen hash browns
- 1 large cauliflower, cut into small florets (about 4 cups)
- 2 cups grated Cheddar cheese, divided
- 1 cup fresh or frozen chopped onion
- ¼ cup diced red bell pepper
- 1¾ cups Hidden Valley Original Ranch Dressing, divided
- ½ cup sour cream
- ½ cup plain dry bread crumbs

WHAT YOU DO

Preheat oven to 350 degrees Fahrenheit.

Mix together hash browns, cauliflower, 1 cup cheese, onion, and pepper in large bowl.

Whisk 1½ cups dressing and sour cream together in separate bowl. Add to potato mixture. Transfer mixture to 2-quart baking dish.

Mix together remaining 1 cup cheese, remaining ¼ cup dressing, and bread crumbs in separate bowl. Sprinkle on top of casserole. Bake 60 minutes, until browned and bubbly and cauliflower is tender. Let stand 10 minutes before serving.

Ranch Picnic Potato Salad

Makes 8 servings

WHAT YOU NEED

- 6 medium potatoes, peeled, sliced, and boiled (about 3½ pounds)
- ½ cup chopped celery
- ¼ cup sliced green onion
- 2 tablespoons chopped fresh parsley
- 1 teaspoon salt
- ⅛ teaspoon ground black pepper

- 1 tablespoon Dijon mustard
- 1 cup Hidden Valley Original Ranch Dressing
- 2 hard-cooked eggs, finely chopped
- Paprika
- Lettuce (optional)

WHAT YOU DO

In large bowl, combine potatoes, celery, onion, parsley, salt, and pepper.

In small bowl, stir mustard into dressing; pour over potatoes and toss lightly. Cover and refrigerate several hours. Sprinkle with eggs and paprika. Serve in lettuce-lined bowl, if desired.

Savory Baked Fish

Makes 6 servings

WHAT YOU NEED

- 6 boneless fish fillets, such as scrod, (about 8 ounces each)
- ¾ cup Hidden Valley Original Ranch Dressing

WHAT YOU DO

Preheat oven to 375 degrees Fahrenheit. Coat large baking pan with nonstick cooking spray.

Arrange fish fillets in prepared baking pan. Spread each fillet with 2 tablespoons dressing. Bake 10 to 20 minutes, depending on the thickness of the fish, or until fish flakes. Finish under broiler to brown the top.

Turkey and Stuffing Bake

Makes 4 to 6 servings

WHAT YOU NEED

- 1 jar (4½ ounces) sliced mushrooms
- ¼ cup butter or margarine
- ½ cup diced celery
- ½ cup chopped onion
- 1¼ cups Hidden Valley Original Ranch Dressing, divided
- ⅔ cup water
- 3 cups seasoned stuffing mix
- ⅓ cup sweetened dried cranberries
- 3 cups coarsely shredded cooked turkey (about 1 pound)

WHAT YOU DO

Preheat oven to 350 degrees Fahrenheit. Coat 8-inch baking pan with nonstick cooking spray.

Drain mushrooms, reserving liquid; set aside. Melt butter (or margarine) over medium-high heat in large skillet. Add celery and onion; cook 4 minutes, or until soft. Remove from heat and stir in ½ cup dressing, water, and reserved mushroom liquid. Stir in stuffing mix and cranberries until thoroughly moistened.

In separate bowl, combine turkey, mushrooms, and remaining ¾ cup dressing; spread evenly in prepared pan. Top with stuffing mixture. Bake 40 minutes, or until bubbly and brown.

Strange Facts

- In the late 1950s and early 1960s, Steve and Gayle Henson ran the Hidden Valley Guest Ranch, a 120-acre dude ranch, near Santa Barbara, California, attracting throngs of weekend visitors, including lively students from the nearby University of California at Santa Barbara. Gayle frequently cooked up to three hundred steaks each weekend evening. Steve topped the salad with a creamy dressing that blended a dry mix of herbs and spices with mayonnaise and buttermilk.

- Steve Henson had begun developing the dressing during his years living in Alaska and perfected his formula at the Santa Barbara ranch.

- Many Hidden Valley guests fell in love with the salad dressing and brought it home in glass jars given to them by Steve Henson. Others guests urged him to market the tasty mixture.

- When a guest from Hawaii insisted that Steve Henson provide him with nearly three hundred jars of the dressing to take back to his home in Oahu for a party, Henson pre-packaged a bunch of envelopes with the mixture and instructed the guest how to mix up the dressing when he got back to Hawaii. After the party, the guest telephoned Henson to order more packets of the powdered mix. Henson was soon marketing the dressing through mail order, and orders began pouring in from across the nation.

- Steve Henson packaged the initial orders for his salad dressing mix himself. Within months, twelve people were helping him mix the dressing in the main house at the Hidden Valley Ranch. Soon after, the Hensons converted the Hidden Valley Ranch almost entirely into a salad dressing packing center.

- Eventually, Henson moved the salad dressing operation into a factory and had a machine developed that could fill thousands of envelopes in less than an hour. In 1971, Henson moved the company to a larger factory in Sparks, Nevada.

- The Henson family sold the salad dressing business to the HVR Company (later renamed the HV Food Products Company) in 1972. Today, the Clorox Company owns the HV Food Products Company.

For More Recipes

Visit www.hiddenvalley.com

Jell-O® Gelatin

Fourth-of-July Jell-O

Makes 12 (½-cup) servings

WHAT YOU NEED

- 6 cups water
- 2 packages (3 ounces each) cherry Jell-O
- 1 package (3 ounces) blueberry Jell-O
- 2 cups miniature marshmallows
- Whipped cream

WHAT YOU DO

Boil 1 cup water and pour into mixing bowl. Add 1 package cherry Jell-O powder, stirring until dissolved. Add 1 cup cold water and blend well. Pour into mold and top with a single layer of miniature marshmallows. (The marshmallows will float on top of the Jell-O.) Refrigerate for 3 hours until firm.

   Boil 1 cup water and pour into mixing bowl. Add blueberry Jell-O powder, stirring until dissolved. Add 1 cup cold water and blend well. Gently pour into the mold, top with a single layer of miniature marshmallows, and refrigerate for 3 hours until firm.

   Boil 1 cup water and pour into mixing bowl. Add remaining package cherry Jell-O powder, stirring until dissolved. Add 1 cup cold water and blend well. Gently pour into the mold, top with a single layer of miniature marshmallows, and refrigerate for several hours until firm.

Jell-O Vegetable Salad

Makes 12 (½-cup) servings

WHAT YOU NEED

- 4 cups water
- 1 package (6 ounces) lemon Jell-O
- ½ cup shredded carrots
- ½ cup sliced celery
- ½ cup sliced cucumber
- ¼ cup raisins
- 16 romaine lettuce leaves
- Mayonnaise (optional)

WHAT YOU DO

Boil 2 cups water and pour into mixing bowl. Add Jell-O powder, stirring until dissolved. Add 2 cups cold water and blend well. Add the carrots, celery, cucumber, and raisins, mixing the vegetables into the Jell-O solution. (The raisins and carrots will be evenly distributed in the mixture, but the cucumbers and celery tend to float to the top, unless they get tangled in the carrots.) Pour into mold or 9- × 13- × 2-inch glass pan. Refrigerate for several hours until firm. Cut into squares. Serve on lettuce and garnish, if desired, with mayonnaise.

Pineapple and Mandarin Orange Jell-O Salad

Makes 16 (½-cup) servings

WHAT YOU NEED

- 4 cups water
- 1 package (6 ounces) orange Jell-O
- 1 can (20 ounces) pineapple chunks
- 1 can (15 ounces) mandarin oranges

WHAT YOU DO

Boil 2 cups water and pour into mixing bowl. Add Jell-O powder, stirring until dissolved.

Drain the juice from pineapple and mandarin oranges into measuring cup and add cold water to make 2 cups liquid. Pour the liquid into the Jell-O mixture, stirring to blend well. Stir the pineapple and mandarin oranges into the Jell-O mixture, mixing well so the fruit is evenly distributed. Pour into mold. Refrigerate for several hours until firm.

Strawberry Jell-O Surprise

Makes 10 (½-cup) servings

WHAT YOU NEED

- 4 cups water
- 1 package (6 ounces) strawberry Jell-O
- 1 container (1 pound) cottage cheese, small curd, drained
- 1 cup strawberry slices
- Whipped cream

WHAT YOU DO

Boil 2 cups water and pour into mixing bowl. Add Jell-O powder, stirring until dissolved. Add 2 cups cold water and blend well. Slowly spoon the cottage cheese into the Jell-O solution, mixing well until the cottage cheese is evenly distributed. Pour in the strawberries, stirring well. Pour into mold or dishes. Refrigerate for several hours until firm. Top with whipped cream.

Utah Green Ambrosia Jell-O Salad

Makes 16 (½-cup) servings

WHAT YOU NEED

- 4 cups water
- 1 package (6 ounces) lime Jell-O
- ¼ cup sugar (or more, to taste)
- 1 can (20 ounces) crushed pineapple
- 1 teaspoon lemon juice (or more, to taste)
- 1 tub (8 ounces) whipped topping, thawed

WHAT YOU DO

Boil 2 cups water and pour into mixing bowl. Add Jell-O powder and sugar, stirring until dissolved.

Drain pineapple juice into measuring cup, add cold water to total 2 cups liquid, and pour into the Jell-O mixture, stirring to blend well. Stir pineapple into the mixture and mix well so the pineapple is evenly distributed through the mixture. Add more sugar to taste, if desired. Add lemon juice, adding more if desired. Refrigerate 2 hours, or until the liquid has thickened to a syrup-like consistency.

Fold whipped topping into Jell-O mixture. Pour the mixture into 9- x 13- x 2-inch pan. Refrigerate for several hours until firm. Cut into squares.

CRACKING THE EGG BEATER

The first hand-cranked egg beaters powered only one rotating whisk. In 1870, Turner Williams of Providence, Rhode Island, invented a hand-cranked egg beater with two intermeshed, counter-rotating whisks, receiving a patent on May 31, 1870. Williams devised the two revolving whisks to revolve in opposite directions "so that they may cut against each other with a very peculiar shearing action."

"The advantage of having two wheels operating in the same space and revolving in different directions," wrote Williams, "is that the fluid being acted upon is cut and thoroughly beaten almost instantaneously, as it cannot partake of the revolving motion of the beating-frames, and thus escape the beating action of the frames, as it does in other egg-beaters of this class."

Fourteen years later, Willis Johnson of Cincinnati, Ohio, patented an improved mechanical egg beater on February 5, 1884. The egg-beater featured two separate chambers allowing the user to beat batter in one section and eggs in the other section.

Strange Facts

- In 1845, industrialist, inventor, and philanthropist Peter Cooper, inventor of Tom Thumb locomotive and founder of the Cooper Union for the Advancement of Science and Art in New York City, obtained the first patent for a gelatin dessert. Cooper packaged the gelatin in small boxes with directions for use, but he did little to promote the product.

- In 1895, Pearle B. Wait, a carpenter and cough medicine manufacturer from LeRoy, New York, bought the patent for the manufacture of gelatin from Cooper and, two years later, developed a fruit-flavored version of Cooper's gelatin, creating strawberry, raspberry, orange, and lemon gelatin. His wife, May Davis Wait, named the dessert Jell-O.

- In 1899, unable to popularize his flavored gelatin, Wait sold the business to Orator Francis Woodward, a neighbor, for $450.

- In 1902, Woodward ran the first Jell-O advertisement in *Ladies' Home Journal* featuring smiling, fashionably coifed women in white aprons proclaiming Jell-O gelatin "America's Most Famous Dessert."

- In 1904, print ads portraying the Jell-O Girl, the brand's first trademark, debuted. Elizabeth King, the four-year-old daughter of Franklin King, an artist for the Genesee Pure Food Company's ad agency, posed for the painting and was shown playing in her nursery with packages of Jell-O gelatin. The tag line read, "You can't be a kid without it."

- During the first quarter of the twentieth century, immigrants entering Ellis Island in New York City were served Jell-O gelatin as a welcome to America.

- In the 1930s, Jell-O sponsored a "Wizard of Oz" radio program and a series of children's booklets by L. Frank Baum, author of the *Wizard of Oz* books, that included Jell-O recipes in the back.

- In 1942, cola flavored Jell-O was introduced, but it lasted only a year.

- In the 1950s, advertisements for Jell-O promoted "National Trim-Your-Torso-With-Jell-O Week," "National Use-Up-Your-Leftovers-in-a Jell-O-Salad Week," and "National Jell-O-With-Fruit-To-Boot Week."

- In 1991, the Smithsonian Institution held its first and only mock conference on Jell-O history, featuring such topics as "American History is Jell-O History," "The Dialectics of Jell-O in Peasant Culture," "The Semiotics of Jell-O," and "Jell-O Salad or Just Desserts: The Poetics of an American Food." The event included a Jell-O Jell-Off Cooking Contest.
- In 1996, Shannon Lucid, an astronaut on a 140-day mission to the Russian Mir space station, revealed that she marked the passage of time by wearing pink socks and eating Jell-O gelatin on Sundays.
- In 1997, the Jell-O Museum opened its doors in LeRoy, New York (the birthplace of Jell-O). The museum features Jell-O artwork by famous artists such as Maxfield Parrish and Norman Rockwell and displays Jell-O memorabilia, including the original painting of the Jell-O Girl.
- Residents of the state of Utah eat twice as much Jell-O as the national average, enough for every man, woman, and child in Salt Lake City to consume two boxes of Jell-O each year.
- Utah State University is home to an annual Jell-O slide, in which participants cover themselves with Jell-O and then plunge headfirst down a plastic sheet on a hillside.
- On St. Patrick's Day, Flanigan's Inn in Zion National Park, Utah, holds a lime Jell-O sculpting contest.
- Grunts and Postures, a vintage clothing store in Salt Lake City, Utah, features an entire wall of the store decorated with more than 100 vintage Jell-O molds.
- In 2001, the Utah Senate declared Jell-O gelatin the "Official State Snack" of Utah, and Governor Michael O. Leavitt proclaimed the second full week of February to be annual "Jell-O Week." Jell-O spokesperson Bill Cosby delivered a comedy routine before Utah lawmakers in the state capitol, where he was made an honorary Utah citizen.
- During the 2002 Winter Olympics in Salt Lake City, Utah, the most popular Olympic pin design depicted a bowl of cubed lime Jell-O.
- About 300 million boxes of Jell-O gelatin are sold in the United States each year.

For More Recipes

Visit www.jello.com

Jif® Peanut Butter

African Beef-Peanut Butter Stew

Makes 6 servings

WHAT YOU NEED

- ½ cup Jif Creamy Peanut Butter
- 2 cups beef broth
- 2 pounds beef stew meat, cut into 1½-inch cubes
- Salt
- Ground black pepper
- 2 tablespoons canola oil

- 1 cup chopped onion
- 3 or 4 cloves garlic, minced
- 1 cup chopped green bell pepper
- 1 cup chopped carrot
- 1 can (14½ ounces) diced tomatoes
- ½ teaspoon dried thyme
- 1 bay leaf

WHAT YOU DO

In medium bowl, whisk together peanut butter and broth until well blended. Set aside.

Season beef with salt and pepper. In large saucepan or stew pot, heat oil over medium heat. Add onion, garlic, bell pepper, and carrot. Sauté until onion is soft and translucent, but not browned. Add beef and continue to cook, stirring often, until it is browned on all sides. Add peanut butter and broth mixture, tomatoes and liquid, thyme, and bay leaf. Stir well and bring to a boil. Reduce heat to low and simmer, stirring often, about 1 hour, or until the beef is tender. Add salt and pepper to taste. Discard bay leaf. Serve hot.

Serving Suggestion: Serve over rice.

Cream of Peanut Soup

Makes 6 (1-cup) servings

WHAT YOU NEED

- 1 stalk celery, chopped
- ½ medium onion, chopped
- 2 tablespoons butter or margarine
- 1½ tablespoons all-purpose flour

- 4 cups chicken broth
- 1 cup Jif Creamy Peanut Butter
- 1 cup milk
- Snipped fresh chives

WHAT YOU DO

In medium saucepan, cook celery and onion in butter (or margarine) until onion is tender but not brown, Stir in flour until well blended and cook 1 minute. Add broth. Cook and stir until thickened and bubbly. Remove from heat and, with the back of a spoon, pass the broth and vegetables through a fine sieve and into stock pot. Add peanut butter and milk, stirring to blend thoroughly. Heat through, but do not boil. Serve hot or cold. Garnish with chives.

Grilled Salmon with Peanut Hoisin Sauce

Makes 4 servings

WHAT YOU NEED

- ½ cup Jif Creamy Peanut Butter
- ½ cup hoisin sauce
- ½ cup finely chopped onion
- ¼ cup rice wine vinegar
- ½ cup water

- 2 or 3 cloves garlic, minced
- 4 salmon filets (6 ounces each)
- Salt
- Ground black pepper
- ½ cup chopped scallions

WHAT YOU DO

Combine peanut butter, hoisin sauce, onion, vinegar, water, garlic, and scallions in saucepan. Stirring constantly, bring to a boil. Reduce the heat and simmer about 5 minutes, stirring often.

Preheat grill.

Coat salmon with nonstick cooking spray on both sides and season with salt and pepper.

Grill about 5 minutes on each side for 1-inch-thick fillets, or until the fish flakes easily when pierced with a fork.

Top salmon with warm sauce and sprinkle with scallions just before serving.

Note: The sauce can be made several days ahead of time and refrigerated. If it is too thick, add a little water when heating it before serving.

Jif Shakes

Makes 2 servings

WHAT YOU NEED

- 1 cup cold milk
- ¼ cup Jif Creamy Peanut Butter
- 1 cup vanilla ice cream

WHAT YOU DO

Place milk and peanut butter in blender. Cover and blend until smooth. Add ice cream; blend until smooth.

Recipe Variation: Banana Jif Shakes: Prepare recipe as directed, except add a sliced banana to the blender with the peanut butter.

Moroccan Peanut Couscous with Peas

Makes 12 (1-cup) servings

WHAT YOU NEED

- 2 tablespoons canola oil
- ½ cup chopped onions
- ½ cup red or green bell pepper
- 2 or 3 cloves garlic, minced
- 1½ cups chicken or vegetable broth
- ½ cup Jif Extra Crunchy Peanut Butter
- ½ teaspoon ground cumin
- Salt
- Ground black pepper
- 1 package (10 ounces) frozen peas (tiny deluxe, if possible)
- 1 cup couscous

WHAT YOU DO

In 2½- or 3-quart saucepan, heat oil over medium heat. Add onions, bell pepper, and garlic. Sauté until onion is just translucent. Add broth and bring to a boil. Whisk in peanut butter and cumin; blend well. Add salt and pepper to taste. Add peas and bring to a boil. Stir in couscous and return to a boil, stirring constantly. Remove from the heat, cover, and let sit about 5 minutes, until the liquid is absorbed. Fluff with a fork and serve.

Olympic Oatmeal

Makes 3 to 4 servings

WHAT YOU NEED

- 2 cups water
- ½ teaspoon salt
- 1 cup quick-cooking rolled oats

- ⅓ cup packed brown sugar
- ¼ cup Jif Creamy Peanut Butter
- 2 tablespoons butter or margarine

WHAT YOU DO

Bring water and salt to boiling in medium saucepan. Add oats and boil 1 minute. Remove from heat and stir in sugar, peanut butter, and butter (or margarine).

Peanut Butter–Bacon Sandwiches

Makes 8 sandwiches

WHAT YOU NEED

- ½ cup Jif Peanut Butter, creamy or crunchy
- 6 slices bacon, cooked until crispy and crumbled
- ⅓ cup finely chopped celery

- 8 small buns, split and toasted
- Butter or margarine, softened
- 8 lettuce leaves
- 8 tomato slices

WHAT YOU DO

In small bowl, combine peanut butter, bacon, and celery. Spread bun halves with butter (or margarine). Place lettuce on each bun bottom; spread with the peanut butter mixture. Top with tomato and bun tops.

Thai Peanut Burgers

Makes 4 servings

WHAT YOU NEED

- ½ cup Jif Extra Crunchy Peanut Butter
- 1 tablespoon lime juice
- ½ tablespoon soy sauce
- ½ tablespoon grated fresh ginger
- ½ tablespoon chopped fresh cilantro
- ¼ teaspoon cayenne pepper (more or less to taste)
- 1 pound lean ground beef or turkey
- 4 hamburger buns

WHAT YOU DO

Preheat grill or broiler.

In large bowl, whisk together peanut butter, lime juice, and soy sauce. Add ginger, cilantro, and cayenne pepper and blend well. Add beef (or turkey) and mix well. Form into 4 patties. Grill, broil, or pan fry to your liking. Serve on buns.

Serving Suggestion: Top with your favorite Thai hot sauce and other condiments.

Strange Facts

- The average American eats eight pounds of peanuts and peanut products over the course of a year.
- Americans consume 270 million pounds of Jif Peanut Butter every year. That's enough peanut butter to make two billion peanut butter sandwiches or to spread a layer of peanut butter one-inch thick over 660 football fields.
- A 28-ounce jar of Jif Peanut Butter contains an average of 1,218 peanuts.
- Peanuts originated in South America, probably in Brazil and Peru. Spanish explorers brought peanuts back to Europe, and traders subsequently brought peanuts to Africa and Asia.
- In 1896, George Washington Carver began his research at Tuskegee Institute, developing more than 300 uses for peanuts and improving peanut horticulture. Carver

used peanuts to make inks, dyes, soap, face cream, wood stains, plastics, linoleum, metal polish, and synthetic rubber.

- The Jif plant in Lexington, Kentucky, is the largest peanut butter–producing facility in the world.
- In August 1976, Tom Miller, a student at the University of Colorado, pushed a peanut to the top of Pike's Peak (14,100 feet) using his nose. The feat took him four days, twenty-three hours, forty-seven minutes, and three seconds.
- Two peanut farmers were elected president of the United States—Thomas Jefferson and Jimmy Carter.
- The phrase "peanut gallery" originated during the late nineteenth century and referred to the inexpensive seats in a theater (usually in the balcony), from which patrons would throw peanuts, a common movie-theater snack food at the time, at those seated below them.
- The producers of the television show *Mr. Ed,* featuring a "talking" horse, used peanut butter to get the horse to move its lips and mouth.
- A jar of peanut butter can be found in nine out of ten American homes.
- Arachibutyrophobia is the fear of getting peanut butter stuck to the roof of your mouth.
- The Oklahoma Peanut Commission and the Oklahoma Wheat Commission created the world's largest peanut butter and jelly sandwich in Oklahoma City, Oklahoma, on September 7, 2002. The sandwich weighed nearly 900 pounds and contained 350 pounds of peanut butter and 144 pounds of jelly.
- Sixty percent of consumers prefer creamy peanut butter over crunchy. Generally women and children prefer creamy, while most men prefer chunky.

For More Recipes

Visit www.jif.com

COOKING WITH A CLOTHES DRYER

Author Carolyn Wyman, a nationally syndicated columnist who reviews new food products, published this recipe for shrimp cooked in a clothes dryer. Wyman's books include *Better Than Homemade* and *Jell-O: A Biography*.

Clothes Dryer Shrimp

What You Need

- 1½ teaspoons Old Bay Seasoning or other favorite seasoning, optional
- ½ pound extra large unpeeled shrimp
- Lots of aluminum foil
- 1 laundry hosiery bag

What You Do

Sprinkle the seasoning over the unpeeled shrimp, if desired, and toss to distribute evenly.

Wrap the shrimp in aluminum foil. You can put up to four in a package, but put them side by side rather than on top of one another.

Seal tightly, then double or even triple wrap. (Good wrapping is essential to avoid Fishy Dryer Syndrome.)

Place the foil package in the hosiery bag, close, and toss in the dryer alone. Run the dryer at the high setting for 10 to 12 minutes. Peel and eat. Serves 2.

Note: Because dryer temperatures vary, you might want to check the package for doneness at 8 minutes. You can also cook shrimp while clothes are being dried, but it will take quite a bit longer.

Reprinted from *The Kitchen Sink Cookbook: Offbeat Recipes from Unusual Ingredients* by Carolyn Wyman (Birch Lane Press/Carol Publishing)

Jolly Time® Pop Corn

Coconut Honey Balls

Makes about 10 popcorn balls

WHAT YOU NEED

- ¾ cup flaked coconut
- 3 quarts popped Jolly Time Pop Corn
- ⅓ cup honey
- ½ teaspoon ground cinnamon
- Dash salt
- 3 tablespoons butter or margarine

WHAT YOU DO

Preheat oven to 350 degrees Fahrenheit.

Spread coconut in shallow baking pan; toast coconut, stirring once, about 8 to 10 minutes.

Reduce oven temperature to 250 degrees Fahrenheit. Line another shallow baking pan with aluminum foil.

Place popcorn in prepared baking pan and remove any unpopped kernels. Keep warm in oven.

Combine honey, cinnamon, and salt in small saucepan. Heat to boiling; boil 2 to 2½ minutes, stirring constantly. Add butter (or margarine); stir until melted. Pour honey mixture over popcorn. Add coconut. Toss to coat well. To make balls, place 1 cup mixture in center of an 11-inch square of plastic wrap. Shape into balls. Twist wrap and tie securely with ribbon.

Crunchy Popcorn Salad

Makes 6 (1-cup) servings

WHAT YOU NEED

- ½ cup sour cream
- ¼ cup mayonnaise
- 1 tablespoon white wine vinegar
- 1¼ teaspoons dry buttermilk ranch salad dressing mix
- ¼ teaspoon ground dry mustard
- ¼ teaspoon ground black pepper
- ¼ teaspoon salt
- 1 cup shredded carrots
- ½ cup sliced green onion
- ½ cup chopped green bell pepper
- 9 small ripe olives, halved
- 3 slices (¾ ounce each) fat-free sharp Cheddar cheese product
- 1 bag (3 ounces) Jolly Time Healthy Pop 94% Fat Free Microwave Pop Corn, popped

WHAT YOU DO

In medium bowl, combine sour cream, mayonnaise, vinegar, dressing mix, mustard, black pepper and salt; mix well. Add carrots, onion, green pepper, and olives. Slice cheese into thick strips, add to vegetable mixture, and mix well (may be covered and refrigerated overnight, if desired). Just before serving, place popped popcorn in large bowl, removing any unpopped kernels. Add sour cream and vegetable mixture and gently stir until well mixed. Serve immediately.

Parmesan Popcorn

Makes 12 (1-cup) servings

WHAT YOU NEED

- 3 quarts popped Jolly Time Pop Corn
- 1 to 2 tablespoons olive oil or vegetable oil
- 2 tablespoons dry spaghetti sauce mix
- 2 tablespoons grated Parmesan cheese

WHAT YOU DO

Place popcorn in large bowl and remove any unpopped kernels.

Heat oil in small saucepan. Drizzle over popcorn; add spaghetti sauce mix and cheese. Toss well. Serve immediately.

Popcorn Marshmallow Balls

Makes about 12 popcorn balls

WHAT YOU NEED

- 3 quarts popped Jolly Time Blast O Butter or Butter-Licious Microwave Pop Corn
- ¼ cup butter or margarine
- 1 bag (10 ounces) miniature marshmallows
- Food coloring (optional)

WHAT YOU DO

Put popcorn in large bowl and remove any unpopped kernels; set aside.

In heavy saucepan, heat butter (or margarine) and marshmallows on low heat, stirring constantly, until melted and smooth. If desired, add a few drops of food coloring to the melted marshmallows and stir until the color is blended. Pour mixture over popcorn and mix carefully until popcorn is well coated. Place 1 cup mixture in center of 11-inch square of plastic wrap. Shape into a ball. Twist wrap and tie securely with ribbon.

Microwave Instructions: Put popped popcorn in large bowl; set aside. In large microwave-safe bowl, microwave butter on high until butter is melted, about 30 to 45 seconds. Add marshmallows. Microwave on high until marshmallows look puffy, about 1 to 1½ minutes. Stir to completely melt marshmallows. (Careful: The mixture will be hot.) Pour melted marshmallows over the popcorn and mix carefully until the popcorn is coated. Shape into balls as directed above.

Popcorn Peanut Butter Cups

Makes 20 pieces

WHAT YOU NEED

- Butter
- 2 quarts popped Jolly Time Blast O Butter Microwave Pop Corn
- 1 cup light corn syrup
- ¾ cup creamy peanut butter
- ¼ cup semisweet chocolate pieces
- 20 small peanut butter cups, unwrapped

WHAT YOU DO

Cover baking sheet with waxed paper and lightly butter it.

Place popped popcorn in large bowl and remove any unpopped kernels.

Heat corn syrup in small saucepan to boiling; boil 3 minutes. Remove from heat. Stir in peanut butter and chocolate pieces until almost smooth. Pour syrup mixture over popcorn; toss well to coat. Let cool about 8 minutes. Using a heaping tablespoon, shape popcorn mixture into 20 balls and place on prepared baking sheet. Flatten slightly and make an indentation in the center with your thumb. Place 1 peanut butter cup in the center of each. Store in tightly-covered container.

Recipe Variation: Instead of peanut butter cups, substitute chocolate stars, mini candy-coated chocolates, candy-coated peanuts, or your favorite candy.

THE TOASTER POPS UP

The first electric toasters, invented in the early 1900s, were metal cages that held the slices of bread next to heating coils, without any way to control the temperature. The user had to keep an eye on the slice of bread to make sure the toast did not burn and then flip over the slice to toast the other side. While far from perfect, the early electric toaster enabled people to make a slice of toast without having to fire up the stove.

During World War I, master mechanic Charles Strite, tired of the burnt toast served in the company cafeteria in Stillwater, Minnesota, used springs and a variable timer to create the world's first pop-up toaster. After receiving a patent in 1919, Strite raised enough money from friends to produce one hundred pop-up toasters assembled by hand. The Childs restaurant chain placed an order for the first batch but returned every toaster for mechanical adjustments, eager for Strite to perfect his invention.

In 1926, Strite introduced the Toastmaster, the first pop-up toaster for the home—complete with a dial to adjust to the desired degree of darkness. Unfortunately, the Toastmaster grew hotter with each slice of toast. The first slice popped up underdone, and the sixth slice popped up burnt. Still, advertisements for the Toastmaster boasted, "This amazing new invention makes perfect toast every time! Without watching! Without turning! Without burning!" Strite eventually worked out the bugs, and by 1930, Americans had bought more than 1.2 million toasters.

- Ancient Egyptians toasted bread to remove moisture, impede the growth of molds and spores, and improve shelf life.
- Before the invention of the toaster, people toasted bread on prongs held over fires.
- In the nineteenth century, people used a product called the Toaster Over, a hollow tin box with wire cages on each of its four sides to hold slices of bread over the opening in a cast-iron coal-burning stove.
- The cover of the Jefferson Airplane's 1973 album *Thirty Seconds Over Winterland* depicts toasters with wings.
- In the 1987 children's film, *The Brave Little Toaster*, a talking toaster embarks on an adventure, accompanied by a vacuum cleaner, a blanket, a lamp, and a clock.
- In 1996, Berkeley Systems animated flying toasters for a computer screensaver in their *After Dark* product.

Popcorn Starlets

Makes about 16 pieces

WHAT YOU NEED

- 1½ quarts popped Jolly Time Blast O Butter or Butter-Licious Microwave Pop Corn
- 1 package (14 ounces) caramels, about 48, unwrapped
- 3 tablespoons half-and-half

- 1 tablespoons butter or margarine
- 1 teaspoon rum flavoring
- ⅔ cup pecan halves (about 48)
- ½ cup canned ready-made chocolate fudge frosting

WHAT YOU DO

Coat baking sheet with nonstick cooking spray.

Place popcorn in large bowl and remove any unpopped kernels.

In medium saucepan over low heat, heat caramels, half-and-half, and butter (or margarine) until caramels are melted, stirring frequently. Remove from heat. Stir in rum flavoring. Pour caramel mixture over popcorn and toss to coat well.

Arrange pecan halves in groups of 3 on prepared baking sheet. Working quickly, spoon heaping tablespoons of popcorn mixture onto the center of each pecan group.

In small saucepan, heat frosting over low heat until softened. Spoon over each mound of popcorn. Store in an airtight container in a cool place.

Rocky Road-Peanut Butter Popcorn Bars

Makes 36 bars

WHAT YOU NEED

- 3 quarts popped Jolly Time Blast O Butter or Butter-Licious Microwave Pop Corn
- ½ cup raisins
- 1 cup light corn syrup
- 1 tablespoon butter or margarine, plus more to butter pan
- ½ cup peanut butter pieces
- ⅓ cup chunky or creamy peanut butter
- ¾ cup miniature marshmallows
- ½ cup peanuts
- ½ cup semisweet chocolate pieces
- 1 teaspoon vegetable shortening

WHAT YOU DO

Coat 9-inch square baking pan with nonstick cooking spray.

Place popcorn and raisins in large bowl and remove any unpopped kernels.

In saucepan, heat corn syrup and butter (or margarine) to a boil; boil 3 minutes. Remove from heat. Stir in peanut butter pieces and peanut butter until smooth. Pour mixture over popcorn, tossing gently to coat all pieces. Press into prepared baking pan. Sprinkle marshmallows and peanuts over top, pressing lightly into popcorn mixture.

In saucepan, melt chocolate pieces and shortening over very low heat. Drizzle over top. Cool several hours before serving. Cut into 2¼- × 1-inch bars.

Strange Facts

- Around 80,000 b.c.e., cave men and women in prehistoric America placed maize kernels too close to the fire, accidentally creating the world's first popcorn.
- In 1492, the Native Americans who greeted Christopher Columbus enjoyed eating popcorn and wearing popcorn necklaces.
- Native Americans in Massachusetts brought bowlfuls of popcorn to the first Thanksgiving feast in 1620.
- In 1700, women from Boston to the Carolinas made the first tasty breakfast cereal by pouring milk and sugar over popcorn.

- Charles Cretors of Chicago, Illinois, invented the first popcorn machine in 1885—an enormous, cumbersome cart with a gasoline burner. Street vendors were soon pushing steam or gas-powered poppers through fairs, parks, and expositions—following crowds. Today, most popcorn poppers operating at movie theaters and fairs are made by the Cretors family.
- In 1914, Cloid Smith and his son, Howard Smith, set up American Pop Corn Company in the basement of their home in Sioux City, Iowa, shelling, cleaning, and packaging Jolly Time Pop Corn, the first branded popcorn in the United States.
- In 1924, Jolly Time obtained the Good Housekeeping Seal of Approval on all of its products.
- In 1925, Jolly Time began packaging popcorn in a metal can developed by the American Can Company to seal in the product's freshness.
- In 1957, Jolly Time became available in a plastic bag.
- In 1968, Jolly Time started advertising on television during the popular game show *Let's Make a Deal*.
- In 1984, Jolly Time introduced its first microwave popcorn.
- In 1997, Jolly Time launched its best-selling product—Blast O Butter Microwave Pop Corn.
- Today, the American Pop Corn Company is run by Cloid Smith's great-grandsons, Carlton and Garrett Smith.
- The American Pop Corn Company exports its products to twenty-five countries around the globe.

For More Recipes

Visit www.jollytime.com

Chip Veal Parmigiana

Makes 6 servings

WHAT YOU NEED

- 1 can (15 ounces) pureed tomatoes, undrained
- 1 can (8 ounces) tomato sauce
- ¼ cup chopped onion
- 1 teaspoon dried basil
- ½ teaspoon sugar

- Salt
- Ground black pepper
- 1½ cups crushed Lay's Classic Potato Chips
- ¾ cup grated Parmesan cheese
- 1½ pounds boneless veal, pounded thin
- 2 eggs, beaten

WHAT YOU DO

In saucepan, combine pureed tomatoes, tomato sauce, onion, basil, and sugar. Add salt and pepper to taste. Simmer 5 minutes; set aside.

Combine chips and cheese in shallow bowl. Dip veal in egg, then chip mixture to coat.

Coat skillet with nonstick cooking spray.

Fry veal in skillet over medium-high heat until golden and just cooked through, about 1 minute per side. Serve with reserved sauce.

Crispy Fish 'n Chips

Makes 4 servings

WHAT YOU NEED

- 2 pounds frozen cod or haddock fillets
- ½ cup evaporated milk
- 1 teaspoon lemon juice

- 1 teaspoon salt
- ½ cup crushed Lay's Classic Potato Chips
- 1 tablespoon butter

WHAT YOU DO

Preheat oven to 450 degrees Fahrenheit. Coat shallow baking pan with nonstick cooking spray.

Allow fish to stand at room temperature 15 minutes. Cut each fillet into three equal portions.

In small bowl, combine milk, lemon juice, and salt.

Pat fish gently with paper towel to absorb excess moisture; dip in milk mixture; roll in chips to coat. Place in prepared pan; dot with butter. Bake about 25 minutes per inch of thickness, until fish flakes.

Japantown Tempura

Makes 4 servings

WHAT YOU NEED

Ginger Dipping Sauce:
- 1 cup chicken broth
- 3 tablespoons soy sauce
- 3 tablespoons dry sherry
- 1 teaspoon sugar
- 2 teaspoons grated fresh ginger or ¼ teaspoon ground ginger

Batter:
- 1 cup all-purpose flour
- ¼ cup cornstarch

- 1¼ cups water
- 1 egg white, stiffly beaten

Tempura:
- Canola oil
- 1 pound thick fish fillets, such as halibut, haddock, cod, or red snapper, cut into 2-inch squares
- 4 cups raw vegetables, such as sliced zucchini, mushrooms, or snow peas
- 2 cups crushed Lay's Classic Potato Chips

WHAT YOU DO

To make the Ginger Dipping Sauce: In bowl, combine broth, soy sauce, sherry, sugar, and ginger. Set aside.

To make the Batter: In medium bowl, combine flour, cornstarch, and water. Fold in egg white.

To make the Tempura: In deep saucepan, heat 3 inches oil to 350 degrees Fahrenheit. Dip fish and vegetable pieces in tempura batter, drain, then coat lightly with chips. Deep fry fish and vegetables a few pieces at a time about 3 minutes until golden and crisp. Drain on paper towels. Serve hot with individual bowls of Ginger Dipping Sauce.

BLOWING THE WHISTLE ON THE TEAKETTLE

In 1921, Joseph Block, a retired cookware executive from New York, toured a teakettle factory in Westphalia, Germany. Seeing so many teakettles at once suddenly triggered a childhood memory in Block's mind. He remembered watching his father design a pressurized potato cooker that emitted a whistling sound when the cooking cycle finished. Block suggested that the teakettle manufacturer create a teakettle that whistled when the water boiled. The simple idea of combining a teakettle with a whistle intrigued the factory owner, who immediately produced thirty-six whistling teakettles, put them on sale at Wertheim's department store in Berlin, and sold out in less than three hours.

The next year, Block came out of retirement to debut his whistling teakettle in the United States at a Chicago housewares fair. He kept at least one kettle whistling throughout the weeklong show, prompting bewitched store buyers to place huge orders for the one-dollar item. Before long, Block was selling 35,000 whistling teakettles a month to department stores across the United States.

Lay's Potato Chip Cookies

Makes 5 dozen cookies

WHAT YOU NEED

- 5 cups crushed Lay's Classic Potato Chips
- 1 cup firmly packed brown sugar
- 1 cup granulated sugar
- 2 eggs, slightly beaten
- ½ cup milk
- 2 teaspoons vanilla extract
- 2 cups all-purpose flour
- 3 teaspoons baking powder
- ½ cup chopped pecans

WHAT YOU DO

Preheat oven to 375 degrees Fahrenheit. Coat baking sheet with nonstick cooking spray.

Combine potato chips, brown sugar, granulated sugar, eggs, milk, and vanilla in bowl and mix well.

In separate bowl, sift together flour and baking powder. Add to the potato chip mixture and mix well. Stir in pecans. Drop by teaspoonfuls onto prepared baking sheet, allowing space for the cookies to spread. Bake 10 to 15 minutes, or until lightly browned.

✳

Potato Chip Quiche Lorraine

Makes 6 servings

WHAT YOU NEED

- 1½ cups finely crushed Lay's Classic Potato Chips
- 1 teaspoon paprika
- 1 cup half-and-half
- 1 cup whipping cream
- 3 eggs, beaten

- 6 slices bacon, cooked crisp and crumbled
- 2 tablespoons sliced green onions
- ¼ teaspoon salt
- Dash ground black pepper
- Dash ground nutmeg
- 2 cups grated Swiss cheese

WHAT YOU DO

Preheat oven to 375 degrees Fahrenheit.

Combine chips and paprika in bowl; gently press into bottom and 1½ inches up sides of 8-inch springform pan.

In small saucepan, warm half-and-half and cream, but do not boil; beat into eggs to blend. Stir in bacon, green onions, salt, pepper, nutmeg, and cheese. Pour into crust. Bake 30 to 35 minutes, until custard is set and golden.

✳ Strange Facts ✳

- In 1853, George Crum, an American Indian working as a chef at Moon Lake Lodge in Saratoga Springs, New York, cooked up crisp, paper-thin french fries to poke fun at a guest who kept sending his order of french fries back to the kitchen. The guest loved Crum's potato chips, which became known as Saratoga Chips on the menu and were soon packaged and distributed across New England.

- In 1932, Herman W. Lay, a drop-out from Furman University living in Nashville, Tennessee, started using his 1929 Model A Ford to distribute potato chips made by a company in Atlanta, Georgia. By 1934, with six snack food routes, Lay was on his way to becoming a major distributor. In 1938, Lay bought the financially-ailing company, changed its name to H.W. Lay & Company, and made Lay's Potato Chips the company's flagship product. H.W. Lay & Company became one of the largest snack and convenience food companies in the Southeast.

- In 1961, Herman W. Lay merged his company with the Frito Company of Dallas, Texas, (founded in 1932 by ice cream maker Elmer Doolin) to form Frito-Lay.

- As chairman of the new Frito-Lay company, Herman Lay worked swiftly toward national distribution of Lay's Potato Chips and Fritos Corn Chips. In 1965, Frito-Lay, Inc. merged with the Pepsi-Cola Company to become PepsiCo, Inc, with Herman Lay as its chairman.

- Americans eat more potato chips than the citizens of any other country in the world.

- In 1960, animated cartoon character Deputy Dawg promoted Lay's Potato Chips.

- In 1963, actor Bert Lahr, who played the Cowardly Lion in the 1939 movie *The Wizard of Oz,* starred in commercials for Lay's Potato Chips, dressed as a devil and tempting viewers with the line, "Betcha can't eat just one."

- In 1968, Buddy Hackett starred in commercials for Lay's Potato Chips and told viewers, "You Can Eat a Million of 'Em, but Nobody Can Eat Just One."

For More Recipes

Visit www.fritolay.com

Lea & Perrins® Worcestershire Sauce

Bloody Mary

Makes 1 serving

WHAT YOU NEED

- ½ cup tomato juice
- 1 ounce tequila or vodka

- 2 teaspoons Lea & Perrins Worcestershire Sauce
- Twist lime peel

WHAT YOU DO

Combine all ingredients and serve in a tall elegant glass over ice.

Cheese 'n Herb Toast

Makes 4 servings

WHAT YOU NEED

- 4 thick slices French bread
- 2 tablespoons olive oil
- 1 clove garlic, halved
- 1 cup grated strong-flavored cheese, such as mature Cheddar or Gruyère
- 1 tablespoon Lea & Perrins Worcestershire Sauce

- 2 teaspoons chopped fresh sage or ½ teaspoon dried sage
- 1 teaspoon course grain mustard
- 1 egg yolk

WHAT YOU DO

Rub bread on both sides with some of the oil and then with garlic. Set bread on baking sheet and broil to toast the bread on one side.

Combine cheese, Worcestershire sauce, sage, mustard, and egg in bowl and spread on untoasted side of bread.

Sprinkle with remaining oil and broil until bubbling and golden, about 1 to 2 minutes.

Cowboy Marinade

Makes approximately 1¼ cups

WHAT YOU NEED

- Steak of your choice
- ½ cup Lea & Perrins Worcestershire Sauce
- ¼ cup olive oil or vegetable oil
- ¼ cup apple cider vinegar

- 1 onion, chopped
- ½ teaspoon garlic powder
- ½ teaspoon chili powder
- ¼ teaspoon salt

WHAT YOU DO

Place steak in shallow non-aluminum baking dish or resealable plastic food-storage bag.

Combine Worcestershire sauce, oil, vinegar, onion, garlic powder, chili powder, and salt in bowl. Pour ¾ cup marinade over steak; turn to coat.

Cover dish or close bag and marinate in refrigerator for at least 30 minutes. (See *Note*.) Refrigerate the remaining marinade.

Preheat grill or broiler.

Remove steak from marinade, discarding any marinade left in bag or dish.

Grill or broil steaks, turning occasionally and brushing frequently with refrigerated marinade, until steaks are cooked.

Note: Marinate 30 minutes to 2 hours for 4 boneless beef loin steaks, 1 inch thick (about 1½ to 1¾ pounds); 4 beef rib-eye steaks, 1 inch thick (about 8 ounces each); 2 beef porterhouse steaks, 1 inch thick (about 1¼ pounds each); or 1 boneless beef top sirloin steak, 1 inch thick (about 1¼ pounds).

Marinate 6 to 24 hours for 1 beef top round steak, 1 inch thick (about 1½ pounds).

Serving Suggestion: This marinade is great with your favorite beef steak

Lea & Perrins Cosmic Cookies (Sesame Seed Biscuits)

Makes 15 to 20 biscuits

WHAT YOU NEED

- 3 tablespoons sesame seeds
- ¾ cup all-purpose flour
- 1 teaspoon salt
- 1 teaspoon ground paprika
- Pinch chili powder
- ¾ cup unsalted butter

- 1 tablespoon Lea & Perrins Worcestershire Sauce, plus more to brush later
- ¼ cup finely grated Parmesan cheese
- ¾ cup finely grated cheese (American, Swiss, or Cheddar)

WHAT YOU DO

Preheat oven to 350 degrees Fahrenheit.

In small pan over medium-high heat, gently toast sesame seeds. Remove from heat; set aside.

Sift together flour, salt, paprika, and chili powder.

Cream together butter, Worcestershire sauce, Parmesan cheese, cheese, and 2 tablespoons toasted sesame seeds.

Combine the flour and the cheese mixtures together to make a soft dough. Roll the dough into a log shape, about 1½-inches in diameter, and wrap in a sheet of aluminum foil

Coat two baking sheets with nonstick cooking spray.

Chill the wrapped dough in refrigerator until firm, then slice into rounds about ¼-inch thick and place onto prepared baking sheets.

Brush each biscuit with additional Worcestershire sauce, then sprinkle on the remaining 1 tablespoon toasted sesame seeds. Bake 10 to 12 minutes, or until golden brown.

Cool biscuits on wire racks and store in an airtight container.

Lea & Perrins Macaroni and Cheese

Makes 4 servings

WHAT YOU NEED

- ¼ cup melted butter
- ¼ cup all-purpose flour
- 2 cups milk
- 2 cups grated Cheddar cheese

- 3 cups cooked macaroni
- 3 tablespoons Lea & Perrins Worcestershire Sauce

WHAT YOU DO

Preheat oven to 350 degrees Fahrenheit. Coat 13- × 9-inch baking dish with nonstick cooking spray.

Whisk butter and flour together in microwave-safe bowl. Add milk and microwave on high for 6 minutes, or until bubbling, stirring 2 or 3 times.

Add cheese and stir until melted.

Stir in macaroni and Worcestershire sauce. Place in prepared baking dish.

Bake 20 minutes, or until hot and bubbling.

Oysters Rockafella

Makes 24 servings

WHAT YOU NEED

- 24 fresh oysters in the shells
- 1 package (8 ounces) frozen chopped spinach, thawed
- 1 cup sour cream
- 2 tablespoons Lea & Perrins Worcestershire Sauce
- 2 cloves garlic, crushed

- Salt
- Ground black pepper
- 3 tablespoons finely grated Cheddar cheese
- 2 tablespoons fresh bread crumbs
- Rock salt

WHAT YOU DO

Preheat oven to 450 degrees Fahrenheit.

Remove oysters from their shells. Discard the top shells. Clean the bottom shells and set aside.

Drain spinach well, pressing through a sieve with the back of a spoon to remove as much moisture as possible.

In large bowl, mix sour cream with Worcestershire sauce, garlic, and spinach. Season with salt and pepper.

Put a teaspoon of the spinach mixture in each oyster shell, return the oysters to their shells, then top with another teaspoon of the mixture.

Mix the cheese with the bread crumbs. Sprinkle this over the oysters.

Fill baking pan with an even layer of rock salt. Arrange the oysters in the rock salt to steady them on a baking pan. Bake 10 minutes until cooked through, and then broil until golden brown.

✳Strange Facts✳

- In the early 1800s, nobleman Lord Sandys returned to his home in the county of Worcester, England, from his travels in Bengal, India. Determined to duplicate a recipe he had acquired for an Indian sauce, Lord Sandys asked John Lea and William Perrins, owners of a chemist shop, to blend the concoction.
- Lea and Perrins prepared a few extra gallons of the sauce for themselves, but they found the taste revolting. They stored the sauce in jars in the cellar. A few years later, they found the abandoned jars and, before throwing them out, tasted the sauce again. They were amazed to discover that the aged concoction now tasted wonderful.
- Lea and Perrins began bottling the sauce, and through word of mouth, Worcestershire sauce (named after the county of its origin) was soon being used across Europe.
- In 1886, a volcanic eruption destroyed and engulfed the Maori village of Te Wairoa in New Zealand. During excavations in the 1970s, archeologists found a bottle of Lea & Perrins Worcestershire Sauce buried in the rubble.
- From 1903 to 1904, Lieutenant Colonel Sir Francis Edward Young journeyed to Tibet, finally arriving at the forbidden city of Lhasa on August 3, 1904. At the monastery, he spotted a bottle of Lea & Perrins Worcestershire Sauce on the refectory table.

For More Recipes

Visit www.leaperrins.com

Barbecued Meat Loaf

Makes 8 servings

WHAT YOU NEED

- 1 envelope (1 ounce) Lipton Recipe Secrets Onion Soup Mix
- 2 pounds ground beef
- 1½ cups fresh bread crumbs

- 2 eggs
- ¾ cup water
- ⅔ cup barbecue sauce, divided

WHAT YOU DO

Preheat oven to 350 degrees Fahrenheit.

In large bowl, combine soup mix, beef, bread crumbs, eggs, water, and ⅓ cup barbecue sauce.

In 13- x 9-inch baking or roasting pan, shape into loaf. Top with reserved barbecue sauce. Bake 1 hour. Let stand 10 minutes before serving.

Green Bean Casserole

Makes 6 servings

WHAT YOU NEED

- 1 envelope (1 ounce) Lipton Recipe Secrets Onion Mushroom Soup Mix
- 1 tablespoon all-purpose flour
- 1 cup milk

- 2 packages (10 ounces each) frozen cut green beans, thawed
- 1 cup shredded Cheddar cheese, divided
- ¼ cup plain dry bread crumbs

WHAT YOU DO

Preheat oven to 350 degrees Fahrenheit.

In 1½-quart ovenproof casserole, combine soup mix, flour, and milk; stir in green beans and ½ cup cheese.

Bake 25 minutes.

Sprinkle with bread crumbs and remaining ½ cup cheese. Bake an additional 5 minutes, or until cheese is melted.

Lipton Onion Dip

Makes 2 cups

WHAT YOU NEED

- 1 envelope (1 ounce) Lipton Recipe Secrets Onion Soup Mix
- 1 container (16 ounces) sour cream

WHAT YOU DO

In medium bowl, blend all ingredients; chill if desired.

Serving Suggestion: Serve with your favorite dippers.

Oniony Braised Short Ribs

Makes 4 servings

WHAT YOU NEED

- 2 tablespoons olive oil
- 3 pounds beef chuck short ribs
- 1 envelope (1 ounce) Lipton Recipe Secrets Onion Soup Mix
- 3½ cups water, divided
- ¼ cup ketchup
- 2 tablespoons firmly packed brown sugar
- 2 tablespoons sherry (optional)
- ½ teaspoon ground ginger
- 1 tablespoon all-purpose flour
- ¼ teaspoon ground black pepper

WHAT YOU DO

In 6-quart Dutch oven or saucepot, heat oil over medium-high heat and brown ribs in two batches. Return all ribs to Dutch oven.

Stir in soup mix combined with 3¼ cups water, ketchup, sugar, sherry (if desired), and ginger. Bring to a boil. Reduce heat to low and simmer covered 2 hours, or until ribs are tender.

Remove ribs to serving platter and keep warm.

In small bowl, whisk together flour and remaining ¼ cup water. Add to Dutch over with pepper. Bring to a boil over high heat. Boil, stirring occasionally, 2 minutes, or until thickened. Pour sauce over ribs.

COOKING WITH A CLOTHES IRON

Sunnyside-Up Eggs

Turn a clothes iron upside down, positioned between two bricks to keep the ironing surface level. Set the iron on heat. Melt a slice of butter on the metal surface, then crack open an egg on the metal surface and, using a spatula, fry the egg.

Toast

To make toast using an iron, preheat the iron to wool setting, place a slice of bread on a wooden cutting board, and iron for 20 seconds.

Grilled Cheese Sandwich

Preheat the iron to the wool setting, place a Kraft Single between two slices of Wonder Bread, place the sandwich on a wooden cutting board, and iron the top piece of bread for 20 seconds. Flip the sandwich over and iron for another 20 seconds.

- In the 1983 movie *Mr. Mom,* Michael Keaton cooks a grilled cheese sandwich using a clothes iron—as does Johnny Depp in the 1993 film *Benny & Joon.*
- In the fifteenth century, upper class Europeans owned irons with compartments that held heated coals. The lower classes used flat irons heated over fires.
- In the nineteenth century, inventors created gas-heated irons, but the devices, connected to gas lines, frequently leaked, exploded, and ignited fires.
- In 1882, Henry W. Weely invented the first electric iron. When plugged into its stand, the iron heated up. While being used, the iron cooled down rapidly, requiring the user to continually reheat the iron.
- At the turn of the twentieth century, manufacturers produced a variety of electric irons—all weighing more than ten pounds. Unfortunately, most consumers could use this laborsaving device only at night because until 1905, most electric companies only ran their generators between sunset and sunrise.
- In the early 1900s, Earl Richardson, a meter reader for an electric company in Ontario, California, devised a homemade lightweight iron and persuaded the power company to generate electricity all day on Tuesdays, the day most homemakers on his route ironed clothes.

Oven Baked Stew

Makes 8 servings

WHAT YOU NEED

- 2 pounds boneless beef chuck or round steak, cut into 1-inch cubes
- ¼ cup all-purpose flour
- 1⅓ cups sliced carrots
- 1 can (14½ ounces) whole peeled tomatoes, undrained and chopped
- 1 bay leaf
- 1 envelope (1 ounce) Lipton Recipe Secrets Onion Soup Mix
- ½ cup dry red wine or water
- 1 cup fresh or canned sliced mushrooms
- 1 package (8 ounces) medium or broad egg noodles, cooked and drained

WHAT YOU DO

Preheat oven to 425 degrees Fahrenheit.

In 2½-quart shallow ovenproof casserole, toss beef with flour, then bake uncovered 20 minutes, stirring halfway.

Reduce heat to 350 degrees Fahrenheit.

Add carrots, tomatoes, and bay leaf.

In small bowl, blend soup mix with wine (or water). Pour over beef.

Bake covered 1½ hours, or until beef is tender. Stir in mushrooms and bake covered an additional 10 minutes. Remove bay leaf. Serve over noodles.

Potato Latkes

Makes 15 latkes

WHAT YOU NEED

- 1 envelope (1 ounce) Lipton Recipe Secrets Onion Soup Mix
- 6 medium potatoes, peeled and finely grated
- ¼ cup all-purpose flour
- 2 eggs, slightly beaten
- Vegetable oil

WHAT YOU DO

In large bowl, combine soup mix, potatoes, flour, and eggs.

In large skillet over high heat, heat ¼ inch oil. Drop potato mixture by heaping tablespoonfuls into hot oil. Cook, turning once, until golden brown; drain. Add additional oil to skillet as needed, heating well after each addition.

Serving Suggestion: Serve with sour cream, cream cheese, or warm applesauce.

Savory Lo Mein

Makes 4 servings

WHAT YOU NEED

- 2 tablespoons vegetable oil
- 1 medium clove garlic, minced
- 1 small head bok choy, cut into 2-inch pieces (about 5 cups), or 5 cups coarsely shredded green cabbage
- 1 envelope (1 ounce) Lipton Recipe Secrets Onion Soup Mix
- 1 cup water

- 2 tablespoons sherry (optional)
- 1 teaspoon soy sauce
- ¼ teaspoon ground ginger (optional)
- 8 ounces linguine or spaghetti, cooked and drained
- Toasted sesame seeds (optional)

WHAT YOU DO

In 12-inch skillet, heat oil over medium heat and cook garlic and bok choy, stirring frequently, 10 minutes, or until crisp-tender. (If substituting cabbage, decrease cooking time to 3 minutes.)

In small bowl, blend soup mix with water, sherry (if desired), soy sauce, and ginger (if desired). Stir mixture into skillet containing garlic and bok choy and bring to a boil over high heat. Reduce heat to low and simmer, stirring occasionally, 5 minutes. Toss with hot linguine. Sprinkle with sesame seeds, if desired.

Southwestern Pork Roast

Makes 8 servings

WHAT YOU NEED

- 1 tablespoon vegetable oil
- 2½- pound boneless pork roast
- 2 cans (4 ounces each) chopped green chilies, undrained
- 1 can (14½ ounces) diced tomatoes, undrained
- 1 envelope (1 ounce) Lipton Recipe Secrets Onion Soup Mix
- 1 tablespoon firmly packed dark brown sugar
- 2 to 3 teaspoons chili powder
- 1 teaspoon ground cumin

WHAT YOU DO

In Dutch oven, heat oil over medium-high heat and brown pork on all sides. Stir in remaining ingredients.

Bring to a boil over high heat. Reduce heat to low and simmer covered 50 minutes, or until pork is done. Let stand 10 minutes.

Serving Suggestion: Serve with hot cooked noodles or rice.

Strange Facts

- Born in 1850 in Glasgow, Scotland, Sir Thomas J. Lipton sold cured meats, eggs, butter, and cheeses from a small store that grew into a chain of stores throughout Scotland and England. In 1888, Lipton entered the tea trade, and two years later the company entered the American market, pioneering packaged tea with the famous Flo-Thru bag.
- Thomas J. Lipton was knighted in 1898 and made a baronet in 1902.
- A yachting enthusiast, Lipton made five unsuccessful attempts to win the America's Cup. His portrait, complete with nautical attire, adorns most Lipton Tea packages.
- The Thomas J. Lipton Company launched Recipe Soup Mix in 1953, featuring easy recipes printed directly on the pouch.

- The onion originated in Mongolia.
- The leading onion-growing state is California, followed by Washington, Oregon, Texas, and Colorado.
- The odor of onions is caused by an oil that forms a vapor when onions are cut or peeled.
- According to *The Guinness Book of World Records*, the largest onion ever grown in recorded history weighted 10 pounds, 14 ounces and was grown by V. Throup of Silsden, Great Britain, in 1990.
- Washing a cutting board or your hands with lemon juice eliminates the smell of onions.

For More Recipes

Visit www.recipesecrets.com

Marshmallow Fluff®

Fluff Seven-Minute Frosting

Makes 3 to 4 cups

WHAT YOU NEED

- 1 cup Marshmallow Fluff
- 2 egg whites, at room temperature
- 1 cup sugar
- ¼ teaspoon cream of tartar
- ⅛ teaspoon salt
- ¼ cup water
- 1 teaspoon vanilla extract

WHAT YOU DO

In large double-boiler over hot, not boiling, water combine Fluff, egg whites, sugar, cream of tartar, salt, and water. With hand mixer, beat until soft peaks form, about 7 minutes. Remove from heat and continue beating until stiff. Beat in vanilla.

Note: This recipe makes enough frosting to fill and frost two 8-or 9-inch cake layers.

Harvard Squares

Makes 24 squares

WHAT YOU NEED

- ⅓ cup butter or margarine, melted
- 1½ cups graham cracker crumbs
- 1 jar (7½ ounces) Marshmallow Fluff
- ⅓ cup milk
- 1 package (6 ounces) semisweet chocolate pieces
- 3½ ounces flaked coconut
- 1 cup chopped walnuts

WHAT YOU DO

Preheat oven to 350 degrees Fahrenheit.

In small bowl, combine butter (or margarine) and graham cracker crumbs. Press buttered crumbs into the bottom of 13- x 9-inch baking pan.

In small saucepan over low heat, combine Fluff and milk, stirring until smooth. Pour over crumbs. Top evenly with chocolate pieces, coconut, and walnuts; press down gently. Bake 25 to 30 minutes, or until lightly browned. Cool completely; cut into 2-inch squares.

Holiday Sweet Potatoes

Makes 6 to 8 servings

WHAT YOU NEED

- 4 large sweet potatoes, peeled, cooked (see *Note*), and cut into chunks, or 1 can (40 ounces) sweet potatoes, well drained
- 1 can (8 ounces) pineapple chunks, well drained
- ¼ teaspoon ground cinnamon
- 1 jar (7½ ounces) Marshmallow Fluff
- ¼ cup butter or margarine
- 1 cup coarsely chopped walnuts

WHAT YOU DO

Preheat oven to 325 degrees Fahrenheit.

Arrange sweet potatoes and pineapple in shallow 2-quart baking dish; sprinkle with cinnamon.

In small saucepan, combine Fluff and butter (or margarine). Heat to boiling over high heat, stirring constantly. Pour over sweet potatoes; sprinkle with walnuts. Bake 15 to 20 minutes, or until hot and bubbly.

Note: To cook fresh sweet potatoes quickly, arrange them on microwave-safe plate, cover with plastic wrap, and cook on high 10 to 12 minutes, or until tender.

Lynne's Cheesecake

Makes 12 to 14 servings

WHAT YOU NEED

- 24 ounces cream cheese, softened
- 3 tablespoons all-purpose flour
- 1 jar (7½ ounces) Marshmallow Fluff
- 2 eggs
- 1 unbaked Graham Cracker Crust (see recipe on page 178) or 1 ready-to-use crust (9 ounces)

WHAT YOU DO

Preheat oven to 350 degrees Fahrenheit.

Mix cream cheese with flour and Fluff in bowl until smooth. Add eggs just until blended. Pour into pie crust. Bake 45 minutes, or just until edges begin to brown. Turn off heat and let cool in oven with door cracked open about 1 hour. Remove to wire rack and cool completely. Refrigerate at least 4 hours before serving.

Graham Cracker Crust:

24 2-inch graham crackers, crushed

⅓ cup butter or margarine, melted

¼ cup sugar

Mix cracker crumbs with butter (or margarine) and sugar in bowl until blended. Pour into 8- or 9-inch springform pan and, using the back of a spoon, press onto bottom and side of pan up to 1 inch of top. Or press crumbs into deep-dish 9-inch or 10-inch pie plate.

Never-Fail Fudge

Makes 2½ pounds

WHAT YOU NEED

- 2½ cups sugar
- ½ stick (4 tablespoons) butter or margarine
- 1 can (5.33 ounces) evaporated milk (¾ cup)
- 1 jar (7½ ounces) Marshmallow Fluff

- ¾ teaspoon salt
- ¾ teaspoon vanilla extract
- 1 package (12 ounces) semisweet chocolate pieces
- ½ cup chopped walnuts

WHAT YOU DO

Coat 9-inch square baking pan with nonstick cooking spray.

In large saucepan combine sugar, butter (or margarine), milk, Fluff, and salt. Stir over low heat until blended. Heat to a full-rolling boil being careful not to mistake escaping air bubbles for boiling. Boil slowly, stirring constantly, 5 minutes. Remove from heat, stir in vanilla and chocolate until chocolate is melted. Add nuts. Turn into prepared pan and cool.

Popcorn Fluff Puffs

Makes 9 puffs

WHAT YOU NEED

- 1 jar (7½ ounces) Marshmallow Fluff
- ¼ cup butter or margarine
- 8 cups popped unsalted, unbuttered popcorn

WHAT YOU DO

Coat 9-inch square baking pan with nonstick cooking spray.

Combine Fluff and butter (or margarine) in microwave-safe dish. Cook on high 2 minutes; stir and cook 1 minute more. (Or combine Fluff and butter in medium saucepan over medium-high heat, stirring constantly until fluff boils.) Stir in popcorn. Using a spatula or waxed paper, pat into prepared pan. Cool. Cut into 3-inch square puffs.

Strange Facts

- In 1920, in Lynn, Massachusetts, H. Allen Durkee and Fred L. Mower, two veterans of World War I who had been making candies together in the kitchen at night and selling them door to door by day, bought the recipe for Marshmallow Fluff for five hundred dollars from Archibald Query, a candy manufacturer from Sommerville, Massachusetts. Within ten years, Durkee and Mower boasted the largest distribution of marshmallow cream in New England.
- In the 1930s, Durkee-Mower sponsored the weekly *Flufferettes* radio show in New England. The fifteen-minute show, which aired on Sunday evenings just before Jack Benny, included live music and comedy skits and served as a steppingstone to national recognition for a number of talented performers. The show continued through the late forties.
- The sugar shortages during World War II forced Durkee-Mower to cut Marshmallow Fluff production back considerably.
- Marshmallow Fluff requires no refrigeration.
- Marshmallow Fluff contains no preservatives of any kind.

- In 1956, Durkee-Mower teamed up with Nestlé to publish a recipe for an easy-to-make fudge in *Ladies Home Journal* and other magazines. The recipe featured Marshmallow Fluff and Nestlé Chocolate Bits, and the nationwide ad campaign won the Promotion-of-the-Year Award. The same Never-Fail Fudge recipe can still be found on the backs of Fluff labels and on page 178 of this cookbook.
- In 1966, Durkee-Mower teamed up with the Kellogg's Company to promote a new Rice Krispies Treats recipe featuring Rice Krispies cereal and Marshmallow Fluff.
- Marshmallow Fluff is available in the United States, Canada, the United Kingdom, France, Germany, Holland, Israel, South Africa, Belgium, and the United Arab Emirates.

For More Recipes

Visit www.marshmallowfluff.com

*Mc Cormick®

*Food Coloring

All-American Pasta Salad

Makes 10 (1-cup) servings

WHAT YOU NEED

- 12 cups water, divided
- 1½ teaspoons McCormick Red Food Coloring
- 6 cups (16 ounces) uncooked rotini (twists), divided
- 1½ teaspoons McCormick Blue Food Coloring

- 1 bottle (8 ounces) Italian salad dressing
- 4 tablespoons McCormick Salad Supreme Seasoning
- 5 cups assorted raw vegetables, such as tomatoes, carrots, cucumbers, yellow squash, and red onions, cut into bite-size pieces

WHAT YOU DO

In large saucepan, bring 2 cups water to a boil. Add red food coloring and 1 cup pasta. Cook according to package directions. Drain and rinse under cold water to stop cooking. Repeat with 2 cups fresh water, blue food coloring and 1 cup pasta. Repeat with 8 cups fresh water and remaining 4 cups pasta.

Place pasta in large salad bowl, add dressing and seasoning, and toss gently to coat.

Add vegetables to pasta and mix gently. Cover and refrigerate at least 4 hours.

Colored Sugar

Makes ½ cup sugar

WHAT YOU NEED

- ½ cup sugar

- McCormick Assorted Food Colors & Egg Dye

WHAT YOU DO

Place sugar in resealable plastic food-storage bag. Add 5 drops of one food coloring to create a pale color. Add more of the same food coloring a drop or two at a time to create a more intense color. Seal bag and knead gently to disburse color throughout the sugar.

Spread sugar in a thin layer on baking sheet and break up any large lumps. Allow to dry thoroughly, about 15 to 20 minutes. Sift or press through sieve to return sugar to its original texture, if needed.

Serving Suggestion: Sprinkle colored sugar onto cookies or cakes before baking or sprinkle onto cooled, freshly iced baked goods or your favorite cookies or cakes. (Allow baked goods to cool thoroughly before glazing or frosting. Fresh icing helps sugar stick to baked goods.)

Easter Eggs

Makes 12 colored eggs

WHAT YOU NEED

- 1 dozen large eggs
- 1 package McCormick Assorted Food Colors & Egg Dye

- Vinegar

WHAT YOU DO

Gently place eggs in a single layer in saucepan. Add enough cold water to cover eggs with 1 inch of water. Cover pan and bring just to a boil, over high heat. Remove from heat and let stand about 15 minutes (Adjust time up or down by 3 minutes for each size larger or smaller.)

After 15 minutes, pour off the hot water and rapidly cool eggs by running them under cold water (or place in ice water) until completely cooled.

Combine ½ cup boiling water, 1 teaspoon vinegar, and specified number of food coloring drops, listed below, in a cup to achieve desired colors. Repeat for each color. Dip hard-cooked eggs in dye for about 5 minutes. Use a slotted spoon, wire egg holder, or tongs to add and remove eggs from dye. Allow eggs to dry.

Color Suggestions: Lime: 24 yellow, 4 green; Purple: 15 blue, 5 red; Cantaloupe: 24 yellow, 2 red; Jade: 17 green, 3 blue; Plum: 10 red, 4 blue; Raspberry: 14 red, 6 blue; Watermelon: 25 red, 2 blue; Teal: 15 green, 5 blue; Fuchsia: 18 red, 2 blue; Spearmint: 12 green, 6 yellow, 2 blue; Maize: 24 yellow, 1 red; Grape: 17 blue, 4 red; Orange Sunset: 17 yellow, 3 red; Jungle Green: 14 green, 6 yellow.

Recipe Variations:
- *Painting eggs: Combine 20 drops food coloring and ½ teaspoon vinegar in small container. Paint hard-cooked eggs with a paintbrush or cotton swab.*

- *Two-tone: Dip top half of hard-cooked egg in 1 color and the bottom half in another.*
- *Designing eggs: Place rubber bands, stickers, or reinforcements on the egg before dyeing to create the design of choice. Once dry, remove the rubber bands, etc., to view the design.*
- *Personalize eggs: Write names or draw pictures on the egg with a white or light-colored crayon before dyeing.*

Festive Mashed Potatoes

Makes 6 servings

WHAT YOU NEED

- McCormick Food Coloring
- 4 cups mashed potatoes

WHAT YOU DO

Add a few drops food coloring to mashed potatoes to make festive holiday food.

Note: Try green for St. Patrick's Day, orange for Halloween, and red for Valentine's Day.

Glazed Sugar Cookies

Makes 30 cookies

WHAT YOU NEED

Sugar Cookies:
- 1 cup butter or margarine, softened
- 1½ cups sugar
- 2 teaspoons cream of tartar
- 1 teaspoon baking soda
- ¼ teaspoon salt
- 2 eggs
- 1 teaspoon vanilla extract
- 2¾ cups all-purpose flour

Glaze:
- 3 to 4 teaspoons milk
- ½ teaspoon vanilla extract
- 1 cup confectioners' sugar, plus more as needed
- McCormick Assorted Food Colors & Egg Dye

WHAT YOU DO

To make the Sugar Cookies: Cream butter (or margarine) for 30 seconds in large mixer bowl. Blend in sugar, cream of tartar, baking soda, and salt. Beat in eggs and vanilla. Mix in as much of the flour as possible with mixer. Use wooden spoon to stir in any remaining flour.

Cover and chill 1 hour, or until dough is firm.

Preheat oven to 375 degrees Fahrenheit.

Shape dough into 1-inch balls and place 2 inches apart on ungreased baking sheet.

Bake 8 to 10 minutes, or until edges are lightly brown. Transfer to wire rack; let cool.

To make the Glaze: Combine milk and vanilla; stir in sugar. Adjust the consistency as needed by adding a bit more water to thin or more confectioners' sugar to stiffen. Blend in 3 or 4 drops food coloring until evenly distributed and glaze is smooth. (If desired, divide the icing among separate small bowls and tint each one with a different color by stirring in 1 to 2 drops food coloring.) Decorate cooled cookies with colored glaze as desired. Allow glaze to set up or dry before storing in airtight container.

Shamrock Pudding

Makes 4 servings

WHAT YOU NEED

- 3½ cups milk
- 1 teaspoon Green McCormick Food Coloring
- 2 packages (3.4 ounces each) vanilla instant pudding mix
- 1 tub (8 ounces) frozen whipped topping, thawed
- 1 package (18 ounces) chocolate sandwich cookies, coarsely crushed

WHAT YOU DO

Pour milk into large bowl. Stir in food coloring. Add pudding mixes. Beat with wire whisk 2 minutes, or until well blended. Let stand 5 minutes. Gently stir in whipped topping.

Layer crushed cookies and pudding mixture in 3-quart bowl, beginning and ending with crushed cookies.

Refrigerate 1 hour, or until ready to serve.

Serving Suggestion: Garnish with shamrock candies.

Strange Facts

- In the eighteenth and nineteenth centuries, unscrupulous food manufacturers used colorings to disguise spoiled foods.

- In the United States, the first federal regulation concerning food colors was an 1886 act of Congress allowing butter to be colored.

- The ancient Aztecs used cochineal, a red dye prepared from the dried bodies of female *Dactylopius coccus*, an insect that lives on cactus plants in Central and South America. Cochineal is still used today in food coloring, medicinal products, cosmetics, inks, and artists' pigments.

- Studies show that people judge the quality of food by its color. In fact, the color of a food actually affects a person's perception of its taste, smell, and feel. Researchers have concluded that color even affects a person's ability to identify flavor.

- In 1976, after scientists determined that Red Dye Number 2 caused cancer in rats, M&M's Chocolate Candies stopped making red M&M's (which did not contain Red Dye Number 2) and replaced them with tan M&M's, sparking protests from the Society for the Restoration and Preservation of Red M&M's. In 1987, the company brought back red M&M's, using FD&C Red Number 40.

- An extensive survey conducted by the National Academy of Sciences in 1977 estimated that every day each American consumes an average of 100 milligrams of FD&C Red Dye No. 40, 43 milligrams of FD&C Yellow Dye No. 5, and 37 milligrams FD&C Yellow Dye No. 6.

For More Recipes

Visit www.mccormick.com

McCormick®
Pure Vanilla
Extract

IGNITING THE STOVE

In the 1790s, British statesman and inventor Count von Rumford, born Benjamin Thompson, designed the first practical cooking stove—a box built from bricks with holes in the top to hold pots.

In 1802, British iron founder George Bodley invented and patented a compact cast-iron, closed-top, even-heating cooking range, fueled by coal, with a modern flue. That same year, German inventor Frederick Albert Winson produced a makeshift gas cooking range. Unfortunately, more permanent gas range models tended to leak fumes and explode. In 1855, German chemist Robert W. Bunsen invented the first practical gas burner, and the following decade, Americans who had gas piped into their homes to fuel gaslights began embracing the gas range.

In 1890, manufacturers introduced the first electric stoves. Unfortunately, these contraptions, equipped with crude thermostats, tended to incinerate meals and send electric bills through the roof. Luckily for consumers, most homes in America were not yet wired for electricity.

In 1910, gas became available in pressurized containers, enabling people living in rural areas to use gas ranges. Twenty years later, manufacturers introduced the modern electric range.

Guava-Cheese Flan

Makes 8 servings

WHAT YOU NEED

- 1 cup sugar
- ¼ cup water
- 1 can (14 ounces) sweetened condensed milk
- 1 can (12 ounces) evaporated milk
- 5 large eggs
- ½ cup guava paste (available in the international aisle)
- 4 ounces cream cheese
- 1 tablespoon McCormick Pure Vanilla Extract

WHAT YOU DO

Preheat oven to 350 degrees Fahrenheit.

Place sugar and water into 9-inch cake pan. Stir until sugar is slightly dissolved. Place pan on stove over medium heat. Caramelize sugar, without stirring, until sugar turns a golden to golden-brown color, about 10 minutes. Use an oven mitt to hold pan and swirl pan to coat bottom and sides with caramel. Place pan on cooling rack to cool and harden caramel slightly.

Meanwhile, place condensed milk, evaporated milk, eggs, guava paste, cream cheese, and vanilla in blender. Blend until smooth.

Pour mixture into cooled and hardened caramelized pan; cover with aluminum foil. Set pan into large shallow baking pan or bottom of broiler pan containing about 1-inch hot water. Bake 1 hour, or until knife inserted in center comes out clean.

Remove pan from water bath and cool on wire rack. Carefully loosen sides of custard from pan with a knife. Cover and refrigerate 3 hours, or until chilled. (May be chilled overnight.) To unmold, invert pan onto large shallow plate or pie dish.

Vanilla-Almond Torte

Makes 6 servings

WHAT YOU NEED

- 1 sheet frozen puff pastry, thawed
- ½ cup whipping cream
- 4 ounces cream cheese, softened
- ¼ cup sugar
- 1 teaspoon McCormick Pure Vanilla Extract
- ⅛ teaspoon almond extract
- 3 tablespoons sliced almonds
- Ground cinnamon

WHAT YOU DO

Preheat oven to 350 degrees Fahrenheit. Coat baking sheet with nonstick cooking spray.

Unfold pastry sheet on floured surface. Press dough together at folds. Cut in half lengthwise. Place on prepared baking sheet. Bake 15 minutes. Let cool. Slice cooled pastry in half horizontally.

Whip cream in bowl until stiff peaks form. Set aside.

Mix cream cheese, sugar, vanilla, and almond extract in bowl until creamy. Gently fold in whipped cream.

Assemble 4-layer torte by alternating layers of pastry and cream using ⅓ cup cream mixture between layers. Begin with pastry and end with cream mixture. Sprinkle with almonds and cinnamon. Refrigerate 2 hours or overnight.

Vanilla French Toast

Makes 4 (2-slice) servings

WHAT YOU NEED

- 2 eggs, slightly beaten
- 2 tablespoons sugar
- 1 tablespoon McCormick Pure Vanilla Extract
- ½ teaspoon ground cinnamon

- ⅛ teaspoon salt
- 1 cup milk
- 1 tablespoon butter
- 8 slices sandwich bread

WHAT YOU DO

Combine eggs, sugar, vanilla, cinnamon, and salt in shallow bowl. Stir in milk. Mix well with a fork or whisk.

Melt just enough butter to lightly coat nonstick skillet, over medium heat, reserving remaining butter for additional batches. Dip 2 or 3 bread slices (or as many as will fit into the skillet) into egg mixture one at a time, coating well. Drain excess.

Place bread in skillet; cook 3 minutes each side, or until lightly browned. Repeat for remaining bread slices.

✳

Vanilla Green Beans Amandine

Makes 6 servings

WHAT YOU NEED

- 1 pound fresh green beans, trimmed, or 16 ounces frozen green beans
- 2 tablespoons butter
- 1 tablespoon dry white wine
- 1½ teaspoons McCormick Pure Vanilla Extract

- ½ teaspoon onion powder
- ¼ teaspoon salt
- ⅛ to ¼ teaspoon ground black pepper
- ¼ cup sliced almonds, toasted (see Note)

WHAT YOU DO

Fill large stockpot with water and bring to a boil. If using fresh green beans, add the green beans and cook, uncovered, on medium-high heat 7 to 8 minutes. Drain. (For frozen green beans, cook following package directions. Drain.)

Melt butter in small saucepan; stir in wine, vanilla, onion powder, salt, and pepper. Simmer 2 minutes.

Toss butter sauce with green beans. Top with almonds.

Note: To toast sliced almonds, spread in a single layer on baking sheet; bake at 350 degrees Fahrenheit 3 to 5 minutes.

✳

Vanilla Vinaigrette

Makes 4 (2-tablespoon) servings

WHAT YOU NEED

- ⅓ cup olive oil
- 3 tablespoons white wine vinegar
- 1 teaspoon McCormick Pure Vanilla Extract
- 1 teaspoon tarragon leaves

- ¼ teaspoon ground black pepper
- ½ teaspoon salt
- ½ teaspoon sugar

WHAT YOU DO

Mix all ingredients until well blended. Refrigerate.

Serving Suggestion: Serve over mixed greens. Add fresh strawberries and toasted almonds, if desired.

Strange Facts

- Vanilla extract is prepared by chopping vanilla beans into small pieces and then percolating them with alcohol and water.
- Vanilla bean, the fruit of a unique species of orchid with aerial roots, fruit pods, and fragrant flowers, is native to the tropical rainforests of Mexico and Central America. Vanilla is the only orchid known to bear edible fruit.
- Indigenous peoples discovered that the tasteless and odorless vanilla bean, when dried by months of tropical heat and humidity, produced a rich taste and aroma.
- When Aztecs conquered the nations of southeastern Mexico in the 1500s, they named the vanilla bean *tlilxochitl*, meaning "black flower."
- In 1520, Aztec emperor Montezuma served Spanish explorer Hernán Cortez a thick, syrupy mixture of cocoa beans, ground corn, honey, and black vanilla pods in a golden goblet. Cortez conquered the Aztecs, killed Montezuma, and brought vanilla to Europe, where it achieved great popularity.
- No one could get vanilla plants to produce pods outside of Mexico—until 1836, when Belgian botanist Charles Morren discovered that a tiny bee, the Melipone, found only in the Vanilla districts of Mexico, is the only insect equipped to pollinate vanilla plants. The bee did not survive outside Mexico, so Morren developed a method of hand-pollinating *Vanilla* blossoms.
- Vanilla is the world's most popular flavor.
- The vanilla bean requires approximately nine months to reach maturity, growing six to ten inches long like a overgrown string bean.
- Vanilla is the second most expensive flavoring in the world to produce, preceded only by saffron.
- Queen Elizabeth I loved vanilla so much that she eventually refused all foods prepared without it.
- Thomas Jefferson, having acquired a taste for vanilla in France, was the first person to import it to the United States.

For More Recipes

Visit www.mccormick.com

*Mott's®
Apple Sauce

Apple-Banana Smoothie

Makes 2 (8-ounce) servings

WHAT YOU NEED

- 2 bananas, peeled and frozen
- ½ cup buttermilk
- 1 cup Mott's Natural Apple Sauce

WHAT YOU DO

Place bananas, buttermilk, and apple sauce in blender. Puree and pour into chilled mugs.

Apple Pasta Salad

Makes 6 servings

WHAT YOU NEED

Dressing:
- 2 cups Mott's Natural Apple Sauce
- ¼ cup apple cider vinegar
- 2 tablespoons Dijon mustard
- 2 tablespoons chopped fresh dill or 1 tablespoon dry dill
- Dash salt

Pasta:
- 1 pound cooked fusilli pasta, cooled
- ¾ cup grape tomatoes, halved
- ½ cup quartered and sliced cucumbers
- ½ cup sliced red onion
- ½ cup feta cheese
- ¼ cup black pitted olives, halved

WHAT YOU DO

To make the Dressing: Combine the dressing ingredients in medium mixing bowl.

To make the Pasta: Add pasta to the dressing. Toss with all other ingredients.

Appledillas

Makes 1 serving

WHAT YOU NEED

- 1 (8-inch) flour tortilla
- 1 tablespoon light cream cheese
- ¼ cup Mott's Natural Apple Sauce
- Pinch ground cinnamon

WHAT YOU DO

Spread one side of tortilla evenly with cream cheese. Spread apple sauce evenly over cream cheese and sprinkle with cinnamon. Fold tortilla in half.

Coat sauté pan with nonstick cooking spray and heat over medium heat. Place folded tortilla in pan, cook 12 minutes on each side until lightly browned. Remove to serving plate. Allow to cool slightly before cutting.

Breakfast Bread Pudding

Makes 9 servings

WHAT YOU NEED

Streusel Topping:
- ⅔ cup quick-cooking oats
- 3 tablespoons brown sugar
- ½ teaspoon ground cinnamon

Bread Pudding:
- 1 cup Mott's Natural Apple Sauce
- 1 cup 2 percent low-fat milk
- 2 large eggs
- ¼ cup brown sugar
- 4 slices cinnamon raisin bread, cut into cubes (about 4 cups)

WHAT YOU DO

Preheat oven to 350 degrees Fahrenheit. Lightly coat 8- × 8-inch baking pan with nonstick cooking spray.

To make the Streusel Topping: In small bowl, combine oats, sugar, and cinnamon. Set aside.

To make the Bread Pudding: Combine apple sauce, milk, eggs, and sugar in medium bowl. Whisk until well combined. Gently stir in bread cubes until well moistened. Pour mixture into prepared pan. Top with Streusel Topping. Bake 30 minutes, or until wooden pick inserted into center comes out clean. Serve warm.

Choco-Bloc Pudding

Makes 6 servings

WHAT YOU NEED

- 1 cup 2 percent low-fat milk, divided
- 2 tablespoons cornstarch
- 1 cup Mott's Natural Apple Sauce
- ½ cup semisweet chocolate chips
- ⅓ cup sugar

WHAT YOU DO

Combine ¼ cup milk and cornstarch in small bowl, mixing until cornstarch is thoroughly dissolved.

Combine apple sauce, remaining ¾ cup milk, chocolate chips, and sugar in heavy saucepan over medium heat. Stir until chocolate is melted and mixture is smooth and simmering. Stir in cornstarch mixture. Cook, stirring constantly, 1 to 2 minutes. Remove from heat and cool. Cover and chill until ready to serve.

Nuts-for-Apples Cookies

Makes about 2 dozen cookies

WHAT YOU NEED

- 1 cup Mott's Natural Apple Sauce
- 1 cup sugar
- ½ cup chunky peanut butter
- 1 large egg
- 1 cup all-purpose flour
- 1 cup rolled oats
- 1 cup shredded coconut, lightly toasted
- ½ cup raisins
- 1 teaspoon ground cinnamon
- ½ teaspoon baking soda

WHAT YOU DO

Preheat oven to 350 degrees Fahrenheit. Lightly coat baking sheet with nonstick cooking spray.

Combine apple sauce, sugar, peanut butter, and egg in large bowl. Mix until smooth. Stir in flour, oats, coconut, raisins, cinnamon, and baking soda. Spoon dough by rounded tablespoons onto prepared baking sheet. Bake 15 minutes, or until lightly browned. Allow to cool slightly before removing cookies to cool completely.

Upside-Down Double Apple Coffee Cake
Makes 10 servings

WHAT YOU NEED

- 1 medium apple
- ¼ cup brown sugar
- 1 tablespoon water
- ½ cup fresh or frozen cranberries
- ¼ cup butter or margarine, softened
- 1 cup granulated sugar

- 1 cup Mott's Natural Apple Sauce
- 1 egg
- 1¾ cup all-purpose flour
- 1 teaspoon baking soda
- ½ teaspoon ground cinnamon

WHAT YOU DO

Preheat oven to 350 degrees Fahrenheit.

Cut apple in half and remove core. Cut each half into slices approximately ⅛-inch thick.

Stir together brown sugar and water in medium saucepan. Add apple slices. Cook, stirring gently, over medium heat, until apple slices are softened, about 5 minutes.

Sprinkle cranberries in bottom of nonstick or greased 9-inch cake pan. Arrange apple slices over cranberries, drizzling with brown sugar sauce. Set aside.

In large bowl or mixer, beat butter (or margarine) with granulated sugar until thoroughly combined. Add apple sauce and egg.

In separate bowl, mix together flour, baking soda, and cinnamon. Gently blend into apple sauce mixture. Spoon batter over apples and cranberries, spreading evenly. Bake 30 minutes, or until wooden pick inserted into center comes out clean. Remove from oven and cool 15 minutes before turning cake out onto wire rack to cool completely.

Strange Facts

- In 1842, Samuel R. Mott of Bouckville, New York, made cider with the help of hitched horses that walked slowly in a circle, crushing apples between two large stone drums at the center of the sweep. The crushed apples were shoveled into a crib with slatted sides, packed in straw, and pressed together to squeeze out the juice, which ran off into a tank beneath and was ready for bottling.

- Mott's cider and vinegar caught the fancy of his neighbors and, as demand grew, so did the size of his mill. Water power and steam replaced his horses, and his son helped him distribute his products beyond the local market. Long before the turn of the century, Clipper ships were carrying 1,000 case lots of Mott's champagne cider and casks of Mott's vinegar around Cape Horn to California.

- In 1900, the Mott Company merged with the W.B. Duffy Cider Company of Rochester, New York. Duffy had also started his business in 1842. He had been the first to perfect a method for preserving apple cider in wood, a discovery that vastly increased its market.

- In 1938, the company introduced Mott's Apple Juice.

- In 1958, the Duffy-Mott Company sold its stock publicly.

- Duffy-Mott extended its Mott's lines west of the Rockies in 1960, when the company leased the 407,000-square-foot plant and purchased all the processing equipment of the Pratt-Low Preserving Corporation from Thriftimart Inc., a West Coast food chain.

- In the 1960s, Duffy-Mott introduced apricot juice, apple prune juice, and apricot nectar under the Sunsweet label, as well as Mott's apple cranberry sauce and apple raspberry sauce.

- In 1966, Duffy-Mott purchased the trademark and rights for Clamato and reformulated it as a clam and tomato flavor cocktail.

- In 1982, Cadbury Schweppes, the famous candy and soft drink company based in London, England, purchased the Duffy-Mott Company.

For More Recipes

Visit www.motts.com

Nestea®

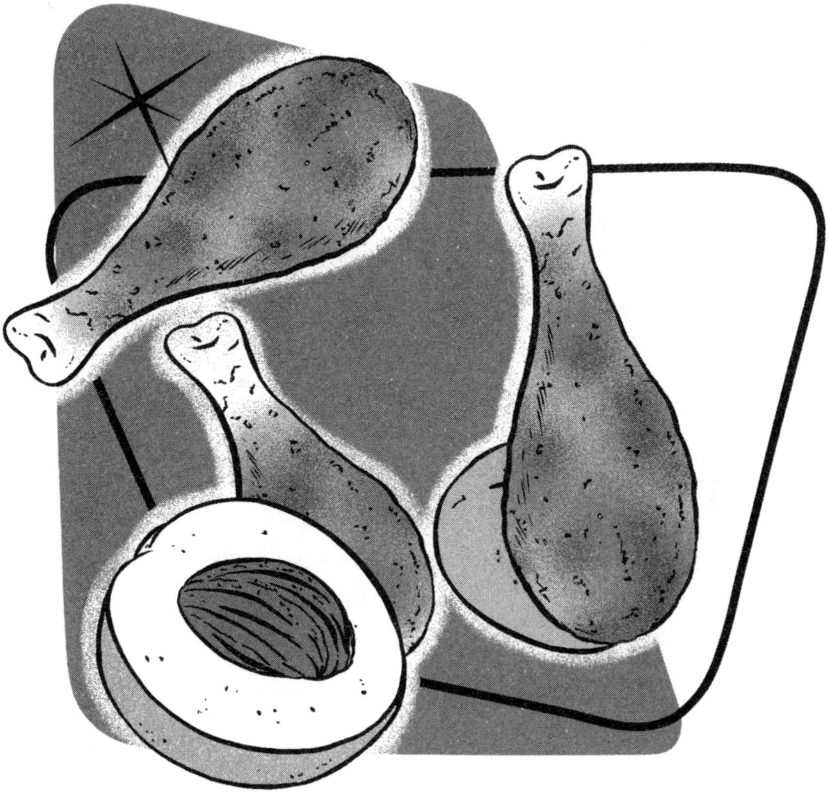

Apricot and Tea-Glazed Drumettes

Makes 6 servings

WHAT YOU NEED

- ⅔ cup apricot preserves
- 1 tablespoon Nestea Unsweetened Instant 100% Tea
- 12 chicken drumettes

WHAT YOU DO

Line baking sheet with foil.

Combine preserves and Nestea in blender; cover. Blend until smooth. Place drumettes on prepared baking sheet; brush heavily with glaze.

Broil drumettes, brushing frequently with glaze, for 12 to 15 minutes on each side, or until no longer pink near bone.

Honey Tea Bread

Makes 1 loaf

WHAT YOU NEED

- 2 cups all-purpose flour
- 1 tablespoon baking powder
- ½ teaspoon salt
- ½ teaspoon ground cinnamon
- ¼ teaspoon ground ginger
- ¾ cup low-fat milk
- ½ cup honey
- ¼ cup Nestea Unsweetened Instant 100% Tea
- ¼ cup vegetable oil
- 1 egg
- 1 teaspoon vanilla extract

WHAT YOU DO

Preheat oven to 350 degrees Fahrenheit. Coat 9- x 5-inch loaf pan with nonstick cooking spray.

Combine flour, baking powder, salt, cinnamon, and ginger in small bowl.

Beat milk, honey, tea, oil, egg, and vanilla in large bowl until tea is dissolved. Gradually stir in flour mixture until moistened. Pour into prepared pan.

Bake 45 to 60 minutes, or until wooden pick inserted into center comes out clean. Cool in pan on wire rack for 10 minutes; remove to wire rack to cool completely.

Iced Tea Cookies

Makes 24 cookies

WHAT YOU NEED

Cookies:

- 1¼ cups butter or margarine (2½ sticks), softened
- 1 cup firmly packed brown sugar
- 6 tablespoons Nestea Unsweetened Instant 100% Tea
- 1 egg yolk
- 2 teaspoons vanilla extract
- 2¼ cups all-purpose flour

Glaze:

- 1 cup sifted confectioners' sugar
- 5 teaspoons hot water
- ¼ teaspoon vanilla extract

WHAT YOU DO

Preheat oven to 350 degrees Fahrenheit.

To make the Cookies: Beat butter (or margarine) and sugar in large mixer bowl until light and fluffy. Beat in tea, egg yolk, and vanilla. Gradually stir in flour. Drop by heaping teaspoon 2 inches apart onto ungreased baking sheets.

Bake 12 to 15 minutes, or until lightly golden around edges and centers are set. Cool on baking sheets for 2 to 4 minutes; remove to wire racks.

To make the Glaze: Combine sugar, hot water, and vanilla in small bowl; stir until smooth.

Brush cookies with glaze; cool completely.

Pork with Savory Raspberry Tea Sauce

Makes 4 servings

WHAT YOU NEED

- 1 cup chicken broth
- ⅓ cup raspberry preserves
- ⅓ cup packed brown sugar
- 2 tablespoons Nestea Unsweetened Instant 100% Tea
- 2 tablespoons fresh lemon juice
- 1 tablespoon cornstarch
- 1 tablespoon Dijon mustard
- 4 (½-inch-thick) pork loin chops, grilled and kept warm

WHAT YOU DO

Whisk broth, preserves, sugar, tea, lemon juice, cornstarch, and mustard in small saucepan. Cook, whisking occasionally, until mixture comes to a boil. Boil, whisking occasionally, until sauce is thickened. Strain, if desired. Serve over pork.

Razzy Tea Vinaigrette

Makes 4 servings

WHAT YOU NEED

- ¼ cup raspberry wine vinegar
- 3 tablespoons olive oil
- 3 tablespoons water
- 2 tablespoons Nestea Unsweetened Instant 100% Tea
- 2 teaspoons sugar
- 1 teaspoon Dijon mustard
- ¼ teaspoon salt
- ¼ teaspoon ground white pepper

WHAT YOU DO

Combine vinegar, oil, water, tea, sugar, mustard, salt, and pepper in small bowl; whisk until blended.

Serving Suggestion: Serve with about 8 cups mixed salad greens.

Sugared Apple Tea Muffins

Makes 18 muffins

WHAT YOU NEED

- 2 cups all-purpose flour
- ½ cup plus 3 tablespoons sugar, divided
- 3 teaspoons baking powder
- ½ teaspoon ground cinnamon
- ½ teaspoon salt
- 1¼ cups 1 percent low-fat milk
- 6 tablespoons Nestea Unsweetened Instant 100% Tea
- ⅓ cup vegetable oil
- 1 large egg
- 1 teaspoon vanilla extract
- 1 cup peeled, cored, and finely chopped baking apple (about 1 medium), such as Granny Smith or Rome

WHAT YOU DO

Preheat oven to 350 degrees Fahrenheit. Coat 18 muffin cups with nonstick cooking spray or paper-line.

Combine flour, ½ cup sugar, baking powder, cinnamon, and salt in small bowl.

Beat milk, tea, oil, egg, and vanilla in large mixer bowl until tea is dissolved. Stir in apple. Gradually stir in flour mixture until moistened. Spoon into prepared muffin cups, filling ⅔ full. Sprinkle evenly with remaining 3 tablespoons sugar.

Bake 20 to 25 minutes, or until wooden pick inserted into center comes out clean. Cool in pans on wire racks for 10 minutes; remove to wire racks to cool completely.

✴ Strange Facts ✴

- Tea is the most ancient beverage in the world and is second only to water in worldwide consumption.
- According to legend, Chinese Emperor Shen Nung discovered tea in 2737 b.c.e. The emperor was purportedly sitting beneath a *Camellia sinensis* tree while his servant boiled drinking water. Some leaves from the tree blew into the pot of water. Shen Nung, a celebrated herbalist, decided to try the hot beverage that his servant had inadvertently brewed.
- On December 16, 1773, to protest the English taxation on tea, forty to fifty Boston colonists disguised themselves as Native Americans, raided three British ships, broke open 240 chests of tea, and threw hundreds of pounds of tea into Boston Harbor. In response to the Boston Tea Party, the British closed the port of Boston and stationed troops throughout the city, prompting colonial leaders to convene and declare a revolution against British rule.
- Eighty-five percent of the tea consumed in the United States is served over ice.
- Englishman Richard Blechynden, the India Tea Commissioner attempting to publicize India and Ceylon tea in the United States, popularized iced tea at the 1904 World's Fair in St. Louis, Missouri. Blechynden was selling hot India tea at the fair, but a heat wave devastated his sales, so he cleverly dumped ice into the tea and served the first iced tea, which became an instant hit.
- Much of the world's tea is grown in mountainous areas usually 3,000 to 7,000 feet above sea level, situated between the Tropic of Cancer and the Tropic of Capricorn.

For More Recipes

Visit www.nestea.com

Nestlé® Carnation® Nonfat Dry Milk

Banana-Nut Bread

Makes 2 loaves

WHAT YOU NEED

- 4 cups all-purpose flour
- 1¼ cups Nestlé Carnation Instant Nonfat Dry Milk powder
- 4 teaspoons baking powder
- 1 teaspoon ground cinnamon
- 4 large eggs
- 3½ cups (about 7 medium) mashed very ripe bananas
- 2 cups sugar
- 1 cup vegetable oil
- 1 cup chopped walnuts

WHAT YOU DO

Preheat oven to 350 degrees Fahrenheit. Coat two 9- × 5-inch loaf pans with nonstick cooking spray.

Combine flour, dry milk, baking powder, and cinnamon in medium bowl.

Beat eggs, bananas, sugar, and oil in large mixer bowl on medium speed. Gradually beat in flour mixture; stir in walnuts. Spoon into prepared pans.

Bake 60 to 65 minutes, or until wooden pick inserted into centers comes out clean. Cool in pans on wire racks for 10 minutes; remove to wire racks to cool completely.

Cream of Broccoli Soup

Makes 6 servings

WHAT YOU NEED

- 3 cans (14.5 ounces each) chicken or vegetable broth
- 9 cups (about 1½ pounds) broccoli florets
- 1 small onion, coarsely chopped
- 2 cloves garlic, finely chopped
- 1½ cups Nestlé Carnation Instant Nonfat Dry Milk powder
- ½ cup water
- ¼ cup all-purpose flour
- ¼ teaspoon salt
- ¼ teaspoon ground black pepper

WHAT YOU DO

Boil broth in large saucepan. Add broccoli, onion, and garlic. Return to a boil; reduce heat to low. Cover; cook 5 to 7 minutes, or until broccoli is tender. Remove from heat; cool slightly.

Transfer half of vegetable-broth mixture to blender or food processor (in batches, if necessary); cover. Blend until desired consistency. Return to remaining mixture in saucepan.

Combine dry milk, water, and flour in medium bowl; mix well. Stir into soup; add salt and pepper. Heat to serving temperature.

Creamy Garlic Dip

Makes 1¼ cups

WHAT YOU NEED

- 1 cup sour cream
- ½ cup Nestlé Carnation Instant Nonfat Dry Milk powder
- 2 tablespoons sliced green onion
- 1 tablespoon cider vinegar

- 1 clove garlic, minced
- ½ teaspoon salt
- ¼ teaspoon ground black pepper

WHAT YOU DO

Combine sour cream, dry milk, green onion, vinegar, garlic, salt, and pepper in small bowl; stir until smooth.

Serving Suggestion: Serve with assorted cut-up fresh vegetables.

Svelte Blue Cheese Dressing and Dip

Makes 8 servings

WHAT YOU NEED

- ½ cup plain fat-free yogurt
- ¼ cup Nestlé Carnation Instant Nonfat Dry Milk powder
- ½ cup chopped green onions
- 2 ounces crumbled blue cheese
- 1 small clove garlic, minced
- ¼ teaspoon crushed dried basil
- ¼ teaspoon crushed dried rosemary
- ⅛ teaspoon salt

WHAT YOU DO

Combine yogurt and dry milk in small bowl. Add green onions, cheese, garlic, basil, rosemary and salt; mix well. Cover; refrigerate for 30 minutes before serving.

Whipped Nestlé Carnation Nonfat Dry Milk Topping

Makes 3 cups

WHAT YOU NEED

- ½ cup ice water
- ½ cup Nestlé Carnation Instant Nonfat Dry Milk powder
- 1½ teaspoons unflavored gelatin
- 2 tablespoons cold water
- 2 tablespoons boiling water
- ¼ cup confectioners' sugar
- 1 teaspoon vanilla extract

WHAT YOU DO

Combine ice water and dry milk in large mixer bowl. Freeze bowl, milk mixture, and beaters for 15 minutes.

Combine gelatin and cold water in small bowl. Let stand for 3 minutes. Add boiling water; blend well. Cool to room temperature.

Whip chilled milk mixture until stiff peaks form. Add gelatin mixture, sugar, and vanilla. Whip just until blended.

If whipped topping develops an airy appearance, simply stir vigorously to restore smooth appearance. For best results, prepare same day as serving.

Zesty Potato Salad

Makes 8 servings

WHAT YOU NEED

- ¼ cup Nestlé Carnation Instant Nonfat Dry Milk powder
- ¼ cup water
- ¼ cup Dijon mustard
- ½ teaspoon salt
- ¼ teaspoon freshly ground black pepper
- 2 pounds red-skinned potatoes, cut into 1-inch cubes, cooked, drained, and cooled

- 2 cups green beans, cut into 1-inch pieces, blanched
- 1 cup chopped red bell pepper
- ¼ cup sliced green onions

WHAT YOU DO

Combine dry milk, water, mustard, salt, and black pepper in small bowl until well mixed.

Combine potatoes, green beans, bell pepper, and onions in large bowl; add milk dressing and toss well to coat. Serve immediately or refrigerate.

Serving Suggestion: Serve over lettuce leaves.

Strange Facts

- On September 6, 1899, grocer E.A. Stuart and a fellow business partner founded the Pacific Coast Condensed Milk Company in Kent, Washington, utilizing the relatively new process of evaporation. Two years later, Stuart's partner sold out, leaving Stuart the company and $105,000 in debt.

- While walking in downtown Seattle, Stuart passed a tobacconist's store with a window display featuring Carnation cigars and decided to use the name for his new milk product.

- Having learned as a boy on his father's farm that quality cows produced quality milk, Stuart distributed purebred bulls to the farmers who were suppliers for his factory, enabling the farmers to breed better milk-producing cows.

- Stuart eventually established his own breeding farm, called Carnation Farm, and Carnation cows held the world milk production record for thirty-two consecutive years.

- One Carnation Farm cow, Segis Pietertje Prospect, produced 37,381 pounds of milk during 1920, and Stuart erected a statue of Segis Pietertje Prospect, whose record went unbroken for sixteen years.

- In 1907, Carnation introduced the advertising slogan, "Carnation Condensed Milk, the Milk from Contented Cows." The company used this slogan for decades and sponsored a radio variety show called "The Contented Hour," which featured Dinah Shore, Jane Powell, and George Burns and Gracie Allen.

- Introduced as "magic crystals" by Carnation in 1954, nonfat dry milk was an immediate hit for its fresh milk flavor when mixed with ice-cold water.

- Whether used in dry form or reconstituted with water, Nestlé Carnation Instant Nonfat Dry Milk is rich in calcium, protein, and vitamins, with no fat.

- To boost your calcium intake, add 1 tablespoon nonfat dry milk to many of the foods you eat every day.

- You can use Nestle Carnation Instant Nonfat Dry Milk to make your own buttermilk substitute for cooking. Combine ⅓ cup dry Nonfat Dry Milk with 1 cup water in small measuring cup. Add 1 tablespoon vinegar or lemon juice; stir. Let stand 5 minutes before using in recipe. Makes 1 cup.

For More Recipes

Visit www.verybestbaking.com

Quaker Oats®

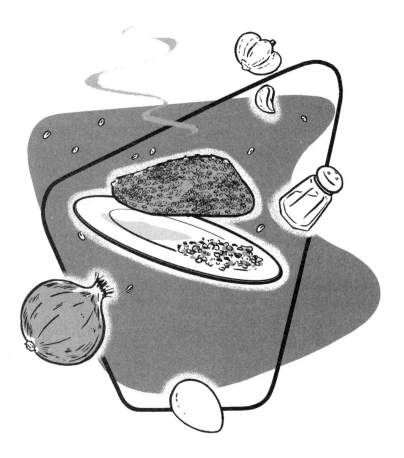

Classic Meat Loaf

Makes 6 to 8 servings

WHAT YOU NEED

- 1½ pounds lean ground beef or turkey
- ¾ cup Quaker Oats (Quick or Old Fashioned), uncooked
- ¾ cup finely chopped onion
- ½ cup ketchup
- 1 egg, lightly beaten
- 1 tablespoon Worcestershire sauce or soy sauce
- 2 cloves garlic, minced
- ½ teaspoon salt
- ¼ teaspoon ground black pepper

WHAT YOU DO

Preheat oven to 350 degrees Fahrenheit.

Combine all ingredients in large bowl; mix lightly but thoroughly. Shape meat loaf mixture into 10- × 6-inch loaf on rack of broiler pan.

Bake 50 to 55 minutes, or until meat loaf is to medium doneness (160 degrees Fahrenheit for beef, 170 degrees Fahrenheit for turkey), until not pink in center and juices show no pink color. Let stand 5 minutes before slicing.

'90s Lazy Daisy Oatmeal Cake

Makes 12 servings

WHAT YOU NEED

Cake:

- 1¼ cups boiling water
- 1 cup Quaker Oats (Quick or Old Fashioned), uncooked
- 5 tablespoons butter or margarine, softened
- 1 cup granulated sugar
- 1 cup firmly packed brown sugar
- 2 egg whites or 1 egg
- 1 teaspoon vanilla extract
- 1¾ cups all-purpose flour
- 1 teaspoon baking soda
- 1 teaspoon ground cinnamon
- ¼ teaspoon ground nutmeg (optional)
- ¼ teaspoon salt (optional)

Topping:

- ½ cup shredded coconut
- ½ cup firmly packed brown sugar
- ½ cup Quaker Oats (Quick or Old Fashioned), uncooked
- 3 tablespoons fat-free milk
- 2 tablespoons butter or margarine, melted

WHAT YOU DO

Preheat oven to 350 degrees Fahrenheit. Lightly coat 8- or 9-inch square baking pan with nonstick cooking spray and dust lightly with flour.

To make the cake: pour boiling water over oats in medium bowl; mix well.

In large bowl, cream butter (or margarine), granulated sugar, and brown sugar until well blended. Add egg whites (or egg) and vanilla; beat well. Add reserved oat mixture.

In bowl, combine flour, baking soda, cinnamon and, if desired, nutmeg and salt; mix well. Stir into oat mixture. Pour batter into prepared pan.

Bake 55 to 65 minutes (8-inch pan) or 50 to 60 minutes (9-inch pan), or until wooden pick inserted into center comes out clean. Transfer cake in pan to wire rack.

To make the topping: combine all ingredients in small bowl; mix well. Spread evenly over top of warm cake. Broil about 4 inches from heat 1 to 2 minutes, or until topping is bubbly. (Watch closely; topping burns easily.) Cool cake in pan on wire rack. Store tightly covered at room temperature.

Oatmeal-Raisin Cookies

Makes about 3 dozen cookies

WHAT YOU NEED

- 1 cup all-purpose flour
- 1 teaspoon baking soda
- ½ teaspoon ground cinnamon
- ¼ teaspoon salt (optional)
- 4 tablespoons (½ stick) butter or margarine, softened
- 3 tablespoons sugar
- ¼ cup egg substitute or 2 egg whites, lightly beaten
- ¾ cup unsweetened applesauce
- ¼ cup frozen unsweetened apple juice concentrate, thawed
- 1 teaspoon vanilla extract
- 1½ cups Quaker Oats (Quick or Old Fashioned), uncooked
- ⅓ cup raisins, chopped

WHAT YOU DO

Preheat oven to 350 degrees Fahrenheit. Lightly coat baking sheets with nonstick cooking spray.

In small bowl, combine flour, baking soda, cinnamon, and salt (if desired); mix well. Set aside.

In large bowl, beat butter (or margarine) and sugar until creamy. Add egg substitute (or egg whites); beat well. Add applesauce, apple juice concentrate, and vanilla; beat well.

Add flour mixture; mix well. Add oats and raisins; mix well. Drop dough by rounded teaspoonfuls onto prepared baking sheets.

Bake 15 to 17 minutes, or until firm to the touch and light golden brown. Cool 1 minute on baking sheets; remove to wire rack. Cool completely. Store tightly covered.

Old-Fashioned Oatmeal Pie

Makes 10 servings

WHAT YOU NEED

- 2 eggs
- ¾ cup sugar
- ¾ cup dark corn syrup
- 4 tablespoons (½ stick) butter or margarine, melted
- 1 teaspoon vanilla extract

- ¾ cup Quaker Oats (Quick or Old Fashioned), uncooked
- ⅓ cup shredded coconut
- 2 tablespoons all-purpose flour
- 1 prepared 9-inch pie shell, unbaked
- Ice cream or whipped cream (optional)

WHAT YOU DO

Preheat oven to 350 degrees Fahrenheit.

In large bowl, beat eggs until foamy. Gradually add sugar; mix well. Add corn syrup, butter (or margarine, and vanilla; mix well.

In bowl, combine oats, coconut, and flour; mix well. Stir into egg mixture. Pour into prepared pie shell.

Bake 40 to 45 minutes, or until center is set. (Center should be firm when touched lightly with finger.) Cool completely on wire rack. Serve with ice cream (or whipped cream), if desired. Store tightly covered in refrigerator.

Quaker's Oatmeal Soup

Makes 4 (1½-cup) servings

WHAT YOU NEED

- 1 onion, finely chopped (about ¾ cup)
- ½ cup shredded carrots
- 3 tablespoons butter or margarine, divided
- ½ cup Quaker Oats (Quick or Old Fashioned), uncooked
- 6 cups chicken broth

- 1 cup Quaker Oats (Quick or Old Fashioned), cooked according to package directions
- Salt
- Ground black pepper
- 3 tablespoons finely chopped fresh parsley or 1 tablespoon dried parsley flakes

WHAT YOU DO

In large skillet or saucepan, cook onion and carrots in 2 tablespoons butter over medium-low heat, stirring often, 5 minutes, or until onion is tender. Add ½ cup uncooked oats and remaining 1 tablespoon butter. Cook, stirring often for 3 minutes, or until oats are golden brown.

Stir in broth; bring to a low boil. Stir in cooked oatmeal, stirring until well mixed. Cook over medium heat 5 minutes. Season to taste with salt and pepper. Serve sprinkled with parsley.

Spicy Oat-Crusted Chicken with Sunshine Salsa

Makes 4 servings

WHAT YOU NEED

Sunshine Salsa:
- ¾ cup prepared salsa
- ¾ cup coarsely chopped orange sections

Chicken:
- 2 tablespoons canola oil
- 1 tablespoon butter or margarine, melted
- 2 teaspoons chili powder
- 1 teaspoon garlic powder

- 1 teaspoon ground cumin
- ¾ teaspoon salt
- 1½ cups Quaker Quick Oats, uncooked
- 1 egg, lightly beaten
- 1 tablespoon water
- 4 boneless, skinless chicken breast halves (5 to 6 ounces each)
- Chopped fresh cilantro (optional)

WHAT YOU DO

To make the Sunshine Salsa: In small bowl, combine salsa and orange sections. Refrigerate, covered, until serving time.

To make the Chicken: Preheat oven to 375 degrees Fahrenheit. Line baking sheet with foil.

In flat, shallow dish, stir together oil, butter (or margarine), chili powder, garlic powder, cumin, and salt. Add oats, stirring until evenly moistened.

In second flat, shallow dish, beat egg and water with fork until frothy. Dip chicken into egg mixture, then coat completely in seasoned oats. Place chicken on prepared baking sheet. Pat any extra oat mixture onto top of chicken.

Bake 30 minutes, or until chicken is cooked through and oat coating is golden brown. Serve with Sunshine Salsa. Garnish with cilantro, if desired.

Star Spangled Muffins

Makes 12 muffins

WHAT YOU NEED

- 1½ cups all-purpose flour
- 1 cup Quaker Oats (Quick or Old Fashioned), uncooked
- ½ cup granulated sugar
- 1 tablespoon baking powder
- 1 cup 1 percent low-fat milk
- ¼ cup vegetable oil
- 1 egg, lightly beaten
- 1 teaspoon vanilla extract
- ½ cup fresh blueberries
- ½ cup sliced fresh strawberries
- 4 tablespoons cinnamon-sugar, divided

WHAT YOU DO

Preheat oven to 400 degrees Fahrenheit. Line 12 medium muffin cups with paper baking cups.

In large bowl, combine flour, oats, granulated sugar, and baking powder; mix well.

In small bowl, combine milk, oil, egg, and vanilla; blend well. Add to dry ingredients all at once; stir just until dry ingredients are moistened. (Do not overmix.) Gently stir in blueberries and strawberries.

Fill muffin cups three-fourths full. Sprinkle batter in each muffin cup with 1 teaspoon cinnamon-sugar.

Bake 18 to 20 minutes, or until golden brown. Cool muffins in pan on wire rack 5 minutes; remove from pan. Serve warm.

Veggie Burgers

Makes 8 servings

WHAT YOU NEED

- 3 teaspoons vegetable oil, divided
- 1 cup sliced mushrooms
- 1 cup shredded carrots (about 2)
- ¾ cup chopped onion (about 1 medium)
- ¾ cup chopped zucchini (about 1 small)
- 2 cups Quaker Oats (Quick or Old Fashioned), uncooked
- 1 can (15 ounces) kidney beans, rinsed and drained

- 1 cup cooked white or brown rice
- ½ cup chopped fresh cilantro or chives (optional)
- 2 tablespoons soy sauce or ½ teaspoon salt
- 1 teaspoon minced garlic
- ⅛ teaspoon ground black pepper
- Hamburger buns and toppings (optional)

WHAT YOU DO

Heat 1 teaspoon oil in large nonstick skillet. Add mushrooms, carrots, onion, and zucchini; cook over medium-high heat 5 minutes, or until vegetables are tender.

Transfer vegetables to food processor bowl. Add oats, beans, rice, cilantro (or chives), soy sauce (or salt), garlic, and pepper. Pulse for about 20 seconds, or until well blended. Divide into eight ½-cup portions. Shape into patties between waxed paper. Refrigerate at least 1 hour, or until firm.

Heat remaining 2 teaspoons oil in same skillet over medium-high heat. Cook patties 3 to 4 minutes on each side, or until golden brown. Serve on buns with toppings, if desired.

Strange Facts

- Oats, the *only* major grain proven to reduce blood cholesterol, are also a source of soluble fiber, which benefits the heart, and insoluble fiber, which benefits the digestive system.
- Oats, one of the earliest cereals cultivated by humans, were known in ancient China as long ago as 7,000 b.c.e.
- The ancient Greeks were the first people known to have made porridge from oats.
- January is Oatmeal Month, during which Americans buy more oatmeal than any other month of the year.
- In January 2001, Americans bought enough oats to make 346 million bowls of oatmeal.
- The most popular oatmeal toppings are milk, sugar, and fruit such as raisins and bananas.
- Oatmeal cookies are the most popular non-cereal use for oatmeal, followed by meat loaf.
- Eighty percent of U.S. households have oatmeal in their cupboards.
- Quaker Oats was the first U.S. breakfast cereal to receive a registered trademark, the first to offer a recipe *and* a premium on its package, and the first to offer trial-size samples.
- An 18-ounce canister of Old Fashioned Quaker Oats contains approximately 26,000 rolled oats.
- Instant Oats, Old Fashioned Oats, Quick Oats, and Steel Cut Oats are different forms of the exact same thing—whole grain oats. On an equal weight basis, there is no nutritional difference between the four forms of oats. The only difference is the way the groat (the oat after the inedible outer hull has been removed) has been cut and/or rolled, which merely affects the cooking time and baking use.

For More Recipes

Visit www.quakeroats.com

Ragú®
Old World Style®
Pasta Sauce

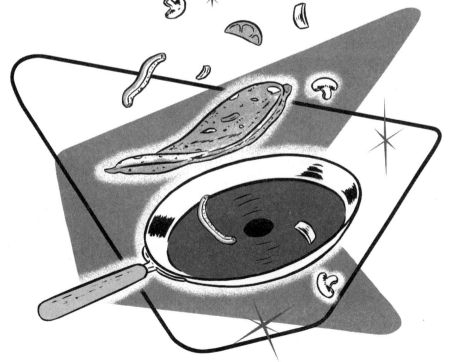

A-B-C Minestrone

Makes 8 servings

WHAT YOU NEED

- 1 tablespoon olive oil
- 1 medium onion, chopped
- 2 medium carrots, chopped
- 1 small zucchini, chopped
- ½ teaspoon dried Italian seasoning
- 4 cups chicken broth

- 1 jar (1 pound, 10 ounces) Ragú Old World Style Pasta Sauce
- 1 can (15½ ounces) cannellini or white kidney beans, rinsed and drained
- 1 cup alphabet pasta

WHAT YOU DO

In 4-quart saucepan, heat oil over medium heat and cook onion, carrots, and zucchini, stirring frequently, 5 minutes, or until vegetables are tender. Add Italian seasoning and cook, stirring occasionally, 1 minute. Add broth and pasta sauce and bring to a boil. Stir in beans and pasta. Cook, stirring occasionally, 10 minutes, or until pasta is tender.

Serving Suggestion: Serve with chopped parsley and grated Parmesan cheese.

Baked Manicotti

Makes 4 servings

WHAT YOU NEED

- 1 jar (1 pound, 10 ounces) Ragú Old World Style Pasta Sauce
- 8 fresh or frozen prepared manicotti

- ½ cup shredded mozzarella cheese (about 2 ounces)
- 2 tablespoons grated Parmesan cheese

WHAT YOU DO

Preheat oven to 450 degrees Fahrenheit.

In 13- x 9-inch baking dish, spread half of the pasta sauce. Add manicotti, then top with remaining pasta sauce and sprinkle with cheeses. Bake covered 20 minutes. Remove cover and continue baking 5 minutes, or until heated through.

Campfire Hot Dogs

Makes 8 servings

WHAT YOU NEED

- ½ pound ground beef
- 2 cups Ragú Old World Style Pasta Sauce
- 1 can (10¾ to 16 ounces) baked beans
- 8 frankfurters, cooked
- 8 frankfurter rolls

WHAT YOU DO

In 12-inch skillet, brown ground beef over medium-high heat; drain.

Stir in pasta sauce and beans. Bring to a boil over high heat. Reduce heat to low and simmer, stirring occasionally, 5 minutes.

To serve, arrange frankfurters in rolls and top with sauce mixture.

Serving Suggestion: Garnish with Cheddar cheese.

Recipe Variation: For Chili Campfire Hot Dogs, simply stir 2 to 3 teaspoons chili powder into sauce mixture.

Creamy Tomato Soup

Makes 6 servings

WHAT YOU NEED

- 1 jar (1 pound, 10 ounces) Ragú Old World Style Pasta Sauce
- 2½ cups milk
- Croutons
- Grated Parmesan cheese

WHAT YOU DO

In 3-quart saucepan, cook pasta sauce and milk, over medium heat, stirring occasionally, 10 minutes, or until heated through. Garnish with croutons and cheese.

Oven Garden Omelette

Makes 6 servings

WHAT YOU NEED

- 10 eggs
- ¾ cup milk
- 3½ cups fresh or frozen assorted vegetables (any combination of broccoli florets, spinach, sliced red or green bell peppers, zucchini, mushrooms, or onions), cooked
- 2 cups shredded mozzarella cheese (about 8 ounces)
- 1 cup Ragú Old World Style Pasta Sauce
- 2 tablespoons chopped fresh basil (optional)

WHAT YOU DO

Preheat oven to 350 degrees Fahrenheit. Coat 11- × 7-inch baking dish with nonstick cooking spray.

In large bowl, beat eggs and milk. Stir in vegetables, cheese, pasta sauce, and basil, if desired.

Pour egg mixture into prepared baking dish. Bake uncovered 45 minutes, or until knife inserted into center comes out clean.

Ragú Extra Saucy Sloppy Joes

Makes 8 servings

WHAT YOU NEED

- 2 pounds ground beef
- 1 medium onion, sliced
- 1 jar (1 pound, 10 ounces) Ragú Old World Style Pasta Sauce
- 2 tablespoons firmly packed brown sugar
- 8 hamburger buns

WHAT YOU DO

In 12-inch skillet, brown ground beef with onion over medium-high heat; drain. Stir in pasta sauce and sugar. Simmer, stirring occasionally, 10 minutes. Serve on hamburger buns.

Simmered Tuscan Chicken

Makes 6 servings

WHAT YOU NEED

- 2 tablespoons olive oil
- 1 pound boneless, skinless chicken breasts, cut into 1-inch cubes
- 2 cloves garlic, minced
- 2 medium potatoes, cut into 1-inch cubes (about 2 cups)
- 1 medium red bell pepper, cut into large pieces
- 1 jar (1 pound, 10 ounces) Ragú Old World Style Pasta Sauce
- 1 teaspoon dried basil leaves, crushed

WHAT YOU DO

In 12-inch skillet, heat oil over medium-high heat and cook chicken with garlic until chicken is thoroughly cooked. Remove chicken and set aside.

In same skillet, add potatoes and pepper. Cook over medium heat, stirring occasionally, 5 minutes. Stir in pasta sauce and basil. Bring to a boil over high heat. Reduce heat to low and simmer, covered, stirring occasionally, 35 minutes, or until potatoes are tender. Return chicken to skillet and heat through.

Spaghetti Cupcakes

Makes 12 servings

WHAT YOU NEED

- 8 ounces spaghetti, cooked and drained
- 4 eggs, slightly beaten
- ½ cup grated Parmesan cheese
- ¼ teaspoon ground black pepper
- 1½ cups Ragú Old World Style Pasta Sauce
- 2 cups shredded mozzarella cheese (about 8 ounces)

WHAT YOU DO

Preheat oven to 375 degrees Fahrenheit. Coat 12-cup muffin pan with nonstick cooking spray; set aside.

In large bowl, combine spaghetti, eggs, Parmesan, and pepper. Evenly press into muffin cups to form a "crust." Top each cup with 2 tablespoons pasta sauce, then mozzarella.

Bake 15 minutes, or until bubbling. Let stand 5 minutes before serving.

Serving Suggestion: For a fun twist, add faces using broccoli florets for hair, eyebrows for nose, sliced pimiento-stuffed olives for eyes, and pepperoni for mouths. Bake an additional 10 minutes.

Strange Facts

- Ragú started as a door-to-door operation in 1937 and grew into one of the biggest brands in the category—the Ragú packing company. When his parents retired, Ralph Cantisano took over operations of the company and helped build it into a $22-million-a-year business.

- Ralph Cantisano sold Ragú Foods to Chesebrough Ponds in 1970, which was eventually purchased by Unilever. After selling Ragú Foods, Cantisano teamed up with several former Ragú employees, including Mr. John LiDestri, to found Cantisano Foods. In 1982, Mr. Edward P. Salzano, joined Cantisano Foods, bringing with him the Francesco Rinaldi name, marketing Rinaldi sauces. In 2002, Mr. Cantisano's family business was passed on to his extended family of nearly thirty years, and the Cantisano Foods name was officially changed to LiDestri Foods.

- For Ragú Tomato and Rich & Meaty sauces, once the jar is opened you can store them in your refrigerator for up to 7 days.

- You may freeze unused portions of the Ragú Tomato and Rich & Meaty sauces in a freezer-safe container for up to 3 months.

- Ragú Pasta Sauce is a natural source of lycopene, the most common carotenoid in the human body and a potent antioxidant.

For More Recipes

Visit www.eat.com

Fried Onion Rings

WHAT YOU NEED

- 1 cup all-purpose flour
- ¾ teaspoon salt
- ¼ teaspoon baking powder
- ¼ teaspoon baking soda
- ¾ cup 7 UP
- 3 tablespoons vegetable oil, plus more for frying
- 2 medium onions, sliced

WHAT YOU DO

Combine flour, salt, baking powder, and baking soda in shallow dish. Add 7 UP and oil and mix well. Separate onion slices into rings. Dip into batter. Fry in deep hot oil until golden, turning once. Drain well on absorbent paper.

Lemon Pound Cake

Makes 12 servings

WHAT YOU NEED

- 1½ cups butter or margarine, softened
- 3 cups sugar
- 4 teaspoons lemon extract
- 5 eggs
- 3 cups all-purpose flour
- ¾ cup 7 UP

WHAT YOU DO

Preheat oven to 325 degrees Fahrenheit. Coat tube or Bundt pan with nonstick cooking spray.

Combine butter (or margarine), sugar, and lemon extract in large bowl; beat until light and fluffy. Add eggs, one at a time, beating well after each addition. Add flour, mixing well. Stir in 7 UP. Spoon into prepared pan. Bake 1 hour and 25 minutes, or until wooden toothpick inserted into the center comes out clean. Cool on wire rack 10 minutes. Remove from pan and cool completely.

Peppy Barbecue Sauce

Makes 1¼ cups

WHAT YOU NEED

- 1 small onion, minced
- 2 tablespoons butter or margarine, melted
- 1 cup 7 UP
- ¼ cup ketchup
- 1 teaspoon dry mustard

- 1 teaspoon salt
- ⅛ teaspoon chili powder
- ⅛ teaspoon ground black pepper
- 4 cloves garlic

WHAT YOU DO

In saucepan, sauté onion in butter (or margarine) until soft but not browned. Stir in 7 UP, ketchup, mustard, salt, chili powder, pepper, and garlic. Bring to a boil; reduce heat and simmer 5 minutes. Remove and discard garlic cloves.

Serving Suggestion: Use as a basting sauce for grilled meats.

Quick German Potato Salad

Makes 16 servings

WHAT YOU NEED

- 6 slices bacon
- ½ cup chopped onion
- ½ cup chopped green bell pepper
- 2 tablespoons all-purpose flour
- 1 tablespoon salt
- ½ teaspoon dry mustard

- ⅛ teaspoon ground black pepper
- ⅓ cup white vinegar
- 1 cup 7 UP
- 4 pounds potatoes, peeled, cooked, and sliced

WHAT YOU DO

In large skillet over medium-high heat, fry bacon until crisp. Drain bacon on absorbent paper, then crumble. Discard all but 3 tablespoons bacon drippings from the skillet. Sauté onion and bell pepper in the reserved drippings. Stir in flour, salt, mustard, and pepper. Cook over low heat, stirring until smooth and bubbly. Remove from heat. Slowly stir in vinegar and 7 UP. Heat to boiling, stirring constantly. Boil 1 minute. Stir in potatoes and crumbled bacon; heat thoroughly. Serve warm.

7 UP Baked Beans

Makes 8 servings

WHAT YOU NEED

- 2 cans (16 ounces each) pork and beans
- 1 can (10¾ ounces) tomato soup
- 2 strips bacon, cooked and crumbled
- ½ cup 7 UP
- ½ cup chopped bell pepper
- ¼ cup chopped onion
- 2 tablespoons Worcestershire sauce
- 1 tablespoon prepared mustard
- 2 teaspoons liquid smoke (optional)

WHAT YOU DO

Preheat oven to 325 degrees. Coat 2-quart shallow baking dish with nonstick cooking spray.

Combine all ingredients in large bowl, mixing well. Spoon into prepared baking dish. Bake 1½ hours.

7 UP Brisket

Makes 8 servings

WHAT YOU NEED

- 1 cup 7 UP
- 1 cup ketchup
- 1 envelope (1 ounce) dry onion soup mix
- ½ cup dry red wine
- 1 (3 to 4 pound) beef brisket

WHAT YOU DO

Combine 7 UP, ketchup, soup mix, and wine in large, heavy Dutch oven. Add brisket; turn several times to coat well. Bring to a boil over medium heat. Reduce heat, cover, and simmer about 2 hours. Baste frequently with 7 UP mixture. Transfer brisket to serving platter; serve with sauce.

THE DAWN OF THE MR. COFFEE MACHINE

In the 1960s, Vince Marotta presided over North American Systems in Pepper Pike, Ohio, building shopping malls and housing developments. When business slowed in 1968, Marotta fell ill. While recuperating in bed, he realized how fed up he was with percolated coffee and decided to develop a better way to make coffee. He contacted the Pan American Coffee Bureau and discovered that South American coffee growers believed that the best way to extract the oil from coffee beans was to pour water, heated to 200 degrees Fahrenheit, over the ground beans.

Marotta hired engineer Irv Schultze to devise a bi-metal actuator to control the temperature of the water. Observing how restaurants used white cloths in their large coffee percolators to capture loose grounds and eliminate sediment, Marotta decided to use a paper filter in his coffee maker.

Marotta showed up at the 1970 Housewares Convention in Chicago with a prototype for Mr. Coffee. On the spot, he hired Bill Howe, a buyer with Hamilton Beach, to represent his product. Howe invited one hundred buyers up to Marotta's hotel room for coffee, and, within two years, Mr. Coffee was selling 42,000 coffee machines a day. According to Marotta, the paper filters—"the blade to the razor"—were cut and fluted by a paper company from an existing paper stock. Marotta sold the Mr. Coffee Company in 1987, and the company went public in 1990.

- Inventor Vince Marotta, determined to give his coffee maker a simple, catchy name, came up with the name Mr. Coffee off the top of his head.
- In 1972, Marotta single-handedly convinced Joe DiMaggio to be the spokesman for Mr. Coffee. DiMaggio appeared in Mr. Coffee television commercials for the next fifteen years.
- Mr. Coffee machines outsell both Black & Decker and Proctor Silex coffee machines by nearly two to one.
- Mr. Coffee is the best-selling coffee maker in the world.

7 UP Fruit Salad

Makes 12 servings

WHAT YOU NEED

- 1 package (6 ounces) lemon-flavored gelatin
- 2 cups boiling water
- 2 cups 7 UP
- 2 cans (8 ounces each) crushed pineapple, undrained
- 2 bananas, chopped

- 2 cups miniature marshmallows
- ½ cup sugar
- 2 tablespoons all-purpose flour
- 1 egg, slightly beaten
- 2 tablespoons butter or margarine
- ½ cup whipping cream, whipped
- ½ cup grated Cheddar cheese

WHAT YOU DO

Dissolve gelatin in boiling water in bowl; stir in 7 UP. Chill about 45 minutes, or until syrupy. Drain pineapple, reserving juice. Fold pineapple and bananas into gelatin mixture. Pour into 13- × 9- × 2-inch dish. Sprinkle marshmallows over top. Chill until firm.

Combine sugar and flour in small nonaluminum saucepan; stir in egg. Add water to reserved pineapple juice, if necessary, to yield 1 cup; stir into sugar mixture. Cook over medium heat, stirring constantly, until thickened. Remove from heat; stir in butter (or margarine) until melted. Cool completely. Fold in whipped cream. Spread mixture over gelatin salad. Sprinkle with cheese. Cut into squares to serve.

7 UP Meat Loaf

Makes 4 servings

WHAT YOU NEED

- 2 pounds ground beef
- 2 eggs, slightly beaten
- 1½ cups bread crumbs
- ¾ cup ketchup

- ½ cup 7 UP
- 1 envelope (1 ounce) dry onion soup mix
- 1 can (8 ounces) tomato sauce

WHAT YOU DO

Preheat oven to 350 degrees Fahrenheit.

Combine beef, eggs, bread crumbs, ketchup, 7 UP, and soup mix in bowl; mix well. Place in shallow baking pan and shape into a loaf. Top with tomato sauce. Bake 1 hour.

Spaghetti Milano Casserole

Makes 4 servings

WHAT YOU NEED

- 1 pound ground beef
- ½ cup chopped green bell pepper
- ⅓ cup chopped onion
- 1 can (8 ounces) tomato sauce
- 1 can (6 ounces) tomato paste
- 1 cup 7 UP

- 1 cup sliced fresh mushrooms
- 1 teaspoon salt
- 1¼ teaspoons dried oregano
- 8 ounces spaghetti, cooked and drained
- ¾ cup grated Parmesan cheese

WHAT YOU DO

Preheat oven to 350 degrees Fahrenheit. Coat 2-quart baking dish with nonstick cooking spray.

Cook ground beef, pepper, and onion in large skillet until beef is browned. Drain well. Stir in tomato sauce, tomato paste, 7 UP, mushrooms, salt, and oregano. Simmer 20 minutes. Place half of spaghetti in prepared baking dish. Spoon half of meat sauce over spaghetti. Sprinkle with half of cheese. Repeat layers. Bake 30 minutes.

Note: Casserole may be made ahead and refrigerated until needed.

✴ Strange Facts ✴

- In 1920, Charles L. Grigg, banking on his thirty years of experience in advertising and merchandising, founded the Howdy Corporation in St. Louis, Missouri, and created the successful Howdy Orange drink. Determined to create a new lemon-flavored soft-drink for national distribution, Grigg spent more than two years testing eleven different formulas, finally introducing "Bib-Label Lithiated Lemon-Lime Soda" two weeks before the stock market crash of October 1929.

- Grigg's pricey caramel-colored lemon-lime soda, marketed as a soft drink that "takes the 'ouch' out of grouch," sold amazingly well during the Depression—possibly because it contained lithium, a strong drug now prescribed to treat manic-depression. Grigg soon changed the soda's cumbersome name to 7 UP, possibly referring to the soda's original seven-ounce bottle and the bubbles rising from the soda's original heavy carbonation, which was later reduced.

- In 1936, Grigg changed the name of the Howdy Corporation to the Seven-Up Company. The label on the bottle listed lithium as an ingredient until the mid-1940s. By the end of the decade, 7 UP had become the third best-selling soft drink in the world.

- In 1967, the Seven-Up Company began advertising 7 UP as "the UnCola."

- In 1978, Philip Morris acquired the Seven-Up Company. In 1986, an investment company bought the Seven-Up Company and merged it with the Dr Pepper Company. In 1995, Cadbury Schweppes bought Dr Pepper/Seven-Up, Inc.

- The earliest advertisement for 7 UP featured a winged 7 UP logo and described the soft drink as "seven natural flavors blended into a savory, flavory drink with a real wallop."

- The 1973 movie *The Seven-Ups*, starring Roy Schneider, was a disappointing sequel to the 1971 Academy Award–winning movie *The French Connection*.

- In 1996, Dr Pepper/Seven Up, Inc., began advertising the tagline, "7 UP. It's an Up Thing."

For More Recipes

Visit www.brandspeoplelove.com/csab

SPAM Luncheon Meat

Baked SPAM Classic

Makes 6 servings

WHAT YOU NEED

- 1 can (12 ounces) SPAM Classic
- Whole cloves
- ⅓ cup firmly-packed brown sugar
- 1 teaspoon water
- 1 teaspoon prepared mustard
- ½ teaspoon vinegar

WHAT YOU DO

Preheat oven to 375 degrees Fahrenheit.

Place SPAM on rack in shallow baking pan. Score surface; stud with cloves.

Combine sugar, water, mustard, and vinegar in bowl, stirring until smooth. Brush over SPAM. Bake 20 minutes, basting often. Slice to serve.

Cajun-Coconut SPAM Fritters

Makes 32 appetizer servings

WHAT YOU NEED

- 1 can (12 ounces) SPAM Classic
- 1½ cups complete pancake mix
- 2 teaspoons Cajun seasoning
- 1 cup milk
- 1½ cups shredded coconut
- Sweet and sour sauce

WHAT YOU DO

Preheat oven to 375 degrees Fahrenheit. Lightly coat baking sheet with nonstick cooking spray.

Cut SPAM into 32 spears. Place a wooden toothpick lengthwise into each spear.

In bowl, combine pancake mix and Cajun seasoning and gradually add milk, stirring until smooth.

Place coconut in separate bowl. Dip each spear into batter; roll in coconut until lightly coated. Place on prepared baking sheet. Bake 10 to 13 minutes, turning halfway through baking, until golden brown and batter is cooked through. Serve warm fritters with sweet and sour sauce on the side for dipping.

Fancy SPAM Musubi

Makes 4 servings

WHAT YOU NEED

- 1 can (12 ounces) SPAM Classic
- 1 clove garlic, minced
- 1 teaspoon grated fresh ginger
- ⅓ cup brown sugar
- ⅓ cup soy sauce
- 2 tablespoons olive oil
- 3 cups cooked white sushi rice
- 1 package hoshi nori (Japanese dried seaweed)

WHAT YOU DO

Slice SPAM lengthwise into 8 equal pieces.

In shallow dish, combine garlic, ginger, sugar, and soy sauce. Place SPAM in the mixture and let sit for 30 minutes. Remove and pat dry.

In skillet, heat oil and brown SPAM slices. Moisten hands and mold rice into 8 thick blocks with the same outside dimensions as SPAM slices. Cut nori into 8½-inch strips. Place SPAM slices on rice blocks and wrap individual nori strips around each middle. Moisten one end slightly to fasten together and serve. Use the remaining marinade as a dip.

Maui SPAM Muffins

Makes 8 servings

WHAT YOU NEED

- 4 English muffins, halved
- Butter or margarine
- Prepared mustard
- 8 thin slices SPAM Classic
- 1 can (15¼ ounces) pineapple slices, drained
- 1 small green pepper, seeded and cut into 8 rings
- ¼ cup firmly-packed brown sugar
- 2 teaspoons water

WHAT YOU DO

Preheat oven to 375 degrees Fahrenheit.

Spread muffin halves with butter (or margarine) and mustard. Layer SPAM slices on each muffin half. Place one pineapple slice and one bell pepper ring on each muffin.

Combine sugar and water in bowl; spoon over sandwiches. Place muffins on baking sheet. Bake 10 minutes. Serve hot.

SPAM Cupcakes

Makes 12 servings

WHAT YOU NEED

- 2 cans (12 ounces each) SPAM Classic
- 2 eggs, slightly beaten
- ⅔ cup quick-cooking oatmeal
- ¾ cup milk
- ⅓ cup brown sugar

- 1 teaspoon prepared mustard
- 2 tablespoons white vinegar
- 1 tablespoon water
- 4 cups prepared mashed potatoes
- Snipped fresh chives

WHAT YOU DO

Preheat oven to 350 degrees Fahrenheit. Lightly coat 12-cup muffin pan with nonstick cooking spray.

In large bowl, grate SPAM. Add eggs, oatmeal, and milk; mix well. Fill each muffin cup two-thirds full with SPAM mixture. Using the back of a spoon, lightly press mixture into cup.

In small bowl, whisk together sugar, mustard, vinegar, and water. Lightly spoon glaze mixture over SPAM mixture. Bake 25 to 30 minutes, or until mixture is set.

Remove cupcakes from oven. Place oven rack 2 to 3 inches from heat source and preheat broiler. Top each cupcake with potatoes. Return muffin tin to oven. Broil 2 to 3 minutes, or until potatoes are lightly browned. Garnish with chives and serve.

SPAM Hot Cheesy Party Dip

Makes 16 servings

WHAT YOU NEED

- 1 can (12 ounces) SPAM Classic or any variety, julienned
- 2 packages (8 ounces each) cream cheese, softened
- ⅓ cup milk
- ¼ cup finely chopped onion

- 2 teaspoons prepared horseradish
- 6 to 8 drops hot pepper sauce
- Sliced green onions (optional)
- French bread, sliced

WHAT YOU DO

Preheat oven to 375 degrees Fahrenheit.

In large skillet, sauté SPAM until lightly browned; set aside.

In bowl, combine cream cheese and milk until smooth. Stir in onion, horseradish, hot pepper sauce, and half of the SPAM. Spoon mixture into 11- × 7-inch baking dish. Sprinkle remaining SPAM over the cream cheese mixture. Bake, uncovered, 20 to 25 minutes, or until hot and bubbly. If desired, garnish with onions. Serve with bread for dipping.

SPAM Stroganoff

Makes 6 servings

WHAT YOU NEED

- 1 can (12 ounces) SPAM Classic
- ½ cup chopped onion
- 2 tablespoons butter or margarine
- 1 can (10¾ ounces) cream of mushroom soup

- 1 can (4 ounces) sliced mushrooms, drained
- ⅛ teaspoon ground black pepper
- 1 cup sour cream
- 1 package (12 ounces) egg noodles, cooked and drained

WHAT YOU DO

Cut SPAM into 2- × ½-inch strips. In large skillet, sauté SPAM and onion in butter (or margarine) until onion is tender. Stir in soup, mushrooms, and pepper. Simmer 10 minutes. Stir in sour cream. Heat thoroughly but do not boil. Serve over noodles.

✳ Strange Facts ✳

- Hormel Foods Corporation, the maker of Spam products, has a fleet of three "SPAMMOBILES"—the largest SPAM cans in the world. The company uses the SPAMMOBILE vehicles, first introduced in 2001, to appear at retail stores, concerts, festivals, and sporting events, where the SPAMMOBILE crew uses electric sandwich grills to prepare miniature SPAMBURGER hamburgers.

- The 16,500-square-foot SPAM Museum opened in Austin, Minnesota, in September 2001. The free museum features a variety of interactive and educational games, SPAM exhibits, and video presentations.

- In 2005, *SPAMALOT,* a musical version of *Monty Python and the Holy Grail,* opened on Broadway, starring Tim Curry, David Hyde Pierce, and Hank Azaria. In honor of *SPAMALOT,* Hormel Foods introduced a limited edition flavor, SPAM golden honey grail in a "SPAMALOT collector's edition" can.

- The SPAM Gift Catalog offers such items for sale as pajamas, a camouflage hat, mittens, earrings, a plastic fly swatter, and glow-in-the-dark boxer shorts—all emblazoned with the SPAM logo.

- On the Internet, the term "spamming" refers to the act of sending unsolicited commercial e-mail, nicknamed "spam," a reference to a skit performed by Monty Python's Flying Circus in which a group of Vikings sang a chorus of "spam, spam, spam . . . ," drowning out any other conversation.

- The book *Spam-Ku: Tranquil Reflections on Luncheon Loaf,* published in 1998, features haikus concerning SPAM Luncheon Meat.

- The SPAM family of products are sold in forty-one countries, from Andorra to Zimbabwe.

- In the United States, a can of SPAM is purchased every three seconds.

- The average Hawaiian buys 5.5 cans of SPAM every year. The average Hawaiian consumes more SPAM than Americans from any other state, followed by Alaska, Arkansas, Texas, and Alabama.

- More than 122 million cans of SPAM are sold worldwide each year.

For More Recipes

Visit www.hormel.com

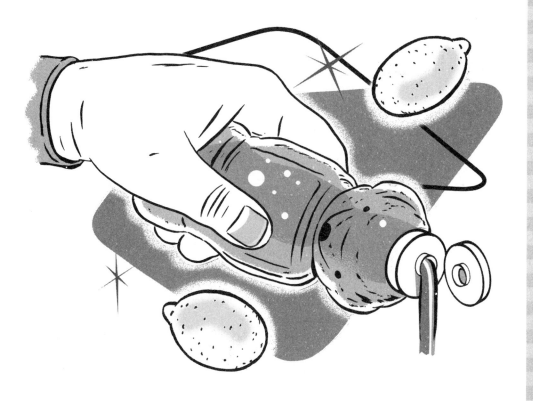

Cashew Chicken

Makes 4 to 6 servings

WHAT YOU NEED

- 1½ cups rice
- ¾ cup orange juice
- ¼ cup soy sauce
- ⅓ cup SueBee Honey
- 1 tablespoon cornstarch
- 1 teaspoon ground ginger
- 1 teaspoon garlic salt
- ½ teaspoon ground black pepper

- 2 tablespoons vegetable oil, divided
- 4 green onions, sliced
- 3 large carrots, peeled and sliced
- 2 ribs celery, sliced
- 1 pound boneless chicken breasts cut into 1-inch strips
- 1 cup cashews

WHAT YOU DO

Cook rice according to package directions.

Combine juice, soy sauce, honey, cornstarch, ginger, salt, and pepper. Set aside.

Heat 1 tablespoon oil in large skillet over high heat until it begins to smoke. Stir-fry onions, carrots, and celery for several minutes until the onions become fragrant. Remove from skillet. Heat the remaining tablespoon oil until smoking and stir-fry chicken until browned and tender. Add cooked vegetables, cashews, and sauce mixture. Continue cooking until sauce bubbles and thickens. Serve over hot rice.

Honey-Lemon-Basil Chicken

Makes 4 servings

WHAT YOU NEED

- ½ cup SueBee Honey
- ¼ cup lemon juice
- ¼ cup diced fresh basil leaves
- 1 teaspoon garlic powder

- ½ teaspoon salt
- 2 tablespoons lemon zest
- 4 boneless, skinless chicken breast halves

WHAT YOU DO

Mix together all ingredients except chicken in a resealable, plastic, food-storage bag. Add chicken and let marinate for at least 2 hours, refrigerated. Transfer chicken to baking dish.

Preheat oven to 350 degrees Fahrenheit.

Bake 35 to 45 minutes, or until juices run clear.

COOKING WITH A COFFEEMAKER

Dr. Peter Mazonson, a physician and vice president of an international health outcomes assessment firm, concocted dozens of recipes for cooking with a coffeemaker, published in his book *Cooking Without a Kitchen: The Coffeemaker Cookbook.*

Chicken Salad in a Coffeemaker

What You Need

- 2 boneless, skinless chicken breasts, halved
- ¼ cup cashews, chopped
- 2 tablespoons mayonnaise
- Salt
- Ground black pepper

- ½ head Boston lettuce (optional)
- 1 medium tomato, cored and cut into wedges (optional)
- 2 slices bread (optional)

What You Do

Place half chicken breast in coffee filter. Run 12 cups of water through filter. Repeat process with a new filter for each half chicken breast.

While chicken is cooking, place cashews in bowl. Shred or dice cooked chicken. Add chicken and mayonnaise to bowl and mix well. Season with salt and pepper. Can be served on bed of Boston lettuce surrounded by tomato wedges or on bread as a sandwich.

Reprinted from *Cooking Without a Kitchen: The Coffeemaker Cookbook* by Peter Mazonson (MCB)

Microwave Honey Peanut Brittle

Makes about 1 pound peanut brittle

WHAT YOU DO

- ¼ cup SueBee Honey
- ¼ cup light corn syrup
- 1 cup sugar
- ⅛ teaspoon salt

- 1 cup raw or roasted peanuts
- 1 teaspoon butter or margarine
- 1 teaspoon vanilla extract
- 1 teaspoon baking soda

WHAT YOU DO

Coat baking sheet with nonstick cooking spray.

Stir honey, corn syrup, sugar, salt, and peanuts into 2-quart microwave-safe dish. (If roasted and salted peanuts are used, omit salt and add peanuts after first 4 minutes of cooking.) Microwave 7 minutes on high, stirring well after 4 minutes. After 7 minutes, add butter (or margarine) and vanilla, blending well. Cook 1 minute more. Add baking soda and gently stir until light and foamy. Pour onto prepared baking sheet. Let cool 30 to 60 minutes. To keep peanut brittle from drawing moisture, store in an airtight container.

Revved-Up Power Smoothie

Makes 4 servings

WHAT YOU NEED

- ½ cup SueBee Honey
- 1 pint fresh strawberries, hulled and sliced, or 2 cups frozen strawberries, slightly thawed
- 1 cup 1 or 2 percent low-fat milk

- 1 cup (8 ounces) plain or vanilla low-fat yogurt
- 1 teaspoon vanilla extract
- 1 cup crushed ice

WHAT YOU DO

In blender or food processor container, combine all ingredients. Blend or process until smooth. Serve immediately.

SueBee Honey-Glazed Carrots

Makes 4 servings

WHAT YOU NEED

- ½ teaspoon salt
- 3 cups sliced carrots or 16 ounces baby carrots
- ¼ cup SueBee Honey
- 2 tablespoons butter or margarine
- 2 tablespoons chopped fresh parsley

WHAT YOU DO

Bring 2 inches water to a boil in medium saucepan over high heat. Add salt and carrots and return to a boil. Reduce heat to medium. Cover and cook 8 to 12 minutes, or until carrots are crisp-tender.

Drain carrots and return to saucepan. Stir in honey, butter (or margarine), and parsley. Cook over low heat, stirring constantly, until carrots are tender and thoroughly glazed.

Strange Facts

- In 1921, with two hundred dollars and three thousand pounds of honey, five bee-keepers located near Sioux City, Iowa, formed the Sioux Honey Association as a cooperative to better market their honey by sharing services, equipment, processing, and packing facilities, and marketing and sales organizations.
- Each of the 315 apiaries that are members of the Sioux Honey Association ship their honey in 55-gallon drums to the organization's processing plants, producing some 40 million pounds of honey annually.
- The Sioux Honey Association has three processing plants: in Sioux City, Iowa; Waycross, Georgia; and Anaheim, California.
- Sioux Honey Association originally marketed its honey under the name "Sioux Bee," but the group changed the name to "SueBee" in 1964 to better reflect the proper pronunciation.
- Worker bees are all female, and during the honey production period, a worker bee's average life span is six weeks.

- The flavor and color of honey depends on the plants used by the bees for the production of honey. Honey flavors include clover, orange, and sage, each with its own distinct color.
- Honey is one of the purest foods available.
- Bees fly an average of thirteen to fifteen miles per hour.
- Honeybees visit approximately two million flowers to make one pound of honey.
- A bee travels an average of 1,600 round trips—from the flowers to the honeycomb—to produce one ounce of honey—flying as far as six miles per round trip.
- To produce one pound of honey, bees travel a distance equal to two times around the earth.
- Bees from the same hive visit approximately 225,000 flowers per day. The average bee visits between fifty and a thousand flowers per day.
- Bees consume approximately eight pounds of honey to produce one pound of beeswax, the sticky material used to build honeycombs.
- A queen bee lays approximately two thousand eggs every day at a rate of five or six per minute.
- The queen bee makes one mating flight in her lifetime, mating with up to seventeen drones over a one to two day period. The queen stores the sperm in her body, giving her a lifetime supply.
- Bees do not sleep, but they can be seen resting in empty honeycomb cells.
- During honey-gathering season, a beehive houses from 40,000 to 60,000 bees.
- Actor Henry Fonda earned his Eagle Scout badge for beekeeping and, as an adult, kept beehives as a hobby, giving away jars of honey labeled "Henry's Honey."
- Honey can be used as a topical dressing for wounds because microbes cannot live in it and an enzyme in honey slowly produces hydrogen peroxide.
- Alexander the Great was embalmed with honey and beeswax.
- In ancient Greece, mead, an alcoholic beverage made with honey, was considered the drink of the Greek gods.
- The word *honeymoon* may have originated with the Norse practice of consuming large quantities of mead during the first month of a marriage.

For More Recipes

Visit www.suebee.com

Swiss Miss® Milk Chocolate Hot Cocoa Mix

Cocoa Pudding Cake

Makes 8 servings

WHAT YOU NEED

- 1 cup all-purpose flour
- ½ cup sugar
- ¼ cup unsweetened cocoa
- 1½ teaspoons baking powder
- ¼ teaspoon salt
- ¾ cup milk

- 2 tablespoons butter or margarine, melted
- 1 teaspoon vanilla extract
- 3 packets (1 ounce each) Swiss Miss Milk Chocolate Hot Cocoa Mix
- 1½ cups boiling water
- Whipped cream

WHAT YOU DO

Preheat oven to 350 degrees Fahrenheit.

Combine flour, sugar, cocoa, baking powder, and salt in large mixing bowl. Add milk, butter (or margarine), and vanilla; mix until blended and smooth. Spoon batter into ungreased 9- × 9-inch baking pan.

Place cocoa mix in medium bowl. Add boiling water; mix well. Pour evenly over batter. Bake 30 minutes, or until top is firm to the touch.

Cool cake 10 minutes. Serve warm with whipped cream.

Easy-to-Please Chocolate Tarts

Makes 6 servings

WHAT YOU NEED

- 1 tub (8 ounces) whipped cream cheese
- ½ cup vanilla yogurt
- 3 packets (1 ounce each) Swiss Miss Chocolate Hot Cocoa Mix

- 1 package (4 ounces) prepared, mini graham cracker crusts (6 shells)
- Whipped cream
- Fresh raspberries (optional)

WHAT YOU DO

Blend cream cheese, yogurt, and cocoa mix in medium bowl until smooth. Divide the cream cheese mixture equally among graham cracker crusts (about ½ cup filling per crust). Cover; chill a minimum of 2 hours. Top each tart with whipped cream immediately before serving. Garnish with raspberries, if desired.

Fudgy Peanut Butter Buttons

Makes 6 dozen buttons

WHAT YOU NEED

- 20 cups hot water
- 1 box (10 ounces) Swiss Miss Milk Chocolate Hot Cocoa Mix or 10 packets (1 ounce each)
- 1 jar (18 ounces) creamy peanut butter
- ½ cup light corn syrup
- 3 cups sifted confectioners' sugar, divided
- 4 cups crushed vanilla wafers
- Bittersweet chocolate morsels

WHAT YOU DO

Coat large piece of waxed paper with nonstick cooking spray.

Combine water and cocoa mix in large bowl; whisk together until smooth. Stir in peanut butter and corn syrup. Add 2 cups sugar; blend. Stir in vanilla wafers.

Drop heaping teaspoonfuls of chocolate mixture onto paper; set aside. Place remaining 1 cup sugar in shallow dish. Roll each piece of chocolate in sugar; shape into balls. Press thumb into the center of each ball until slightly indented; place chocolate morsel in middle (tip side up).

Chill at least 1 hour before serving. Store refrigerated in airtight container.

THE BIRTH OF THE BLENDER

In 1915, Stephen J. Poplawski, a Polish-American from Racine, Wisconsin, began designing a gadget to mix his favorite drink: malted milk shakes. Seven years later, Poplawski patented the "vibrator," the first mixer with a wheel of blades mounted inside the bottom of a pitcher and activated only when the pitcher is placed in a base containing the motor. Picturing every soda fountain in America using his mixer, Poplawski struck a deal with the Racine-based Horlick Corporation, the largest manufacturer of the powdered malt used in soda fountain shakes. Obsessed with malted milk shakes, Poplawski never thought of using his mixer to blend fruits and vegetables.

In 1936, Fred Waring, the famous bandleader of the "Pennsylvanians," witnessed a demonstration of one of Poplawski's blenders. Impressed, he decided to finance the development of a competing food liquefier to be marketed to bartenders to mix daiquiris. The Waring Blendor would be spelled with the letter "o" to make the blender stand out.

At the 1936 National Restaurant Show in Chicago, the Waring Mixer Corporation demonstrated how the new Waring Blendor could mix daiquiris and other drinks, and then gave out sample drinks, making the blender accessible to a wider audience than Poplawski had ever imagined. Soon afterwards, the Ron Rico Rum Company launched an advertising campaign showing how the Waring Blendor could be used to make exotic rum drinks easily and effortlessly.

In 1955, to promote blenders for use in the kitchen, Waring introduced blenders in designer colors. Meanwhile, Poplawski sold his company to Oster Manufacturing. Oster doubled the number of speeds of its blender from two ("Low" and "High") to four (adding "Medium" and "Off"), inadvertently launching a "Battle of the Buttons." Competitors began adding more buttons, including "Chop," "Dice," "Grate," "Liquefy," "Puree," and "Whip." By 1968, blenders boasted as many as fifteen different buttons, despite the fact that most people use only two or three speeds.

No-Bake Peanut Butter Iceberg Pie

Makes 6 to 8 servings

WHAT YOU NEED

- 2 packets (1 ounce each) Swiss Miss Milk Chocolate Hot Cocoa Mix (⅓ cup)
- 2 tablespoons hot water
- 1¼ cups creamy peanut butter, divided
- 1 ready made 9-inch crumb pie crust
- 3 cups vanilla ice cream, softened

WHAT YOU DO

Whisk together cocoa mix and water in bowl until smooth; set aside.

Melt ¾ cup peanut butter in microwave. Brush the inside of pie crust with melted peanut butter. Place crust in freezer 15 minutes, or until set.

Heat remaining peanut butter in microwave until just soft but not melted. Quickly fill pie crust with ice cream. Drizzle peanut butter over ice cream, followed by cocoa mixture.

Freeze pie until firm. Store in freezer.

Rocky Road Popcorn Balls

Makes 16 popcorn balls

WHAT YOU NEED

- 1 bag microwave popcorn, popped
- ½ cup chopped pecans or walnuts, toasted
- ¼ cup (½ stick) butter or margarine
- 1 package (10 ounces) miniature marshmallows
- 1 packet (1 ounce) Swiss Miss Milk Chocolate Hot Cocoa Mix

WHAT YOU DO

Combine popcorn and pecans (or walnuts) together in large bowl; set aside.

Melt butter (or margarine) in medium saucepan over medium heat. Add marshmallows and cook 5 minutes, or until melted, stirring frequently. Stir in cocoa mix.

Pour over popcorn mixture. Stir well with spoon sprayed with nonstick cooking spray. Spray your hands with cooking spray; form popcorn mixture into 16 balls. Store unused portions in airtight container up to 3 days.

✳Strange Facts✳

- In Menomonie, Wisconsin, the Swiss Miss company created the first instant cocoa in 1957 by blending together the imported cocoa powder with milk.
- The ancient Mayans considered cocoa beans to be "the food of the gods" and carved images of cocoa bean pods into the walls of their stone temples. The Mayans created the first beverage from crushed cocoa beans, serving the delicacy to royalty and using the beverage at sacred ceremonies.
- The Aztecs made a drink from cocoa beans called *chocolatl*, meaning "warm liquid," imbibing the unsweetened beverage during special ceremonies. Aztec ruler Montezuma II kept great storehouses filled with cocoa beans and reportedly drank more than fifty portions of chocolatl every day from a golden goblet. The Aztecs also used cocoa beans as currency.
- In 1502, Christopher Columbus brought a handful of cocoa beans back to Spain from the Caribbean islands and presented them to King Ferdinand and Queen Isabella, who never grasped their culinary or commercial potential.
- In 1519, Spanish explorer Hernando Cortes arrived in Mexico, where the Aztecs mistook him for a reincarnation of a former god-king who had been exiled from the land. Unaware that Cortes was seeking gold, Aztec ruler Montezuma greeted Cortez and his men with a large banquet that included cups of a bitter chocolate drink.
- After conquering the Aztecs, Cortes recognized the commercial potential for cocoa beans and added sugar cane to chocolatl to make it more agreeable to Spanish tastes.
- In Spain, chocolatl grew in popularity, especially after someone discovered that the beverage tasted better when served steaming hot, creating hot chocolate.
- In 1847, an English company introduced the first solid eating chocolate made by combining melted cocoa butter with sugar and cocoa powder.
- In 1876 in Vevey, Switzerland, Daniel Peter discovered how to add milk to chocolate, creating milk chocolate.

For More Recipes

Visit www.conagrafoods.com

Tabasco® Pepper Sauce

Chunky Salsa

Makes 3½ cups

WHAT YOU NEED

- 2 tablespoons olive oil
- 1 cup coarsely chopped onion
- 1 cup coarsely chopped green bell pepper
- 1 can (35 ounces) tomatoes (about 4 cups), coarsely chopped
- 1 tablespoon freshly squeezed lime juice
- 2 teaspoons Tabasco Pepper Sauce
- ½ teaspoon salt
- 2 tablespoons chopped fresh cilantro or parsley

WHAT YOU DO

Heat oil in large heavy saucepan over high heat. Add onion and bell pepper and sauté 5 to 6 minutes, or until tender, stirring frequently. Add tomatoes and bring to a boil; reduce heat and simmer until liquid is reduced and salsa is slightly thickened, about 8 minutes, stirring occasionally. Remove from heat and stir in lime juice, pepper sauce, and salt. Cool to lukewarm and stir in cilantro (or parsley). Spoon salsa into clean jars and refrigerate up to 5 days.

Classic Bloody Mary

Makes 6 (6-ounce) servings

WHAT YOU NEED

- 1 quart tomato juice
- 1 cup vodka
- 1 tablespoon Worcestershire sauce
- 1 tablespoon fresh lime juice
- ½ teaspoon Tabasco Pepper Sauce
- Lime slices or celery stalks

WHAT YOU DO

Combine tomato juice, vodka, Worcestershire sauce, lime juice, and pepper sauce in 2-quart pitcher; stir well. Serve over ice. Garnish with lime (or celery).

Fireballs

Makes about 3 dozen fireballs

WHAT YOU NEED

- 1 package (12 ounces) semisweet chocolate chips
- ¼ cup butter or margarine
- ½ cup walnuts, toasted and finely chopped
- 2 tablespoons dark rum
- 1½ teaspoons Tabasco Pepper Sauce
- ⅓ cup sugar

WHAT YOU DO

Melt chocolate and butter (or margarine) in small saucepan over low heat. Stir in walnuts, rum, and pepper sauce and mix well. Refrigerate mixture about 15 minutes. Shape into 1-inch balls, then roll in sugar to coat. Store in refrigerator.

Hot 'n Nutty Cookies

Makes 2 dozen cookies

WHAT YOU NEED

- ¾ cup unsalted butter, softened
- 1 cup granulated sugar
- 1 cup packed brown sugar
- 2 cups smooth or chunky peanut butter
- ½ cup macadamia nuts, chopped (optional)
- 2 eggs
- 1 teaspoon vanilla extract
- 1 teaspoon Tabasco Pepper Sauce
- 3 cups all-purpose flour
- 1 teaspoon salt
- 1 teaspoon baking soda

WHAT YOU DO

Preheat oven to 350 degrees Fahrenheit. Lightly butter and flour baking sheet.

In large bowl, cream together butter, granulated sugar, and brown sugar. Stir in peanut butter and macadamia nuts (if desired); mix until well blended. Add eggs, vanilla, and pepper sauce. Mix until well combined.

In another bowl, mix together flour, salt, and baking soda. Add to nut mixture and stir until blended.

Spoon batter onto prepared baking sheet, using 1 heaping tablespoon for each cookie. Coat tines of fork in flour and score each cookie in crisscross pattern. Bake 15 to 17 minute, or until edges begin to turn golden. Cool on racks.

Peppersass Cookies

Makes about 5 dozen cookies

WHAT YOU NEED

- 2¼ cups all-purpose flour
- ½ teaspoon baking soda
- ½ teaspoon salt
- 1 cup sugar, plus more for coating

- ⅔ cup butter or margarine, at room temperature
- 1 large egg
- 2 teaspoons Tabasco Pepper Sauce
- 1 teaspoon vanilla extract

WHAT YOU DO

In small bowl, combine flour, baking soda, and salt.

In large bowl with mixer at low speed, cream sugar and butter (or margarine) until well blended. Add egg, pepper sauce, vanilla, and flour mixture; beat until smooth.

Divide dough in half. On plastic wrap, shape each dough half into a log, about 1½ inches in diameter. Cover and refrigerate until firm.

Preheat oven to 350 degrees Fahrenheit.

Cut dough rolls into ¼-inch-thick slices. Dip each slice in sugar. Place 1 inch apart on ungreased baking sheets. Bake 10 to 12 minutes, or until cookies are golden around the edges. Cool on wire racks.

Spiced Iced Tea

Makes 4 servings

WHAT YOU NEED

- 4 cups cold water
- 8 tea bags
- 4 whole cloves
- ⅓ cup sugar

- ½ cup fresh orange juice
- 2 tablespoons fresh lemon juice
- 1 teaspoon Tabasco Pepper Sauce
- 1 orange, cut in half and thinly sliced

WHAT YOU DO

Boil water. Place tea bags, cloves, and sugar in heatproof bowl. Stir in bowling water. Cover and steep 5 minutes. Add orange juice, lemon juice, and pepper sauce. Pour into pitcher and cool 30 minutes. To serve, stir in orange slices and pour over ice.

Spiced-Up Apple Cake

Makes 12 servings

WHAT YOU NEED

Cake:
- 1¼ cups all-purpose flour
- 1 teaspoon ground allspice
- ½ teaspoon baking powder
- ½ teaspoon baking soda
- ½ teaspoon salt
- ½ cup butter or margarine, softened
- ½ cup granulated sugar
- ¼ cup packed brown sugar
- 1 large egg
- ½ cup milk
- 1½ teaspoons Tabasco Pepper Sauce

- 1 large Golden Delicious apple, peeled, cored, and diced (2 cups)

Topping:
- 2 tablespoons sugar
- 1 tablespoon all-purpose flour
- 1 tablespoon butter or margarine, cut into pieces
- ½ teaspoon ground cinnamon
- ¾ cup walnuts, coarsely chopped

Glaze:
- ¼ cup confectioners' sugar
- 1 teaspoon milk

WHAT YOU DO

Preheat oven to 350 degrees Fahrenheit. Coat 8- × 8-inch baking pan with nonstick cooking spray.

To make the cake: In small bowl combine flour, allspice, baking powder, baking soda, and salt.

In large bowl with electric mixer at high speed, cream butter (or margarine), granulated sugar, and brown sugar until light and fluffy. Add egg, milk, pepper sauce, and flour mixture. Beat at medium until blended and smooth; stir in apple. Spoon mixture into prepared pan.

To prepare the topping: In small bowl, combine sugar, flour, butter (or margarine), and cinnamon until well mixed. Stir in walnuts.

Sprinkle mixture over top of batter in pan. Bake 45 to 50 minutes, or until wooden pick inserted into center comes out clean. Cool in pan on wire rack.

To prepare the glaze: In small bowl, stir sugar and milk until smooth. Drizzle over cooled cake.

Sweet and Spicy Brownies

Makes 16 brownies

WHAT YOU NEED

- 4 squares (1 ounce each) unsweetened chocolate
- ¾ cup butter or margarine
- 2 cups sugar
- 3 large eggs

- 1 cup all-purpose flour
- 1 tablespoon Tabasco Pepper Sauce
- ½ cup semisweet chocolate chips
- ½ cup chopped walnuts

WHAT YOU DO

Melt unsweetened chocolate and butter (or margarine) in 2-quart saucepan over low heat, stirring frequently; stir in sugar and set aside to cool slightly.

Preheat oven to 350 degrees Fahrenheit. Coat 9- × 9-inch baking pan with nonstick cooking spray.

Add eggs, one at a time, to chocolate mixture in saucepan, beating well after each addition. Stir in flour and pepper sauce and mix well. Stir in semisweet chocolate and walnuts. Pour mixture into pan. Bake 35 to 40 minutes, or until wooden pick inserted into center comes out clean. Cool completely in pan on wire rack; cut into squares.

Strange Facts

- Tabasco products are produced by McIlhenny Company, founded in 1868 at Avery Island, Louisiana.

- Shortly after the McIlhenny family returned to Avery Island from self-imposed exile during the Civil War, Edmund McIlhenny obtained some hot pepper seeds from a traveler who had recently arrived in Louisiana from Central America. McIlhenny planted the seeds on Avery Island, and then experimented with recipes for pepper sauces until he hit upon one he liked.

- According to tradition, McIlhenny first used discarded cologne bottles topped with sprinkler fitments for distributing his sauce informally to family and friends. The sprinkler fitment enabled users to sprinkle—rather than pour—the concentrated pepper sauce on food.

- Acquaintances encouraged McIlhenny to market his pepper sauce commercially, and so in 1868 he did just that, distributing Tabasco Pepper Sauce, now packaged in new cologne bottles, around New Orleans.

- In 1870, Edmund McIlhenny received a patent for his unique formula for processing peppers into a fiery red sauce.

- During the early 1870s, his concoction found its way to New York City, where a major nineteenth-century wholesale grocery firm, E.C. Hazard and Company, helped to introduce the product to the northeastern United States and beyond.

- The McIlhenny Company uses the same process to make Tabasco Pepper Sauce today that Edmund McIlhenny devised in 1868. Avery Island remains the head-quarters for the worldwide company, which is still owned and operated by direct descendants of Edmund McIlhenny.

- Tabasco Pepper Sauce is made with three simple ingredients: fully-aged red pepper, high grain all-natural vinegar, and a small amount of salt mined right on Avery Island. The product is pure pepper sauce with no additives whatsoever.

- In 2002, archeologists discovered a 130-year-old Tabasco Pepper Sauce bottle at an archaeological excavation in Virginia City, Nevada. The artifact appears to be of the earliest surviving form of a bottle used by the company.

- Edmund McIlhenny originally wanted to call his concoction Petite Anse Sauce (after Avery Island, which then was known as Isle Petite Anse). When family members balked at the commercial use of the family island's name, McIlhenny decided to use the name Tabasco as the brand name.
- Some scholars say *Tabasco* is a Central American Indian word that means "land where the soil is hot and humid." Other scholars claim that *Tabasco* means "place of coral or oyster shell."
- Each 2-ounce bottle of Tabasco Pepper Sauce contains at least 720 drops. There are 60 drops per teaspoon.
- When all four production lines at the Avery Island factory are in operation, the factory can produce more than 600,000 2-ounce bottles of Tabasco Pepper Sauce in a single day.

For More Recipes

Visit www.tabasco.com

Tang® Drink Mix

Calcium-Rich Tang Smoothie

Makes 1 (12-ounce) serving

WHAT YOU NEED

- 1 cup cold milk
- ½ cup nonfat dry milk powder
- 2 tablespoons Tang Orange Flavor Drink Mix

- ¼ cup fresh strawberries, hulled
- ¼ cup fresh blueberries
- 1 frozen banana, sliced

WHAT YOU DO

In blender, blend milk, dry milk, drink mix, strawberries, and blueberries. Add banana and blend until thick and creamy.

Orangey Pancakes

Makes 4 (3 to 4 pancake) servings

WHAT YOU NEED

- 6 tablespoons Tang Orange Flavor Drink Mix
- 2 cups instant pancake mix

- 1½ cups water
- 2 tablespoons all-vegetable shortening

WHAT YOU DO

Preheat skillet over medium heat or electric griddle to 275 degrees Fahrenheit.

Mix drink mix, pancake mix, and water in large bowl with wire whisk until large lumps vanish. (Do not overmix, otherwise pancakes may be tough.) Lightly grease skillet or griddle with shortening. Pour approximately ¼ cup batter for each pancake onto the skillet. When pancakes bubble and bottoms are golden brown, flip pancakes.

Serving Suggestion: Serve with maple syrup or fruit preserves.

Orangey Rice

Makes 4 servings

WHAT YOU NEED

- 6 tablespoons Tang Orange Flavor Drink Mix
- 2¼ cups water
- 1 cup rice
- 2 teaspoons butter
- ¼ cup raisins

WHAT YOU DO

Dissolve drink mix in water in bowl.

Combine orange water, rice, and butter in saucepan. Bring to a boil. Reduce heat to medium-low and simmer covered 20 minutes. Remove from heat, add raisins, and let stand covered 5 minutes, or until water is absorbed. Fluff with fork and serve.

✳

Tangy Orange Glaze for Ham

Makes 1½ cups

WHAT YOU NEED

- 6 tablespoons Tang Orange Flavor Drink Mix
- 6 ounces water
- ½ cup molasses

WHAT YOU DO

Stir drink mix and water in bowl until drink mix is dissolved. Add molasses and mix well until blended.

During the last half hour of baking ham, brush glaze over the ham several times.

Tangy Tortilla Wraps

Makes 1 serving

WHAT YOU NEED

- 1 flour tortilla
- 1 teaspoon butter
- 1 teaspoon Tang Orange Flavor Drink Mix
- Pinch ground cinnamon

WHAT YOU DO

Place tortilla on flat surface, smear with butter, and sprinkle drink mix over buttered area. Add cinnamon. Roll up tortilla, place on paper towel, and microwave on high for 30 seconds for a great after-school snack.

Strange Facts

- In 1957, after two years of research, General Foods Corporation launched *Tang* powdered beverage in test markets in the United States. In 1959, General Foods introduced Tang in Canada and Venezuela, and two years later, in Great Britain and Peru. Today Tang is sold in more than sixty countries.
- In 1965, the astronauts aboard Gemini 4 drank Tang during their mission, using a specially designed drink dispenser. Tang was served on all manned Gemini and Apollo space flights.
- Most Tang drinkers in the United States are children aged nine to twelve.
- Kraft sells sour cherry flavored Tang in Turkey, mango flavor in Saudi Arabia and the Philippines, a sweeter orange flavor in Brazil, and a tarter orange flavor in Argentina.

For More Recipes

Visit www.kraftfoods.com

Uncle Ben's® Converted® Brand Rice

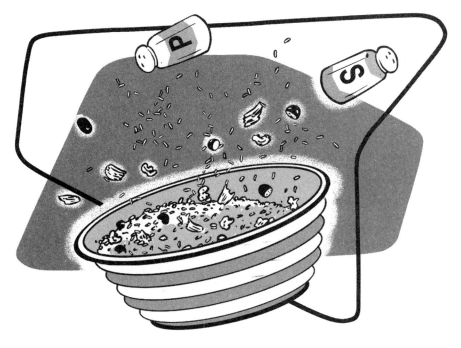

Better-Than-Potato Salad

Makes 6 to 8 servings

WHAT YOU NEED

- 1 cup Uncle Ben's Converted Brand Rice
- 2 cups mayonnaise
- 2 cups sliced celery
- 1 medium onion, finely chopped
- 4 teaspoons prepared mustard

- ½ teaspoon salt
- 4 hard-cooked eggs, chopped
- 8 radishes, sliced
- 1 cucumber, peeled and diced

WHAT YOU DO

Cook rice according to package directions. Place in bowl and chill. Add mayonnaise, celery, onion, mustard, and salt; mix well. Chill. Stir in eggs, radishes, and cucumber before serving.

Curried Chicken and Rice Salad

Makes 12 servings

WHAT YOU NEED

- 3½ cups Uncle Ben's Converted Brand Rice, cooked and cooled
- 1 cup chicken or turkey, cooked and chopped
- 1 cup seedless grapes, halved
- ½ cup walnuts, coarsely chopped

- ½ cup mayonnaise
- ½ cup plain yogurt
- 1 tablespoon curry powder
- Salt
- Ground black pepper

WHAT YOU DO

In large bowl, combine rice, chicken (or turkey), grapes, and walnuts.

In another bowl, combine mayonnaise, yogurt, and curry powder and salt and pepper to taste. Pour dressing over rice/fruit mixture. Toss well and refrigerate.

Serving Suggestion: Serve chilled as is or on a bed of lettuce.

Fried Rice

Makes 5 to 6 servings

WHAT YOU NEED

- 1 cup Uncle Ben's Converted Brand Rice
- 2 cups chopped cooked pork
- ¼ cup vegetable oil
- 2 eggs, lightly beaten
- ¼ teaspoon ground black pepper
- 2 tablespoons soy sauce
- ½ cup chopped green onions

WHAT YOU DO

Cook rice according to the package directions. In large skillet over medium heat, stir fry pork in oil until coated and heated through, about 1 minute, stirring constantly. Add eggs and pepper and cook for 5 minutes, stirring constantly. Add cooked rice and soy sauce. Fry, stirring frequently, about 5 minutes. Sprinkle onions over top and serve.

Gazpacho Salad

Makes 4 servings

WHAT YOU NEED

- 2 cups Uncle Ben's Converted Brand Rice, cooked and chilled
- ½ cup peeled, seeded, and diced cucumber
- ¼ cup fresh parsley, chopped
- ¼ cup shallots
- ¼ cup diced green bell pepper
- 1 tomato, peeled, seeded, and diced
- ⅓ cup olive oil
- Ground black pepper
- 2 cloves garlic, minced
- 3 tablespoons lemon juice
- 1 teaspoon salt
- ½ teaspoon sugar
- Mixed greens

WHAT YOU DO

In large bowl, combine rice, cucumber, parsley, shallots, bell pepper, and tomato and toss lightly.

In jar, combine oil, black pepper, garlic, lemon juice, salt, and sugar, cover, and shake well. Pour over the rice and vegetable mixture and toss lightly.

Chill, covered, for several hours and then serve on a bed of greens.

CLOSING IN ON TUPPERWARE

In 1936, after twenty-nine-year-old Massachusetts tree surgeon and landscaper Earl Silas Tupper went bankrupt, he found a job at Viscoloid, DuPont's plastics division in Leominster, Massachusetts. After one year, Tupper took his newly-acquired design, research, development, and manufacturing experience and founded his own plastics company. The Earl S. Tupper Company, at first a subcontractor for DuPont, began making gas masks and other equipment for American troops during World War II. After the war, Tupper invented a method to transform polyethylene slag (a black, smelly by-product of the crude oil refinement process) into a clean, clear, and translucent plastic that was pliant, solid, and grease-free—a vast improvement over the brittle, slimy, and putrid plastics of the day. Tupper also developed an airtight and watertight seal for containers made of his improved plastic, creating Tupperware—the plastic storage container that still bears his name.

By 1946, Tupper was marketing a wide range of brightly colored Tupperware, but sales were disappointing. In 1948, Tupper learned that two Stanley Home Products salespeople were selling large quantities of his Tupperware. Stanley salespeople, he discovered, introduced their products to homemakers assembled at an in-home sales party. Recalling his own success as a door-to-door salesman as a youth, Tupper teamed up with several Stanley distributors to market Tupperware exclusively through Tupperware Parties. By 1954, sales exceeded twenty-five million dollars. Nine thousand dealers nationwide were arranging Tupperware parties in the homes of housewives who agreed to host the event in exchange for a free Tupperware gift. Tupperware Parties had become a national phenomenon, firmly establishing Tupperware as an American icon.

- The lid and bowl of Tupperware containers lock together with the signature Tupperware "burp."
- In 1958, Earl Tupper sold Tupperware Home Parties, Inc., to Rexall Drugs for sixteen million dollars. Tupper became a citizen of Costa Rica, where he died in 1983.
- In 1996, the Violence Policy Center, a non-profit organization based in Washington, DC, working to stop gun violence, issued a reported titled "Gun Shows In America: Tupperware Parties for Criminals," In a radio address two years later, President Bill Clinton called gun shows "Tupperware parties for criminals."

Old-Fashioned Rice Pudding

Makes 5 to 6 servings

WHAT YOU NEED

- 1¾ cups water
- ½ cup Uncle Ben's Converted Brand Rice
- ½ teaspoon salt
- 2 cups milk
- 2 eggs, beaten
- ⅓ cup sugar
- 1 teaspoon vanilla extract
- ¼ cup raisins, soaked in hot water until soft and drained (optional)
- Ground nutmeg or ground cinnamon (optional)

WHAT YOU DO

Preheat oven to 350 degrees Fahrenheit. Coat 1½-quart casserole dish with nonstick cooking spray.

In large saucepan, bring water to boil. Stir in rice and salt. Cover and simmer until all water is absorbed, about 30 minutes. Add milk and boil gently, stirring occasionally, until mixture thickens slightly, about 5 minutes. Remove from heat.

In small bowl, combine eggs, sugar, and vanilla. Gradually stir into rice mixture; mix well.

Pour into prepared casserole. If desired, stir in raisins and sprinkle nutmeg (or cinnamon) over top. Place casserole in pan containing about 1 inch hot water. Bake, uncovered, 45 to 50 minutes, or until knife inserted near center comes out clean. Serve warm or chilled.

Strange Facts

- During the processing necessary to produce white rice, the bran layer—containing a large part of the nutritive value of rice—is removed. In England, scientists discovered a special steeping and steaming process to force the bran nutrients, under pressure, into the rice grain before the bran is removed, locking the nutrients inside the grain.
- In the early 1940s, George Harwell, a successful Texas food broker, received permission to introduce the process developed in England to the United States but only if he could build a plant immediately. Because the new process improved the nutritional,

cooking, and storage qualities of a food that had remained unchanged for more than five thousand years, Harwell convinced the United States government that this unique product merited war priorities. In 1943, Harwell and his partners shipped the first carload of Converted Brand Rice to an army quartermaster depot.

- Until the end of World War II, Converted Brand Rice was produced for use solely by military personnel. Then in 1946, Harwell's company, Converted Rice, Inc., brought this special rice to American consumers for the very first time using the familiar portrait of Uncle Ben as its trademark. Consumer response was so great that in just six years Uncle Ben's Converted Brand Rice became the number one packaged long grain rice sold in the United States.

- The original Uncle Ben was an African-American rice farmer known to rice millers in and around Houston for consistently delivering the highest quality rice for milling. Uncle Ben harvested his rice with such care that he purportedly received several honors for full-kernel yields and quality. Legend holds that other rice growers proudly claimed their rice was "as good as Uncle Ben's." Unfortunately, further details of Uncle Ben's life (including his last name) were lost to history.

- In the 1980s, the company dropped Uncle Ben from the rice boxes for two years. Sales plummeted, and the company quickly reinstated Uncle Ben's portrait on the boxes.

- Frank Brown, a maître d' in a Houston restaurant, posed for the portrait of Uncle Ben on the brand's packaging

- The world's leading producer of rice is China. The world's second leading exporter of rice is the United States, second only to Thailand. The world's leading importer of rice is Indonesia, followed by Brazil and Iran.

- Adding one tablespoon of butter, margarine, or oil to the water before adding the rice will prevent the rice from becoming sticky.

- To reheat rice, place the cooked rice in a coffee filter and place in a vegetable steamer over boiling water.

- Thrown at weddings, rice is a symbol of fertility.

- Rice is grown on more than 10 percent of the earth's farmable surface.

- Rice is the mainstay for nearly 40 percent of the world's population.

For More Recipes

Visit www.unclebens.com

Calcutta Lamb Curry

Makes 6 to 8 servings

WHAT YOU NEED

- 2 tablespoons vegetable oil
- 2 pounds lamb, cut into 1-inch cubes
- 1 can (10½ ounces) condensed chicken broth, undiluted
- 1 cup Welch's Grape Jelly
- 1 cup chopped onion
- 2 teaspoons curry powder
- 1 teaspoon sugar

- ½ teaspoon dried mint leaves
- 1 medium ripe cantaloupe or honeydew melon, cut into 1-inch pieces
- 1 large ripe mango, cut into bite-size pieces
- ½ cup lime juice
- ½ cup heavy cream
- Peanuts, chopped

WHAT YOU DO

Preheat pressure cooker.

Place oil in pressure cooker; brown lamb. Add broth, jelly, onion, curry powder, sugar, and mint. Close cover securely. Place pressure regulator on vent pipe. Cook 10 minutes. Cool pressure cooker at once. Add cantaloupe (or honeydew) and mango and simmer 5 minutes. Stir in lime juice and cream. Do not allow sauce to boil. Garnish with peanuts.

Grape Crumble Bars

Makes 36 bars

WHAT YOU NEED

- ¾ cup butter or margarine
- 1 cup firmly packed brown sugar
- 1½ cups all-purpose flour
- ½ teaspoon baking soda

- 1 teaspoon salt
- 2 cups ready-to-eat all natural cereal or granola with raisins and dates
- 10 ounces Welch's Grape Jelly

WHAT YOU DO

Preheat oven to 400 degrees Fahrenheit. Coat 13- x 9- x 2-inch pan with nonstick cooking spray.

Cream butter (or margarine) and sugar in bowl until light and fluffy. Add flour, baking soda, and salt and mix well. Stir in cereal (or granola). Press half the dough into prepared pan. Break jelly with a fork and spread over dough in pan, up to ⅛ inch from the edges. With fingers, crumble the remaining dough over top. Bake about 20 minutes, or until brown. Cool, then cut into bars.

Grape Jelly Pudding

Makes 4 to 5 servings

WHAT YOU NEED

- 1 package (3 ounces) vanilla pudding
- 1¼ cups Welch's Grape Jelly, chilled

WHAT YOU DO

Prepare pudding according to package directions. Refrigerate until firm. Alternate layers of pudding and jelly in dessert dishes.

Ham Roll-Ups

Makes 4 sandwiches

WHAT YOU NEED

- 1 package (3 ounces) cream cheese, softened
- ⅓ cup Welch's Grape Jelly
- ¼ cup crushed pineapple, well drained
- ¼ cup chopped peanuts
- 8 slices ham
- 4 hot dog bun
- 2 tablespoons butter or margarine

WHAT YOU DO

Blend cream cheese, jelly, and pineapple in bowl. Stir in peanuts. On a flat surface, overlap 2 slices of ham. Place about ¼ cup pineapple mixture on one end and roll up. Repeat with remaining ham and pineapple mixture. Spread hot dog buns lightly with butter (or margarine); place ham roll-ups inside.

Jelly-Flavored Mayonnaise for Fruit Salad

Makes ¾ cup

WHAT YOU NEED

- ½ cup mayonnaise
- ¼ cup Welch's Grape Jelly
- 1 tablespoon white vinegar

WHAT YOU DO

Beat mayonnaise with jelly and vinegar until well blended.

Serving Suggestion: Combine with prepared fruit and serve in lettuce cups.

✳

Peanut Butter and Jelly Swirl Bundt Cake

Makes 8 servings

WHAT YOU NEED

- 2½ cups all-purpose flour
- 1½ teaspoons baking powder
- 1 teaspoon baking soda
- ½ teaspoon salt
- ½ cup unsalted butter, at room temperature
- 2 cups sugar
- ¾ cup chunky peanut butter
- 2 teaspoons vanilla extract
- 3 large eggs
- 1 cup sour cream
- ½ cup Welch's Grape Jelly

WHAT YOU DO

Place baking rack in bottom third of oven. Preheat oven to 350 degrees Fahrenheit. Coat 12-cup Bundt pan with nonstick cooking spray.

Whisk together flour, baking powder, baking soda, and salt in bowl; set aside.

In large bowl, beat butter and sugar together until light and fluffy. Add peanut butter and vanilla, beating until well combined. Add eggs, one at a time, beating until incorporated. Beat in sour cream. Reduce mixer to lowest speed and gradually add flour mixture, mixing until just blended. Spoon half of the batter (about 3 cups) into prepared pan. Dollop 3 tablespoons jelly over batter, avoiding edges of pan. Partially stir jelly into batter using a skewer or thin-bladed knife. Spoon remaining batter into pan and dollop and swirl remaining jelly into batter. Bake 1 hour, or until wooden pick inserted into center comes out clean. Let cake cool in pan for 10 minutes, then invert onto wire rack. Serve warm or at room temperature.

Special Corn Muffins

Makes 12 muffins

WHAT YOU NEED

- ¾ cup cornmeal
- 1 cup sifted all-purpose flour
- 4 teaspoons baking powder
- 1 teaspoon salt
- 4 tablespoons sugar

- 1 egg, well beaten
- 1 cup milk
- 3 tablespoons shortening, melted
- 12 teaspoons Welch's Grape Jelly

WHAT YOU DO

Preheat oven to 425 degrees Fahrenheit. Coat 12-cup muffin pan with nonstick cooking spray.

Sift cornmeal, flour, baking powder, salt, and sugar together in bowl.

Combine egg, milk, and shortening in separate bowl and stir into dry mixture. Fill prepared pan one-third full of batter. Place 1 teaspoon grape jelly on top of batter in each muffin cup and cover with remaining batter so that cups are not more than two-thirds full. Bake about 25 minutes.

Sweet 'n Smoky Sauce

Makes 2½ cups

WHAT YOU NEED

- 4 strips bacon, diced
- ½ cup chopped onion
- 1 cup Welch's Grape Jelly

- 1 cup ketchup
- 2 tablespoons cider vinegar

WHAT YOU DO

Sauté bacon and onion in saucepan until bacon is crisp. Drain off fat. Add jelly, ketchup, and vinegar and cook over low heat, stirring occasionally, for 10 minutes, or until sauce thickens.

Serving Suggestion: Serve with grilled steak or meatballs.

Walnut Hearts with Jelly Jewels

Makes 2 dozen scones

WHAT YOU NEED

- 1⅔ cups self-rising cake flour
- 2 tablespoons sugar
- ½ teaspoon salt
- ⅓ cup finely ground walnuts
- ¼ cup unsalted butter
- 1 egg

- ½ cup buttermilk
- 1 teaspoon vanilla extract
- Flour for dusting
- ¼ cup Welch's Grape Jelly
- 2 tablespoons milk

WHAT YOU DO

Preheat oven to 425 degrees Fahrenheit. Line baking sheet with parchment paper or coat baking sheet with nonstick cooking spray and dust with flour.

Sift flour, sugar, and salt into mixing bowl. Add walnuts. Cut in butter until mixture resembles coarse meal.

In another bowl, whisk together egg, buttermilk, and vanilla. Combine the wet and dry ingredients until just mixed. (Be careful not to overmix.) Roll dough gently on lightly floured surface. With a heart-shaped cookie cutter, cut scones, reforming dough scraps and gently rolling and cutting until all the dough is used. Transfer scones to prepared baking sheet. With your thumb or the back of a teaspoon, press a shallow indentation into the center of each heart. Spoon jelly into each well. Brush milk onto hearts and bake 10 to 12 minutes. Cool on baking rack.

✳

Western-Style Meatballs

Makes 24 meatballs

WHAT YOU NEED

- 10 ounces Welch's Grape Jelly
- 1 bottle (12 ounce) chili sauce
- 1 pound ground chuck
- 1 egg
- Dash onion salt
- Dash celery salt
- Dash garlic salt
- Dash salt
- Dash ground black pepper

WHAT YOU DO

Slowly heat grape jelly with chili sauce in saucepan over medium heat.

In bowl, combine chuck, egg, onion salt, celery salt, garlic salt, salt, and pepper. Shape into 1-inch-diameter meatballs Place meatballs into the simmering jelly-chili sauce. Cover and cook approximately 20 minutes, or until the meatballs are cooked through. Serve in chafing dish to keep warm.

✳ Strange Facts ✳

- In 1849 in Concord, Massachusetts, after more than ten years and 22,000 cross-breeding experiments on 125 grape vines, Ephraim Wales Bull developed the sweet and palatable Concord grape.
- In 1869, physician and dentist Thomas Bramwell Welch and his son Charles pasteurized Concord grape juice to produce the first "unfermented sacramental wine" for

fellow parishioners at his Methodist church in Vineland, New Jersey, where the elder Welch served as communion steward.

- In 1893, thousands of visitors at the Chicago World's Fair sampled Dr. Welch's Grape Juice. Welch's son Charles quit his dentistry practice to devote his full attention to marketing the grape juice, adopting a new label that dropped the word *Dr.* before the name *Welch's.*

- In 1913, Secretary of State William Jennings Bryan served Welch's Grape Juice instead of wine at a black-tie diplomatic function honoring the retiring British ambassador in Washington, DC. For months afterward, newspaper columnists and political cartoonists mocked "The Grape Juice Incident," making Welch's a household name. One political cartoon showed Uncle Sam drinking "Grape Juice Democracy."

- In 1914, Secretary of the Navy Josephus Daniels banned alcoholic beverages aboard Navy ships, substituting Welch's Grape Juice instead. The Navy became known as "Daniels's Grape Juice Navy."

- In 1918, Welch's develops its first jam product—Grapelade. The United States Army purchased the entire first production run, and soldiers returned to civilian life as loyal customers.

- In 1923, Welch's introduced Concord Grape Jelly.

- In 1949, Welch's launched Welch's Frozen Grape Juice Concentrate, becoming a pioneer in the frozen juice concentrate industry.

- In 1962, Welch's sponsored the animated television series *The Flintstones.*

- Welch's products are sold in more than fifty countries and territories around the world.

For More Recipes

Visit www.welchs.com

Caribbean Jerk Beef Steak

Makes 4 servings

WHAT YOU NEED

- ¾ cup Wish-Bone Italian Dressing
- 1 tablespoon Worcestershire sauce
- 1 tablespoon firmly packed brown sugar
- 1 large jalapeño pepper, seeded and finely chopped
- 1 teaspoon ground allspice
- 1 teaspoon ground ginger
- 1 beef top round steak, 1 inch thick (about 1½ pounds)

WHAT YOU DO

Combine dressing, Worcestershire sauce, sugar, jalapeño, allspice, and ginger in small bowl.

Place steak in large, shallow, nonaluminum baking dish or large, resealable, plastic food-storage bag. Pour ½ cup marinade over steak; turn to coat. Cover dish or seal bag and marinate in refrigerator, turning occasionally, 3 to 24 hours. Refrigerate remaining marinade.

Preheat grill.

Remove steak from marinade, discarding marinade. Grill steak, turning occasionally and brushing frequently with refrigerated marinade, until steak is desired doneness.

Easy Broiled Fish Fillets

Makes 4 servings

WHAT YOU NEED

- ½ cup Wish-Bone Italian Dressing, divided
- 1 pound fish fillets
- ⅓ cup dry bread crumbs
- 1 tablespoon chopped fresh parsley

WHAT YOU DO

Set aside 1 tablespoon dressing. In large, shallow nonaluminum baking dish or large, resealable, plastic food-storage bag, pour dressing over fish. Cover dish or close bag and marinate in refrigerator up to 1 hour. Remove fish from marinade.

In small bowl, combine bread crumbs and parsley.

Preheat broiler.

On broiler pan, arrange fillets. Broil until fish flakes with a fork. Brush with reserved 1 table-spoon dressing, then sprinkle with bread crumb mixture. Continue broiling until crumbs are golden.

Easy Mediterranean Pasta Salad

Makes 8 servings

WHAT YOU NEED

- ¾ cup Wish-Bone Italian Dressing
- ¼ cup chopped fresh parsley
- ¼ teaspoon ground black pepper
- 8 ounces twist pasta, cooked, rinsed with cold water, and drained

- 1 can (14 ounces) artichoke hearts, drained and quartered
- 1 jar (7 ounces) roasted red peppers, sliced
- 1 can (4 ounces) pitted ripe olives, drained
- 4 ounces sliced pepperoni, halved

WHAT YOU DO

In large bowl, blend dressing, parsley, and black pepper. Stir in pasta, artichokes, red peppers, olives, and pepperoni. Serve at room temperature or chilled.

Mediterranean Grilled Steak

Makes 6 servings

WHAT YOU NEED

- ½ cup Wish-Bone Italian Dressing
- 2 large cloves garlic, finely chopped
- 2 teaspoons finely chopped fresh rosemary leaves or ½ teaspoon dried rosemary leaves, crushed (see *Note*)

- 1 top sirloin steak (about 1½ pounds and 1-inch thick)

WHAT YOU DO

Combine dressing, garlic, and rosemary in bowl.

Place steak in large, shallow, nonaluminum baking dish or large, resealable, plastic food-storage bag. Pour ¼ cup marinade over steak; turn to coat. Cover dish or close bag and marinate in refrigerator 30 minutes. Refrigerate remaining marinade.

Preheat grill.

Remove steak from marinade, discarding marinade. Grill steak, turning occasionally and brushing frequently with refrigerated marinade, until desired doneness.

Note: Substitute 1 tablespoon finely chopped fresh basil leaves or 1 teaspoon crushed dried basil leaves for the rosemary.

Pesto Chicken Salad

Makes 4 servings

WHAT YOU NEED

- ½ cup Wish-Bone Italian Dressing
- 1 cup packed fresh basil leaves
- ¼ cup packed fresh parsley leaves
- 1 clove garlic

- 1 tablespoon pignoli (pine nuts) or chopped walnuts (optional)
- 4 boneless skinless chicken breast halves (about 1¼ pounds)
- Salad greens
- Tomato wedges (optional)

WHAT YOU DO

In food processor or blender, process dressing, basil, parsley, garlic, and pignoli (or walnuts, if desired) until basil and parsley are finely chopped.

Place chicken in large, shallow nonaluminum baking dish or large, resealable, plastic food-storage bag. Pour ½ cup pesto over chicken. Cover dish or close bag and marinate in refrigerator, turning occasionally, 30 minutes to 3 hours. Refrigerate remaining ¼ cup marinade.

Preheat grill or broiler.

Remove chicken from marinade, reserving marinade. Grill or broil chicken, turning once and brushing with refrigerated marinade, until chicken is thoroughly cooked. To serve, slice chicken and serve over greens. Garnish, if desired, with tomato wedges.

Shrimp Scampi Italiano

Makes 4 servings

WHAT YOU NEED

- 1 pound uncooked medium shrimp, cleaned
- ⅓ cup Wish-Bone Italian Dressing
- Fresh chopped parsley (optional)

WHAT YOU DO

Place shrimp in large, shallow nonaluminum broiler pan, pour dressing over shrimp. Cover and marinate in refrigerator, turning occasionally, at least 2 hours.

On bottom of broiler pan, without rack, broil shrimp, turning and basting frequently, until shrimp turn pink. Garnish, if desired, with chopped fresh parsley.

Serving Suggestion: Serve with hot cooked rice.

Wish-Bone Marinated Chicken 1-2-3

Makes 6 servings

WHAT YOU NEED

- ¾ cup Wish-Bone Italian Dressing, divided
- 6 boneless, skinless chicken breast halves (about 1½ pounds)

WHAT YOU DO

In large, shallow nonaluminum baking dish or large, resealable, plastic food-storage bag, pour ½ cup dressing over chicken. Cover dish or close bag and marinate in refrigerator, turning occasionally, 30 minutes to 3 hours.

Remove chicken from marinade, discarding marinade. Grill or broil chicken, turning once and brushing frequently with remaining ¼ cup dressing, 12 minutes, or until chicken is thoroughly cooked.

✦ Strange Facts ✦

- In 1945, Phillip Sollomi, a soldier returning from World War II, opened a family-style chicken restaurant in Kansas City, Missouri and named it "The Wish-Bone." Three years later, he asked his mother, an immigrant from Sicily, for the recipe for her spicy salad dressing. When customers at The Wish-Bone asked for bottles of the salad dressing, Phil began mixing the dressing in a fifty-gallon drum while his mother happily applied labels reading "The Kansas City Wish-Bone Famous Italian-Style Dressing."
- In 1957, Sollomi sold his salad dressing business to the T.J. Lipton Company.
- In 1970, Wish-Bone became the best-selling Italian dressing in the United States, a position it holds to this day.
- To this day, Wish-Bone salad dressings are still made in Kansas City, Missouri.

For More Recipes

Visit www.wish-bone.com

Acknowledgments

At Rodale, I am grateful to Margot Schupf for her passion, enthusiasm, and excitement for this book. I am also deeply indebted to my editors Emily Williams and Jennifer DeFilippi, researcher Debbie Green, expert copy editor Jennifer Bright Reich, designer Anthony Serge, illustrator Jason Schneider, and Cindy Ratzlaff.

A very special thanks to my agent, Stephanie Tade; my manager, Barb North; and to the hundreds of people who continually visit my Web site and send me their ingenious ideas.

I am also indebted to Carrie Bruder; Linda Mukhar; Patti Calagna; Bob Blumer (aka The Surreal Gourmet); Carolyn Wyman; Peter Mazonson; Molly Bailey; Charlie Martin at ACH Food Companies, Inc. (maker of Argo Corn Starch); Tracy Boever at American Pop Corn Company (maker of Jolly Time Pop Corn); Jennifer Hayes at Bumble Bee Foods (maker of Bumble Bee Tuna); Erika Marshall at Fleishman-Hillard (public relations firm for Bumble Bee Tuna); Doris Lucas, William Boykan, Megan May, and Telea Stafford at Cadbury Schweppes (maker of Dr Pepper and 7 UP); Jill Johnston at Campbell Soup Company (maker of Campbell's Condensed Cream of Mushroom Soup and Campbell's Condensed Tomato Soup); Bill Lee, Joy Vencill, and Cynthia Birdsong at the Coca-Cola Company; Regina DeMars at ConAgra Foods, Inc. (maker of Hebrew National Beef Franks and Swiss Miss Milk Chocolate Hot Cocoa Mix); Timothy Oswald and Donna Skidmore at Dole Food Company (maker of Dole Pineapple); John L. Casey and Mark Schuessler at Doumak, Inc. (maker of Campfire Marshmallows); Donald Durkee at Durkee-Mower, Inc. (maker of Marshmallow Fluff); Janet Hoppe at Frito-Lay (maker of Fritos Corn Chips and Lay's Potato Chips); Gregory Kaihoi at General Mills (makers of Cheerios and Chex Cereal); Barbara Ellen at the HV Food Products Company (makers of Hidden Valley Original Ranch Dressing); Kevin Jones and Kara Mallory at Hormel Foods (maker of SPAM products); Leonard Cullo, Laura Hillock, and Robin Teets at H. J. Heinz Company (maker of Heinz Ketchup and Heinz Vinegar); Tara Rush at MasterFoods USA (maker of Uncle Ben's Converted Brand Rice); Laurie Harrsen at McCormick & Company, Inc. (maker of McCormick Food Coloring and McCormick Pure Vanilla Extract); Lewis Goldstein and Beth Gaeta at Mott's LLP (maker of Mott's Apple Sauce); Ava Baffoni at Nestlé (maker of Nestea and Nestlé Carnation Nonfat Dry Milk); Janet Silverberg at Pepsico (makers of Quaker Oats); Barbara Yaros at Reckitt Benckiser (maker of French's Mustard and French's Original French Fried Onions); Jim Powell at Sioux Honey Association (make of SueBee Honey); Kevin Jackson, Christopher Resweber, DeAnne Hrabak, and Adam Ekonomon at the J. M. Smucker Company (maker of Jif Peanut Butter and Crisco All-Vegetable Shortening); Jaci Hebert at the McIlhenny Company (maker of Tabasco Pepper Sauce); Mitchell Frank at Unilever (maker of Hellmann's Mayonaisse, Lipton Recipe Secrets Onion Soup Mix, Ragú Old World Style Pasta Sauce, and Wish-Bone Italian Dressing); and Jim Callahan at Welch's (maker of Welch's Grape Jelly).

Above all, all my love to Debbie, Ashley, and Julia.

The Fine Print

Sources

- *Advertising in America: The First 200 Years* by Charles Goodrum and Helen Dalrymple (New York: Harry N. Abrams, 1990)
- *The Blunder Book: Colossal Errors, Minor Mistakes, and Surprising Slipups That Have Changed the Course of History* by M. Hirsh Goldberg (New York: William Morrow, 1984)
- *The Book of Lists* by David Wallechinsky, Irving Wallace, and Amy Wallace (New York: William Morrow, 1977)
- *The Book of Lists, No. 2* by Irving Wallace, David Wallechinsky, Amy Wallace, and Sylvia Wallace (New York: William Morrow, 1983)
- *A Campbell Cookbook: Cooking with Soup: 608 skillet dishes, casseroles, stews, sauces, gravies, dips, soup mates and garnishes* (Camden, New Jersey: Campbell Soup Company)
- *Cooking with Condensed Soups* (Selected Recipe Edition) by Anne Marshall (Camden, New Jersey: Campbell Soup Company)
- *Cooking with Dr Pepper and 7 UP: A Compilation of Recipes Containing Dr Pepper and 7 UP Products* (Plano, Texas: Dr Pepper/Seven Up, Inc, 2003)
- *Cooking Without a Kitchen: The Coffeemaker Cookbook* by Peter Mazonson (San Antonio, Texas: MCB Publishing, 1999)
- *Dictionary of Trade Name Origins* by Adrian Room (London: Routledge & Kegan Paul Books Ltd., 1982)
- *Everybody's Business: A Field Guide to the 400 Leading Companies in America* by Milton Moskowitz, Robert Levering, and Michael Katz (New York: Doubleday, 1990)
- *Famous American Trademarks* by Arnold B. Barach (Washington, D.C.: Public Affairs Press, 1971)
- *Favorite Brand Name Recipe Cookbook* by the Editors of Consumer Guide (New York: Beekman House, 1981)
- *The Film Encyclopedia* by Ephraim Katz (New York: Perigee, 1979)
- *The Guinness Book of Records* edited by Peter Matthews (New York: Bantam, 1993)
- *Hoover's Handbook of American Business 1995* (Austin: Reference Press, 1995)
- *Inventions and Discoveries 1993* by Valérie-Anne Giscard d'Estaing and Mark Young (New York: Facts on File, 1993)
- "It's Utah, It's Good to Be Green (Jell-O)" by Carolyn Wyman, *Los Angeles Times,* February 13, 2002.
- *The Joy of Cooking* by Irma S. Rombauer and Marion Rombauer Becker (New York: Bobbs-Merrill Company, 1975)
- *The Kitchen Sink Cookbook: Offbeat Recipes From Unusual Ingredients* by Carolyn Wyman (New York: Birch Lane Press/Carol Publishing, 1997)
- *Off the Eaten Path: Inspired Recipes for Adventurous Cooks* by Bob Blumer (New York: Ballantine Books, 2000)
- *Oops! A Stupefying Survey of Goofs, Blunders & Botches, Great & Small* by Paul Kirchner (Los Angeles, General Publishing Books, 1996)
- *The Origins of Everyday Things* by the editors of *Reader's Digest* (London: Reader's Digest, 1999)
- *Panati's Extraordinary Origins of Everyday Things* by Charles Panati (New York: HarperCollins, 1987)
- *Reader's Digest Book of Facts* (Pleasantville, New York: Reader's Digest, 1987)
- *Strange Stories, Amazing Facts: Stories That Are Bizarre, Unusual, Odd, Astonishing, and Often Incredible* by the editors of *Reader's Digest* (Pleasantville, New York: Reader's Digest, 1996)
- *The Tabasco Cookbook* by Paul McIlhenny with Barbara Hunter (New York: Clarkson Potter, 1993)
- *Why Did They Name It…?* by Hannah Campbell (New York: Fleet, 1964)
- "Why Use the Oven When the Dishwasher Will Cook Your Meal?" Wall Street Journal, December 3, 1999.

Copyright Information

Trademark Information

"Argo," "Kingsford's" and the Kingsford logo are registered trademarks of ACH Food Companies.

"Aunt Jemima" is a registered trademark of the Quaker Oats Company.

"Bumble Bee" is a registered trademark of Bumble Bee Seafoods, Inc.

"Campbell" is a registered trademark of Campbell Soup Company.

"Campfire" is a registered trademark of Doumak, Inc.

"Canada Dry" is a registered trademark of Cadbury Beverages Inc.

"Cheerios" is a registered trademark of General Mills, Inc.

"Cheez Whiz" is a registered trademark of Kraft Foods.

"Chex" is a registered trademark of General Mills, Inc.

"Coca-Cola" and "Coke" are registered trademarks of the Coca-Cola Company.

"Crisco" is a registered trademark of J. M. Smucker Co.

"Crock-Pot" is a registered trademark of Rival.

"Cuisinart" is a registered trademark of Cuisinart.

"Dole" is a registered trademark of Dole Fruit Company, Inc.

"Dr Pepper" is a registered trademark of Dr Pepper/Seven Up , Inc.

"French's" is a registered trademark of Reckitt Benckiser.

"Fritos" is a registered trademark of Frito-Lay.

"Hebrew National" is a registered trademark of ConAgra.

"Heinz" is a registered trademark of H.J. Heinz Company.

"Hellmann's" is a registered trademark of Unilever.

"Hidden Valley" and "Original Ranch" are registered trademarks of the Clorox Company.

"Jell-O" is a registered trademark of Kraft Foods, Inc.

"Jif" is a registered trademark of the J. M. Smucker Co.

"Jolly Time" is a registered trademark of American Pop Corn Company.

"Lay's" is a registered trademark of Frito-Lay.

"Lea & Perrins" is a registered trademark of H.J. Heinz Company.

"Lipton" and "Recipe Secrets" are registered trademarks of Unilever.

"Marshmallow Fluff" is a registered trademark of Durkee-Mower Inc.

"McCormick" is a registered trademark of McCormick & Company, Incorporated.

"Mr. Coffee" is a registered trademark of Mr. Coffee.

"Mott's" is a registered trademark of Mott's Inc.

"Nestea," "Nestlé," and "Carnation" are registered trademarks of Société des Produits Nestlé S.A., Vevey, Switzerland.

"Quaker Oats" is a registered trademark of the Quaker Oats Company.

"Radarange" and "Amana" are registered trademarks of Maytag Corporation.

"Ragú" is a registered trademark of Unilever.

"7 UP" is a registered trademark of Dr Pepper/Seven-Up, Inc.

"SPAM" is a registered trademark of Hormel Foods Corporation.

"SueBee" is a registered trademark of Sioux Honey Association.

"Sunbeam" and "Mixmaster" are registered trademarks of Sunbeam Corporation.

"Swiss Miss" is a registered trademark of ConAgra.

"Tabasco" is a registered trademark of McIlhenny Company.

"Tang" is a registered trademark of Kraft Foods.

"Toastmaster" is a registered trademark of Salton Inc.

"Tupperware" is a registered trademark of Tupperware Worldwide.

"Uncle Ben's" and "Converted" are registered trademarks of Uncle Ben's, Inc.

"Waring" is a registered trademark of Waring Products, Inc.

"Welch's" is a registered trademark of Welch Foods Inc.

"Wish-Bone" is a registered trademark of Unilever.

Index

Underscored page references indicate boxed text.

About the Author

Joey Green—author of *Polish Your Furniture with Panty Hose, Paint Your House with Powdered Milk, Wash Your Hair with Whipped Cream,* and *Clean Your Clothes with Cheez Whiz*—got Jay Leno to shave with Jif Peanut Butter on *The Tonight Show,* Rosie O'Donnell to mousse her hair with Jell-O on *The Rosie O'Donnell Show,* and Katie Couric to drop her diamond engagement ring in a glass of Efferdent on *Today.* He has been seen polishing furniture with SPAM on *NBC Dateline,* cleaning a toilet with Coca-Cola in the *New York Times,* and washing his hair with Reddi-wip in *People.*

Green, a former contributing editor to *National Lampoon* and a former advertising copywriter at J. Walter Thompson, is the author of more than thirty-five books, including *Marx & Lennon: The Parallel Sayings, Weird Christmas, The Jolly President,* and *Champagne and Caviar Again?* A native of Miami, Florida, and a graduate of Cornell University, he wrote television commercials for Burger King and Walt Disney World and won a Clio Award for a print ad he created for Eastman Kodak. He backpacked around the world for two years on his honeymoon and lives in Los Angeles with his wife, Debbie, and their two daughters, Ashley and Julia. The four of them traveled around the world together for two months in 2006.

Visit Joey Green at www.wackyuses.com